Life on Muskrat Creek

Life on Muskrat Creek

A Homestead Family in Wyoming

Ethel Waxham Love and J. David Love

Edited by
Frances Love Froidevaux and Barbara Love

LEHIGH UNIVERSITY PRESS
Bethlehem

Published by Lehigh University Press
Copublished by The Rowman & Littlefield Publishing Group, Inc.
4501 Forbes Boulevard, Suite 200, Lanham, Maryland 20706
www.rowman.com

6 Tinworth Street, London SE11 5AL, United Kingdom

Distributed by NATIONAL BOOK NETWORK

British Library Cataloguing in Publication Information Available

Library of Congress Cataloging-in-Publication Data Available

ISBN 978-1-61146-264-7 (cloth: alk. paper)
ISBN 978-1-61146-266-1 (pbk. : alk. paper)
ISBN 978-1-61146-265-4 (electronic)

Contents

~

Figure Titles and Captions

and the ranch activities. Water was heated in large copper boilers on the cookstove and carried to the wash and rinse tubs, in warm weather in the yard. Mother did the washing by hand, using a hand agitator and a hand-cranked wringer. The clothes were washed—sheets first, socks last—pressed through the wringer, whose chrome reflected GAT YAM, into two galvanized rinse tubs, then rinsed and hung to dry. In winter, often the clothes froze on the lines. Stiff as boards, they were stacked near the stove until they softened and dried. The next day, Mother ironed. Flatirons were heated on the stove, then clamped onto a wooden handle. As they cooled, they were replaced with others which had been heating. Scottish economy dictated that the stove be cooking something as well—often several loaves of bread and a kettle of soup or stew—to relieve Mother from having to cook supper after a full day's work."   70

Acknowledgments

John McPhee, for throwing down the gauntlet

Linda Hasselstrom, for her help and encouragement

Wilma Slaight, Archivist at the Margaret Clapp Library, Wellesley College, for her insight and initiative

Mrs. Peter Benson, for her willingness to share information about her mother, Winifred Hawkridge

Richard W. Jones, Editor, Wyoming Geological Survey, for providing geographical details of times gone by

Ruth (Sunnye) Fulton Tiedemann, friend and expert sleuth

George I. Johnson, for being there when we couldn't be

Bernie Huebner, for his friendship and literary expertise

Todd Guenther, former Director, The Pioneer Museum, Lander, Wyoming, for his dedication to preserving Wyoming history

Phoebe Love Holzinger, for her calm and free spirit

The editors at Lehigh University Press and Rowman & Littlefield, who believed in this project

Our in-laws, Karen Love, Jane C. Love, and Stephen Cutcliffe, for their editorial advice

Our niece, Jordan Love, for her ancestry research clarifying dates

Our brothers, Charles M. and David W. Love, for their enthusiastic encouragement

Our parents, Jane M. and J. David Love, for their continued love and support

Claude Froidevaux, Frances' husband, for making the maps and keeping the family on course

Our children, Ben, Sarah (Zoë), and Rachel Froidevaux, and Daniel and Nicolas dePeyer for their patience while their mothers lived in another era

All of John and Ethel Love's descendants, who didn't quit

Maps

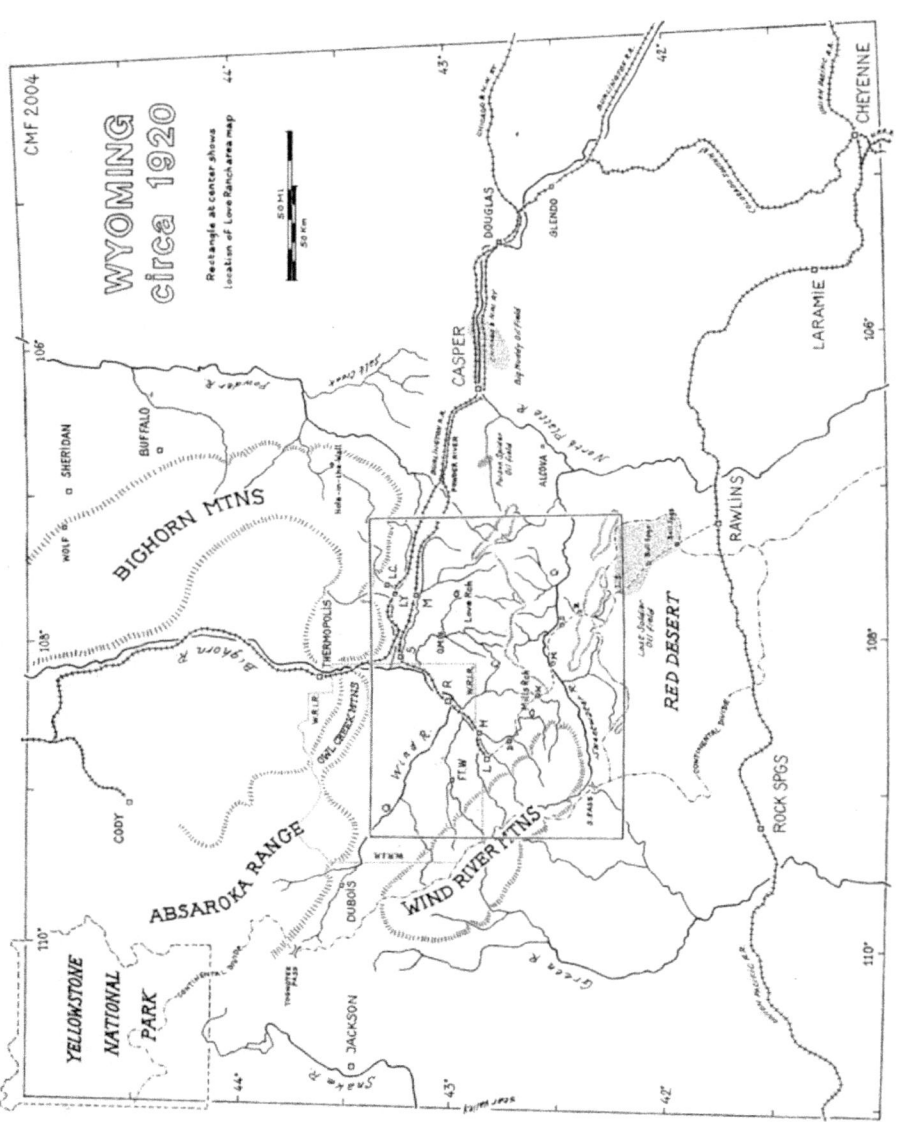

Map of Wyoming
Map drawn by Claude M. Froidevaux.

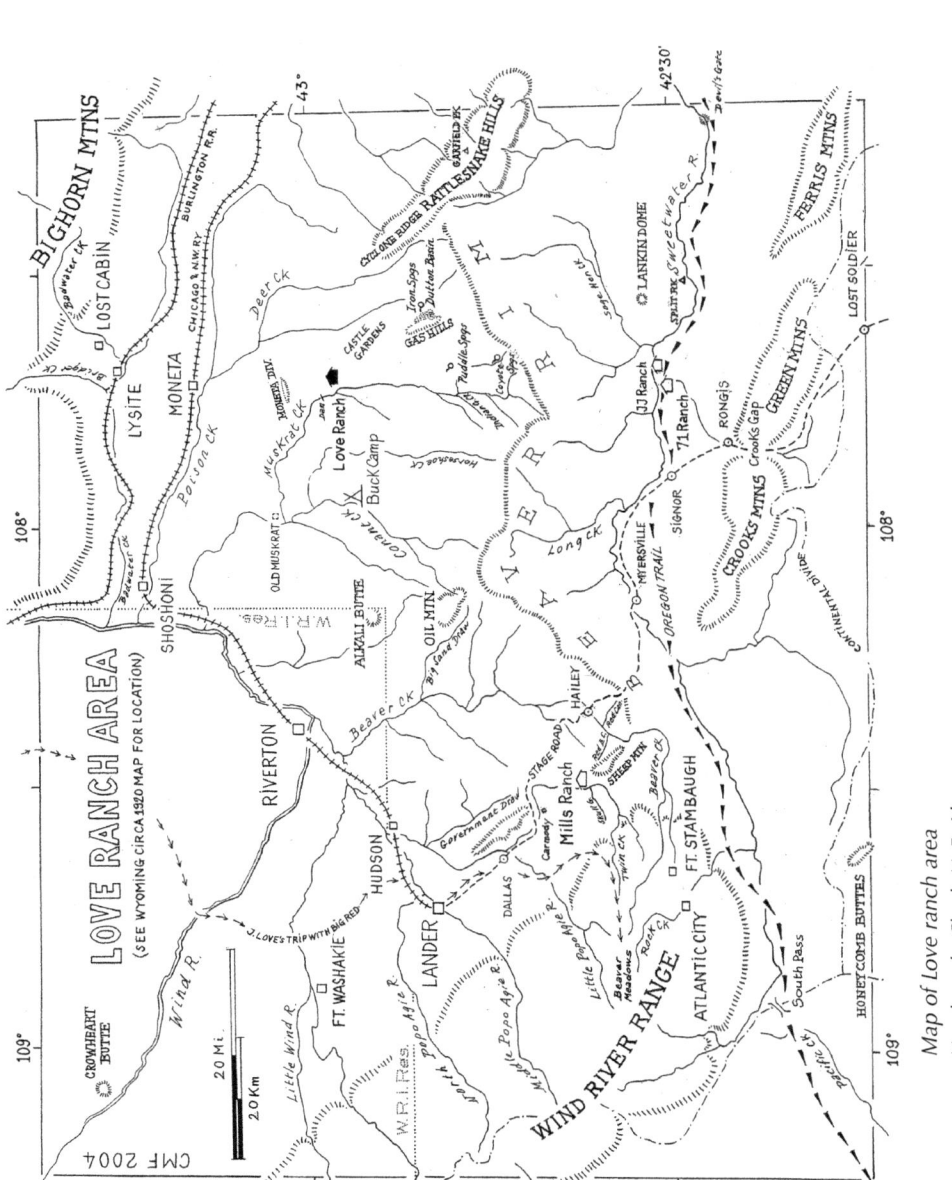

Map of Love ranch area
Map drawn by Claude M. Froidevaux.

~

Preface

July 8th, 1997. The caravan of six vehicles ground to a stop along the dusty road at the top of the Moneta Divide in central Wyoming. Two dozen people, aged five to eighty-four, assembled in the sparse grass around a tall, silver-haired man in brown canvas pants and a sweat-stained Stetson. "Love" was emblazoned on his brass belt buckle. David Love spoke to the circle of faces around him. Descendants of John and Ethel Love, David's parents, were gathered for a first-ever Love Family Reunion. Some of the younger generations were seeing for the first time the land where their forebears had made their home for 37 years.

David gestured expansively at the treeless land bowl stretching around them, then at the mountains shimmering on the western horizon. He explained that 87 years ago, almost to the day, his father, John Galloway Love, arrived here with his bride, Ethel Waxham Love. He pointed out the Wind River Mountains 100 miles away, the highest and longest mountain range in Wyoming, snowcapped even in mid-summer. There, his father had cut many of the logs for his ranch buildings. David noted, "It took two weeks to make each trip." To the northwest he pointed out the Absarokas and, to the north, the low, gray humps of the Owl Creek Mountains. "Nasty in a blizzard," David remembered. Behind them, in a pale shade of blue, was the southeast end of the Bighorns and, to the left, across the waves of sage and buffalo grass, the low, rocky Rattlesnake Hills. Garfield Peak was visible as a little bump, and straight ahead to the south was the Beaver Divide (Map of Wyoming, p. xiv).

Below the group, the meandering ribbon of Muskrat Creek sparkled across the muted palette of the landscape. A life-giver to the grasses and sedges on either side, its water showed little other effect on the parched terrain. Along the northern bank of Muskrat Creek were the ranch buildings, including the ranch house and, to the east of the house, a row of outbuildings for the cowboys, repairs, and maintenance. About 150 yards farther were the corrals and barns, all connected to facilitate work on the ranch. "It was a long walk in winter," David remembered, "but in summer we appreciated the livestock being downwind from the house." A patch of dark green grass east of the corrals was the wild hay meadow, 160 acres of good grass, sub-irrigated by an underground spring—one of the reasons John chose to homestead here. All he had to do to protect the hay was enclose the field with about 2,000 cedar posts, which he brought by horse and wagon, fifteen at a time, from Green Mountain, sixty miles away. John dreamed of developing an irrigation system to make his desert bloom with hay meadows, grain fields, fruit orchards, and shade trees. The hay and grain would feed herds of his cattle, sheep, and horses, which would roam the thousand square miles of uninhabited land surrounding his homestead (Map of Love ranch area, p. xv).

Climbing back into their cars, the descendants of John and Ethel Love drove from the ridge the six miles to the ranch house. As they explored the tired, abandoned buildings, ever alert for the warning of rattlesnakes, they attempted to imagine how it had been to live there: no running water, no electricity, no telephone, the nearest neighbor 13 miles away by buggy, Moneta, the nearest town, 15 miles. The only building still intact was the outhouse, a 180-foot sprint west from the kitchen door. So little but the memories remained of the lives that had occupied this place. "There are ghosts here," David said.

* * *

Life on Muskrat Creek tells the story of the Love family's life on the ranch from 1910 to 1925, and it serves as a sequel to *Lady's Choice: Ethel Waxham's Journals & Letters, 1905–1910* (University of New Mexico Press, 1993). When age and ill health eventually caused John and Ethel to leave the ranch in 1947 and live with David and his family in Laramie, Wyoming, they left most of their household furnishings behind, bringing only a single pickup truckload of their most treasured possessions: a few mementos, books, boxes of notes, photos, and letters. This book compiles many of these unpublished materials, which include narratives and poems that Ethel wrote in the years following her marriage to John in 1910 and her move to his Wyoming ranch.

After John's death in 1950, Ethel took creative writing classes at the University of Wyoming, using this opportunity to develop her notes on experiences in a West that was rapidly disappearing. While a few of her poems and other short writings were published,[1] many of her accounts, as well as ideas and drafts for an uncompleted book, *Life on the Rat*, were found scribbled on notebook paper, on backs of envelopes, and on scraps of paper pinned together with rusty straight pins. Ironically, some material was also discovered in an envelope marked "papers of no importance."

This book selects pieces from Ethel's varied writings that constitute an informal social history describing family life on a Wyoming ranch in the first half of the twentieth century. Ethel was always an astute observer of the people and events around her, but after her marriage, she did not systematically keep a journal and rarely expressed her own innermost thoughts or emotions except in poetry and her letters, some of which her friends returned to her in later years. Taken together, these materials offer a unique account of what it was like to make a home on the ranch. Ethel describes people, events, and activities ranging from the everyday responsibilities of doing laundry and caring for pets to the larger challenges of raising, educating, and providing for children in rural Wyoming. Ethel also creates lively portraits of the people who visited the ranch over the years. As Charles Rankin wrote in the Introduction to *Lady's Choice*, "Ethel's experiences were generally representative, at least for women of her economic class and social status, but . . . her descriptions of them were truly exceptional in their color, depth, insight, and honesty."[2] Ethel's writings in this volume are similarly rich; she did not make light of the difficulties of living in such an isolated place, but described them with courage and grace.

Ethel offers an important view of the family's life on the ranch, and this book enriches her perspective by including relevant anecdotes and memories recorded by David, Ethel's and John's second son. In 1967, David, the editors' father, began writing vignettes and stories about his own experiences of growing up on the isolated ranch, presenting installments to his family nearly every Christmas for more than thirty years. David wanted future generations to understand the challenges his parents had faced as well as his own adventures growing up on Muskrat Creek, a life very different from the urban upbringing he had provided for his own family. David's adult perspective reflects back on his childhood, describing his experiences of growing up with his brother, the family's interactions with friends and outlaws, and the challenges the family faced with weather, livestock, and getting an education. Some of his writing is from his own detailed memories of events he experienced firsthand, whereas in other pieces he recounts events that his parents later described to him.[3]

In presenting the voices and perspectives of both Ethel and David, this book offers a unique opportunity to explore how family members of different generations—and of both genders—experienced a West in transition from the early days of homesteading and free-range livestock, through the devastating echoes of World War I, bank foreclosures, the growing constraints on ranching, and the difficulties of a geographically isolated life. While many authors have written about their experiences in the West and the effects ranch life has had on them,[4] *Life on Muskrat Creek* offers a fresh approach to histories of the West by interweaving the voices of two different yet interconnected family members. Crafting their memories into engaging narratives and poetic forms, Ethel and David make their experiences of the American West come alive. Their use of rhetorical devices, including dialogue, irony, and dramatic structure, enables readers to visualize the action and to share in the emotions of the people living on the ranch.

Ethel and David wrote about people and incidents they felt were important in their ranch experience, and sometimes each wrote a version of the same events, but from distinctive points of view. For example, in David's story of "The Broken Plank," he reconstructs the confrontation, later told to him by his father, between his brave mother and a hunger-crazed bull that could have doomed the family's survival; describing the same event in her notes, Ethel writes simply, "the bull broke into the granary." The facts are the same, but the viewpoints and writing styles differ: whereas Ethel succinctly recorded her experience, David passed along his father's skill at telling a suspenseful story. Together, they provide not only a record of events on Muskrat Creek, but also a range of personal insights into what it meant for many early ranchers to wrest a living from an arid and unforgiving landscape.

Frances Love Froidevaux, David's eldest daughter, meticulously assembled the text, fact-checking details and terminology with our father and published sources. Her work made it possible to fill in our father's anecdotes of oral history and to shape a trove of family archives into a coherent historical narrative. Tragically, Frances's life was cut short by cancer in 2011, before the manuscript could be published. The project then passed back to Barbara Love, David's younger daughter, who continued editing and shepherding the manuscript through the publication process. In order to preserve the sense of history found in Ethel's and David's writings, the editors first selected the pieces of writing that pertained explicitly to the ranch experience and that fit a designated time frame. The book covers material beginning in 1910 with John's and Ethel's marriage, and ending in 1925, when Ethel and the children began spending the school year in Lander so the boys could attend high school. The chapters are thus organized chronologically, exploring events and issues that were important in the family history and ranch life more generally. Each chapter also juxtaposes Ethel's and David's voices so as to create a kind of dialogue as both writers reflect on the same incidents and experiences. The chapter titles are drawn from headings or comments in Ethel's and David's writings, or they derive from major themes that emerge in life on the ranch, a life in which the constant vicissitudes of weather, disease, and luck determined success or failure.

Some of Ethel's and David's shorter vignettes or anecdotes are included in their entirety in the book; however, their longer pieces of writing, which encompass many years, are excerpted in several chapters. In presenting their original material, there only minor editorial adjustments for clarity and consistency. Moreover, the brief contextual information provided in the chapters is set in italics to be readily distinguished from Ethel's and David's primary accounts. For scholars and readers interested in the full range of available source material, David's and Ethel's unabridged writings will eventually be archived in the American Heritage Center at the University of Wyoming.

While both Ethel and David described their personal experiences, they were also aware that they were recording aspects of an existence that extended beyond their lives as individuals. Their writing exhibits a consciousness that an entire way of life was vanishing. As original homesteaders grew old, the rural Wyoming the authors had experienced and described was giving way to developing oil, gas, and mining industries, isolated ranches were being absorbed by conglomerates, and the younger generations were lured away to towns and cities. Every ranch has its own history, and reasons for abandonment range from drought, loss of livestock, financial ruin, ill health, and, as in this case, the younger generation choosing other professions. The history told in this book is a blend of voices and characters that does not simply record the details of a particular family's life; rather, Ethel's and David's stories illuminate the larger experiences common to many settlers living in a West in transition.

Frances Love Froidevaux, 2011
Barbara Love, 2017

Notes

1. Three of Ethel's poems and her description of the "Wyoming Wolf Drive" were published in the 1958 University of Wyoming English Department's publication *Writing at Wyoming*. Her experience of teaching in 1905 "At the Twin Creek School"

was published in the 1965 volume *Let Your Light Shine, Pioneer Women Educators of Wyoming.*

2. Charles Rankin, Introduction to *Lady's Choice: Ethel Waxham's Journals & Letters, 1905–1910*, Barbara Love and Frances Love Froidevaux, eds., University of New Mexico Press, 1993: xix.

3. Excerpts from Ethel's journals and David's memoirs were included in John McPhee's *Rising from the Plains* (Farrar, Straus, Giroux, 1986), a profile of David Love and his career as a geologist, and Episode 8, "One Sky above Us," of the Ken Burns PBS series *The West*, a film by Stephen Ives (The West Film Project, Inc./Greater Washington Educational Telecommunications Association, Inc., 1996).

4. Many authors have written about their experiences in the West and the effects ranch life has had on them. Some, like Elinore Pruett Stewart's *Letters of a Woman Homesteader* (1914), Cecilia Hennel Hendricks's *Letters from Honey Hill: A Woman's View of Homesteading 1914–1922* (1986), and Cathy Healy's *An Improbable Pioneer: The Letters of Edith Holden Healy 1911–1950* (2013), to name just a few, are based on letters written to family and friends in other parts of the country. Other memoirs, such as Judy Blunt's *Breaking Clean* (2002) and Teresa Jordan's *Riding the White Horse Home: A Western Family Album* (1993), describe the authors' conflicted feelings about being members of fourth generation ranch families who eventually leave ranching, even though ranching doesn't leave them. The male perspective on a Western experience is eloquently expressed in much of Wallace Stegner's and Ivan Doig's writing, as well as many other authors.

~

Family Background

Ethel

Ethel Phoebe Waxham was born August 11, 1882, in Rockford, Illinois, the second of the three daughters of Dr. Frank E. Waxham and Elizabeth "Lizzie" Leach Waxham. Ethel and her sisters, Vera and Faith, began their education at Hyde Park School in Chicago but graduated from East Denver High School when the family moved to Colorado in the late 1880s.[1]

Frank Eudorus Waxham, M.D. and Elizabeth "Lizzie" Leach Waxham, Ethel Waxham Love's parents in the mid-1880s.
Love Family Archives

Vera, Faith, and Ethel Waxham, 1888.
Love Family Archives

Dr. Waxham, who specialized in diseases of the lungs and throat, believed that Colorado's high altitude and dry air would be beneficial in curing his wife, but Lizzie died of consumption or asthma in 1898. Although not wealthy, the Waxham family lived comfortably, with a maid, an automobile, electricity, and a telephone. They were regular patrons of Denver's social and cultural events. In 1901, Dr. Waxham married Alice Welles, who, in 1905, gave birth to a daughter, Ruth Eudora. In 1907, when Alice's speculating on the stock market nearly ruined the family's finances, Dr. Waxham divorced her. Alice left Denver, but Ruth remained with her father and half-sisters.

In 1901, Ethel enrolled at Wellesley College in Massachusetts, where she studied classical literature, Greek, French, German, and Latin. Her quest for adventure led her and several classmates to work in a settlement house in New York during the summer of 1904. A keen observer of life, with a passion for history, she took notes, wrote stories, poetry, and a journal. Ethel was awarded one of Wellesley's first Phi Beta Kappa keys before her graduation in 1905. She then returned to Denver.

The autumn following her graduation, Ethel described her life to a friend as "flat, stale, and unproductive." She had spent the summer working without pay in her father's medical office, but, as time passed, she became increasingly restless. Her sister Vera had accepted a contract to teach at the Twin Creek school in central Wyoming, but when Vera decided to get married, Ethel agreed to replace her as a teacher, lodging with the Mills family at their nearby Red Bluff ranch. Anyone with a B.A. was supposed to be able to teach—and so Ethel went.

Ethel Phoebe Waxham, 1905.
Love Family Archives

Ethel Phoebe Waxham on her horse in Denver, 1905.
Love Family Archives

John and Ethel met November 12, 1905, shortly after Ethel's arrival at the Red Bluff ranch, which was sixty miles across country southwest of John's ranch (Map of Love ranch area, p. xv). John, just getting a start, was a sheepman, called a "muttonaire" by his friends. He fell in love with Ethel almost immediately and asked her to marry him. Although she declined, he was undaunted and began to court her, mostly by mail, a courtship that lasted nearly five years. His letters bearing the cancellation "Moneta, Wyoming" across their 2¢ stamps, followed her to Boulder, Colorado, where she earned an M.A. in literature, then to Kenosha, Wisconsin, where she taught Latin for a year in an Anglican girls' school, and to Pueblo, Colorado, for a high school teaching job. At last in 1910, she agreed to be his wife. Many years later, she told their children that she was attracted to him because he had the look of eagles.

John

As Ethel later wrote in "John," a chapter of her unfinished memoir, Life on the Rat:

John was born in Portage, Wisconsin, October 2, 1868,[2] to Scottish parents Barbara Galloway Love and John Watson Love, the youngest child and only boy in the family of five children. Barbara, a sister-in-law of John Muir the naturalist, died within a few days of her son's birth. Two grandmothers, aunts, and four sisters—Arabella, Laura, Georgia, and Amelia—cared for him, unwilling to hear "Barbara's bairn greet," but their father took all the children back to Scotland.[3]

John's father had had his own medical training at the University of Edinburgh,[4] and thought the schools much superior in Scotland. For a time the family lived on a palatial estate at Peacock Bank, County of Fife, until the property was lost by heirs on a greyhound race. Young John was put into the John Watson School in Edinburgh, his sisters in the corresponding school for girls.

Memorization was a key element in their instruction:

> Scots, wha hae wi Wallace bled
> Scots, wham Bruce has aften led;
> Welcome to your gory bed,
> Or to victory! . . .[5]

was a sample characteristic of the dreary ballads John used until the end of his life to pleasantly while away long drives. Sixty years later, he could still recite Walter Scott's "The Lady of the Lake" in its entirety, along with many other Scottish and English ballads. Debates, thunderous and clever, on any

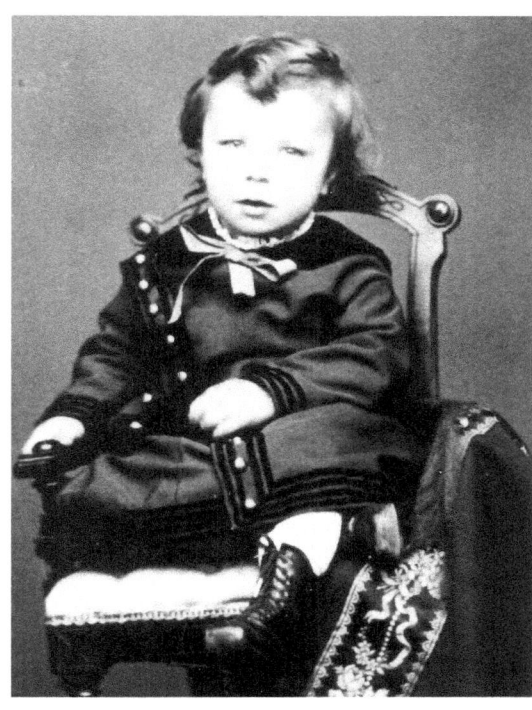

John Galloway Love, 1874.
Love Family Archives

John W. Love, 1882. Barbara Galloway Love and Amelia, 1868.
Love Family Archives

timely subject, rocked the household and taught the children self-expression. Public debates were popular in Scotland then, and John Watson Love participated in them with skill and enthusiasm. One morning[6] after young John, not yet in his teens, had listened to his father take part in a debate—and John said he never spoke better—he awoke to find his father dead beside him. Affairs were settled. Only enough was left to take the children back overseas to Wisconsin to be raised by relatives.

David, drawing on his mother's notes, later wrote in "A Part of Your Heritage":

When Arabella, Georgia, Laura, and Amelia were of college age, they moved to Nebraska to attend the university at Lincoln, teaching school to pay their way. As they reached the age of twenty-one, the girls all filed on homesteads west of Lincoln in the rich farm country near Sargent. Not yet old enough to homestead, young John worked for a time on his sisters' farms. In 1890 John enrolled at the University of Nebraska. The following spring, annoyed that the Dean paid more attention to his flowers than to his students, John planted a post in the administrator's flower garden. When John refused to name his accomplices, he was expelled. He decided to go west. Using all his savings, he bought a buggy and a pair of handsome black horses, packed his possessions in a small trunk, and drove west to Wyoming. Near the present town of Douglas, he camped for the night beside a spring. In the morning, both horses were dead, possibly from bad water, poisonous vegetation with high selenium content, or death camas,[7] all of which are present in that area. Abandoning his buggy and trunk beside his dead horses, John walked westward for a hundred miles to the Sweetwater country in central Wyoming. He was twenty-two years old.

Ethel's description of her husband's start in Wyoming continued:

John found work herding sheep in the Ferris Mountains for a Scotsman named Jack McTurk. There were few fences; central Wyoming was an open pastureland. Grass was long after the disastrous winter of 1888, which had put most of the large cattle companies out of business. John had charge of a herd of 5,000 head of two and three-year-old wethers,[8] moving them to Rawlins for shipping. Sheep wagons had not yet come into frequent use in the area. Herders in winter had side-walled tents or tepees, moving infrequently. Any man grazing sheep within four miles of another was "crowding."

As David wrote in "A Part of Your Heritage":

For seven years, in all seasons, John led a Spartan existence, sleeping on the range with the herds of sheep or cattle he was tending. Too poor or too Scottish to buy a tent, he felt that tents were for pilgrims, people passing through, not from the country. "There might not be one available when ye need it, laddies," he later told my brother and me, so we learned to do with-

John Galloway Love, 1890.
Love Family Archives

out. He slept in a "henskin," a bedroll of quilts in a canvas tarpaulin closed by spring hooks clipped into D-shaped rings. In cold weather he would pick a sheltered draw with a sandy bottom, build a brush fire, let it burn until the sand was hot, scrape away the fire, and lay his bedroll on the hot sand. One year he spent a total of $75.00.

Ethel's account added:

A large black umbrella was John's distinguishing badge on the range during his first years of herding. It made a good walking stick, he said. Braced on a hilltop, it gave him shelter from the sun, rain, and wind. Under it he sat, watching the sheep feed, and working them with his dogs. Through the long days, he read interminably and indiscriminately, and, like many other Scotsmen, he kept a worn copy of Bobby Burns' poems in his "sar sack," along with classics, poetry, novels, history, and trash.

Never had he let sheep get away from him, he boasted, and always had his tally, or the pelts of the few sheep killed by coyotes. For, in addition to the umbrella, wherever he went, he carried within reach a heavy Smith & Wesson .44 caliber pistol. He practiced constantly and was a splendid shot.

As a start in the sheep business, John ran a bunch of bucks for several sheep men. They paid by the head to have him take the bucks to the mountains in summer and return them in the fall. At $35 a month, getting a start was slow—wool at 5¢ a pound was close to giving it away.

David told the family that it was during this time that John met the legendary Shoshone* Chief Washakie. Impressed that his father had known the great chief, David once asked his father about him and later recounted this response:[9]

Wanting to run sheep in the Owl Creek Mountains on land belonging to the Indians, my father had to ask permission of Chief Washakie, and he and the aging Shoshone became friends. Legends abounded about the chief, and finally Dad asked the great man about one of them. Crowheart Butte, a cone-shaped butte southeast of the town of Dubois, Wyoming, was the site of a mortal combat between Chief Washakie and Big Robber, chief of the Crows, with whom the Shoshones had been warring over hunting grounds. Chief Washakie was reputed to have cut out the heart of the vanquished chief and eaten it on the spot.

When my father asked if the story were true, the great chief smiled. "Well, Johnnie, when one is young and full of life, one does foolish things."

Ethel finished her chapter on John by saying:

Eventually, John put the flatiron brand on his own sheep—one, two, then three bands of the woolies—and gradually bought cattle and a few horses. At last he was "on top of the world with a down-hill pull."

In his effort to get ahead, as he later told his sons, John gambled on weather, his own strength, and the endurance of his extraordinary horse, Big Red, on whom he made a grueling ride to deliver sheep to one buyer and then returned to the bank to secure financing for his ranch (Chapter 14). Winters were good, the market rose, and on December 7, 1897, he filed on a homestead site on Muskrat Creek.

Building the Ranch

David wrote of the ranch beginnings in "A Part of Your Heritage":

"Why did you homestead in that God-forsaken, lonesome place?" his friends asked John. With calm assurance he would reply: "Because it has what I want."

The fertile, watered valleys were already settled, and he needed space, lots of space, in which to expand. He had first filed on a site in the Big Sand Draw area, 30 miles southwest of his present ranch, but relinquished it when he found the water to be bad, the snow deep, and the grass sparse. (Twenty years later it became the site of the Big Sand Draw oil and gas field, which

---

*Although both spellings are common, Shoshone is usually used for the tribe and its members in Wyoming; Shoshoni is the spelling for the town, bank, and some geographic features.

has yielded considerably more than 100 million dollars' worth of oil and gas and is still a profitable producer.) He chose instead the treeless bowl of prairie through which Muskrat Creek flowed, 12 miles from the geographical center of the state.

It may have been during this time that Dad became friends with a man named George Leroy Parker, although Dad always called him "Butch Cassidy." This friendship is one of the family mysteries. How did they come to know each other? How did my father finance his ranch? Was it a coincidence that Dad's homestead on Muskrat Creek was mid-way between Butch's hide-out at Hole-in-the-Wall (so named because of the notch in a circular wall of red sandstone rimmed with Alcova limestone) and Crooks Gap, 80 miles to the southwest, where Butch's lady friend lived along the Sweetwater River? It was not unusual for Butch to spend the night at this midpoint.

Shortly after the turn of the century, Butch disappeared, said to have gone to South America. The lady friend died a few years later under mysterious circumstances.

When my parents met in 1905, Butch had been gone for two or three years. How much did Dad tell Mother about this friendship? Did Dad and Butch ever meet again? Mother's notes, undated, said: "Butch Cassidy, rustler and train robber, spent a night with John in sheep camp."

On the few occasions when Butch's name was mentioned at our ranch, Dad always replied: "Butch was a fine man. He never killed anyone as far as I knew, but he may have nicked a few." Years later Mother donated a rawhide rope Cassidy had left behind to the Casper Historical Society.

In 1900, Dad acquired state leases, which, with his other land, gave him control of eight miles of Muskrat Creek, the only intermittently flowing stream in the region. Stough Spring[10] flows a few gallons per day into Muskrat Creek south of the ranch barn, and was then the only potable water in the region.

My parents also filed on two desert claims[11] of 320 acres each. To keep this desert acreage, Dad had to develop a water supply sufficient to grow and harvest enough barley, wheat, or rye to satisfy the legal requirements of "proving up" on his claims. Dad planned his ranch carefully. Fir, cedar, and pine were used for fences and corral posts. Despite being planted in high silica soil, some are still in place after 100 years.

Ethel's notes for Life on the Rat *described the ranch buildings:*

Logs for the ranch house had grown in the forests of the Wind River Mountains, 100 miles away. They were cut, hauled, and built into a house 50 miles away in a lonely draw. John bought the house. He and a hand named Smithy spent one winter taking it to pieces, moving and rebuilding it where it now sits on Muskrat Creek, using, John said, 500 pounds of nails. Many more pounds had been driven in halfway for hanging anything that could hang. Sand from Muskrat Creek mixed with lime and horse manure chinked the logs of the ranch house. The windowpanes were of distorted glass, pocked with random bubbles of air.

The town of Old Muskrat, 18 miles northwest of the ranch, had been a halfway station on the 150-mile stage line between Casper and Lander. The stage road crossed Muskrat Creek 28 miles below where John later put his ranch house. "Near enough," was his opinion. With a permanent population of—not to exaggerate—perhaps half a dozen people, the town had consisted of shearing pens, barn, saloon, hotel, and a store containing a post office.

Old timers said that the Old Muskrat storekeeper kept a monkey, briefly, popular with all the men. On election day, the voters, dissatisfied with one of the candidates, declared that the monkey was the better man, and put up Jocko's name for a county office. He carried the precinct unanimously.

Old Muskrat was abandoned when the stageline, and consequently the post office, were discontinued. My husband bought the town for 50 dollars. That fall his men moved it to our ranch with horses and wagons, although it still appeared on most of the maps of Wyoming, even the one in the *Encyclopædia Britannica International* of 1916. At that time the town had not existed for ten years.

Moneta, established 30 miles northeast of Old Muskrat, thrived and grew, a halfway station when the Chicago-Northwestern Railroad extended its tracks in 1906 from Casper to Lander, passing 15 miles north of the Love ranch. It became our nearest link to the Outside World.

The Old Muskrat saloon became our respectable hay house. A smaller log building was the bunkhouse. Equipped with bunk beds, a pot-bellied stove, and furnishings for eight to ten men, our bunkhouse was the social hub for the working men in the area. A large g-shaped iron meat hook hung from the ceiling. A horizontal stretching bar extended across a door jam, from which tired cowboys hung to stretch out the compacted spaces between their vertebrae and realign their innards after long rides. The four doors of the old Muskrat hotel, which we called the long building, facing south, opened into the men's kitchen, harness, grain, and trunk rooms. The hotel dining room was moved beside the ranch house to make a living room. The post office boxes hung on our storeroom wall for odds and ends of hardware, bolts, and screws. A painting filled the window frame on the west wall, its sheet-iron back holding the outside elements at bay. Salvaged from the Old Muskrat Saloon, and entitled: "Going, Going, Gone!" it depicted three cowboys in various stages of inebriation to advertise the popular Red Top Rye whiskey.

SUPPLY WAGON →

← HIGH WATER MARK ON LITTLE DAM RESERVOIR

LONG BUILDING
↓

BUNK HOUSE →

BUGGY
↑
← BUGGY SHED

STORE HOUSE
↑

← RESERVOIR BEHIND LITTLE DAM

MAIN RANCH HOUSE
↓

SHEEP WAGON
HONEYMOON

← ICE HOUSE

Love ranch in 1910 left to right (west to east): ice house, honeymoon sheep wagon, main ranch house, store house, buggy shed, bunkhouse, long building, two sheep wagons, and supply wagons. In the foreground are Muskrat Creek and the reservoir behind the Little Dam. Ethel wrote: "The ranch buildings, of logs or unpainted boards, facing south, followed the curve of the creek in a long arc, 300 yards long. To the east, beyond the edge of the photograph, against a bank of the creekbed, were the hay house, cow sheds, chicken house, barn and granary, somewhat sheltered by the terrace from the ever-present wind. In front of these buildings were the horse corrals and weaning pen for calves, extending 100 yards south to Muskrat Creek."

Love Family Archives

On the terrace, beyond the cowboys' privy and bunkhouse, were the sheep shearing pens, and a wool-tramping tower ten feet tall. Farther east were the animal buildings and a complex of corrals, a preferred venue for roundup crews in the area. Two 100-foot wings of horizontal poles funneled livestock into the largest corral, to then be culled into a smaller, round or "action" corral, where such violent procedures as horse breaking took place. The corral had pole sides ten feet high and no angles where cowboys or livestock could be injured, its snubbing post in the center as polished from rope burns as a piece of fine furniture. Rarely did John break a horse by force, and seldom did he use a lariat rope. Speaking in a low voice, he could walk up to even a wild range horse, and they did not shy away. However, many cowboys expressed their manhood by "topping off," or trying to ride, a wild bronc in the action corral.

Next to the sod-roofed granary, a gulch, usually dry, drained from the meadow to Muskrat Creek. Some wag had put up a sign, "Bear Creek, look out for steamboats." Beside Bear Creek, the road from Moneta swept down the low hill, circling past the long building, bunkhouse, buggy shed, store house, and blacksmith shop to the ranch house.

David noted in "A Part of Your Heritage":

The patent on the Love ranch was granted August 5, 1905, signed by a functionary in the administration of Theodore Roosevelt, the "real" Roosevelt as Dad called him in later years. At the turn of the century, when the use of federal land had no grazing fees attached, only areas along and adjacent to water were homesteaded, and therefore taxable. The free use of associated federal land made the difference between profit and loss to the livestock industry.[12] Meeting Mother in November of 1905 added impetus to Dad's drive to complete his ranch, and to do that, he needed water.

During the nearly ten years that Dad had been building his ranch, he had carefully observed the volume and depth of Muskrat Creek in all seasons. The perpetual flow of clear alkaline water in Muskrat Creek was about 200,000 gallons per day, enough for ranch use, but not for irrigation. Despite his lack of experience, Dad began to build what he called the Little Dam, about 1,000 feet downstream from the ranch buildings. He laid an oval concrete pipe, four feet in diameter, to bring water from the reservoir side under a steel headgate to a ditch, which would spread water over the valley floor to the west. Of silt, sand, and clay, the completed dam was 700 feet long, with a height of 15 feet.

The reservoir, while it lasted, was the only open water for many miles, and became a haven for migrating wild ducks. The reservoir was a source of ice as well. The spring of 1909, Dad wrote to Mother that he had cut and buried ten tons of ice in sawdust in the ice house to preserve the meat from butchered animals during the summer. The reservoir was also a breeding ground for mosquitoes, which the prevailing southwest winds carried to the house in swarms.

Dad soon discovered that during normal runoff years the Little Dam did not contain enough water to irrigate all the crops downstream. By hand he dug a well fifteen feet deep and eight feet square, boxed it with planks, and installed a steel-towered windmill in the front yard. The windmill could pump 50,000 gallons of alkaline water per day, enough to maintain a small alfalfa field and fruit trees in summer. But this was not enough. He made plans to build a Big Dam and reservoir, two miles downstream from the Little Dam. Ed Crabb, a surveyor from Shoshoni, surveyed the site and filed a Reservoir Application on May 28, 1908. The area of the reservoir was to be 40.3 acres, its estimated cost: $3,500. No motorized earth-moving equipment was available.

Using his need to see a dentist as an excuse, my father visited Mother in Colorado often—at least once a year. Hoping that her "no's" were not "no's," but "maybe's," in 1909, he had his ranch hands dig flowerbeds all around the ranch house, and ordered a new sheep wagon to be built with Mother's comfort in mind.

Dad's livestock survived the winter of 1908–1909 well—until April, when spring storms killed 400 lambs in 40 days. Then a mysterious disease sent several thousand sheep, from one to fifty per day, to join what he called "the silent majority." Frantically, he doctored them with cresoleum dip, sulphate of copper, sulphate of mercury, carbolic acid, and iodine in a vain attempt to cure the leg and lip ulcerations. A veterinary surgeon from Washington ventured that the sheep had eaten plants that caused hydrocyanic acid to form in the fourth stomach. Despite his losses, Dad wrote to Mother that he was starting the winter with 11,500 sheep, 200 cattle, and 100 horses, as well as assorted cats, dogs, chickens, and geese. He anticipated full recovery by the following spring.

However, it was not to be. The winter of 1909–1910 was long and difficult. Teaching and living in rented rooms was becoming wearisome for Mother. For Dad, it was the first of four disastrous winters. Not only did he lose sheep, but one of his herders died of exposure during the storm of New Year's 1910.

In April 1910, Dad visited Mother in Pueblo, and once more asked her to marry him. To his astonished delight, she accepted. When he wrote to Dr. Waxham to formally ask for his daughter's hand, he was able to say not only that he loved her deeply but, despite his losses of the previous year, he had ample resources to provide a good life for her. These resources, wrung from the land by hard work, frugal living, ingenuity, and luck, consisted of the ranch of several thousand acres, its livestock and equipment, all free of debt, with a value in post-F.D. Roosevelt dollars of approximately $5 million. The future looked rosy indeed. Many years later he told us: "She waited until I was going bankrupt to marry me."

No letters or journals explain Ethel's change of heart. She was almost twenty-eight years old, and John was forty-one. In one of her last letters to him before the wedding, she mentioned "the unsettled condition of things at home," referring to the approaching marriage of her father to Helen Welles Elliott, sister of his previous wife, Alice. John Love had remained one of the few constants in her post-college life.

He gave her generous and beautiful gifts: a Tiffany-mounted diamond solitaire ring to wear beside her wide gold wedding band, a gold and diamond starburst brooch for her lapel, a tiny platinum Elgin watch, and a saddle, custom-made for her small frame, with silver-plated safety stirrups, which could open to release her feet in case of trouble. Without question, he provided the references her father requested when he formally asked for her hand. He gave her his promise as well: that if she did not like living on the ranch, they would move wherever she wanted to go, even, perhaps, Europe. But here, together, he was sure they could build a ranch empire.

A flurry of letters passed between them before the wedding. John's tailor in Omaha had lost his measurements, so no new suit could be made. John feared that Ethel would be worn out with the wedding preparations, and was relieved that the ceremony would be simple and short. What would she think of his ranch, which still was not finished to his satisfaction? Ethel was unsure of the spelling of John's middle name for the announcements. She would forego buying "finery" until they could go to Paris, a dream which remained a dream. And not even for him, whom she called nihil nisi bonum [nothing but the best], would she choose July 4th as a wedding date, as that was Independence Day. He was far from being the "best," he replied, but he promised to do his utmost to deserve her love and affection while life lasted, as that would be about as near to heaven as he was likely to get. He then switched to more practical matters: tablecloths for the sheep wagon.

They were married the afternoon of June 20, 1910, Ethel wearing a white "lingerie" gown and her mother's wedding veil. The only surviving photograph of the wedding day, cracked and peeling, shows Ethel in her "going-away" clothes: a high-necked blouse and broad-brimmed hat, and John in a dark suit, white shirt, tie, and the "Old Indestructible," his Stetson hat. After a small reception with only family and a few friends present, they departed on the seven o'clock train to Wyoming.

Notes

1. Much of the information in this section is also found in the prologue to *Lady's Choice*, but with editing and revisions from further research during the years since publication in 1993.

2. The family previously thought John had been born October 2, 1870, the date listed on various official and insurance forms. Subsequent research by Jordan Love on Ancestry.com, however, showed that John's mother Barbara died October 5, 1868. His age recorded in the census records in 1870, 1885, and 1900 is consistent with the 1868 birthdate. After his marriage to Ethel, perhaps to minimize their fourteen-year age difference, he used the 1870 date on all further census records.

3. Infant John evidently stayed with his grandparents and aunts in Wisconsin while his father took the older children back to Scotland. He is listed in the 1870 census, but the others are not. Immigration records show John Sr. returning to America in 1870, presumably to fetch his young son and return with him to Scotland.

4. John Watson Love enrolled in medical studies for two years at the University of Edinburgh, but never graduated. Instead, he became a photographer, lecturer, orator, and world traveler. In "Letter from Jerusalem," published in the *British Millennial Harbinger*, 1853, he describes his travels across Palestine. He gave lectures about his travels, illustrated with glass slides. Unfortunately, any records of these were lost after his death.

5. Robert Burns, "Scots Wha Hae" (1793). In *English Romantic Poetry & Prose*, ed. Russell Noyes. New York: Oxford University Press, 1956: 166.

6. January 3, 1880.

7. *Toxicoscordion venenosum*.

8. Castrated bucks or rams.

9. Oral history, also included in John McPhee's *Rising from the Plains*, pp. 37–38.

10. Named for an early sheriff of Fremont County, rhymes with "plow."

11. Land with no natural water supply.

12. This tenuous balance changed in the 1930s with the passage of the Taylor Grazing Act.

CHAPTER ONE

~

1910

"Rome Was Not Built in a Day"

In a chapter titled "Rome Was Not Built in a Day" from Life on the Rat, *Ethel wrote of her introduction to marriage and life on the ranch:*

"Is it true," I asked John, "that it is necessary to kill a Scotsman or agree with him?"

"No," he answered, whether from guile or innocence I never knew.

It was true that we were married June 20, 1910, at my father's house in Denver, and he took me to his ranch on Muskrat Creek.

Twenty miles of barbed wire fence enclosed roughly the patented and leased land. Through eight miles of it Muskrat Creek meandered northward, flooded, raged, trickled or slowly dried, depending upon the time of year, snow and rain, or lack of them. "Muskrat Creek," John spoke of it with pride. For brevity or invective, he called it, "The Rat."

Salt sage, June grass, red top, grama, and nutritious buffalo grass furnished a variety of feed for his sheep and cattle. Greasewood, whose bright green color belies the nutritional value of its spiny bushes, and sagebrush in the draws gave shelter. A wild hay meadow, in which were springs and swampy bog holes, spread out toward a low bluff, a landmark for miles.

The complete emptiness of the country, treeless, from horizon to horizon, gave me a deeper respect for the men who could endure and make use of the range.

> I am monarch of all I survey,
> My right there is none to dispute . . .[1]

1

John used to chant on our all-day rides that first summer, he on his tall, spirited sorrel, Punch, and I on Kentucky, a lively, little black single-footer.[2]

While the ranch house was being completed, we lived in his new sheep wagon, blue painted and fresh. It was comfortable for two people, but a little small for two people and a dog, especially a wet dog.

A peculiarly offensive smell began to trouble me. Something, perhaps a mouse, had died in the wagon, I thought. In a few days I suspected that it was a cat. When I was sure it must be larger, I asked John hesitantly, "Did a dog die here?"

He sniffed. "Oh," he answered, "Sourdough!" He lifted the lid of a cupboard under a seat, rummaged inside, and brought out a covered pail, with that overpowering odor. "Kept too long," he commented.

David explained more about the early days of his parents' marriage in "A Part of Your Heritage":

The couple had planned to spend their honeymoon taking John's sheep to the Absaroka mountains for summer grazing, and later visiting Yellowstone Park. They would live in the sheep wagon John had had specially built. Afterward, they never discussed their honeymoon with their children, except in some oblique way. At times of chaos, mud, rain, shouting, swearing men, and struggling, frightened horses, Ethel would smile wanly and say, "Just like our honeymoon!" After two weeks of bad weather, they had only just reached the mountains—a trip that normally took four days. The horses were exhausted, the bride and groom disheartened. The annual horse and cattle roundups were imminent and John had to be on hand so, reluctantly, they abandoned their honeymoon and returned to the ranch. Nearly twenty more years would pass before they would visit Yellowstone Park together.

Once back at the ranch, Ethel described some of the other residents in "Rome Was Not Built in A Day":

Peggy Macbeth, whiskered, wooden-legged, and Irish, stumped to the sheep wagon with our meals. He cooked in the bunkhouse for the men John had working on the ranch, George, Lem, Toby, and Rollicky Dick. When John was gone for several days at a time on affairs to do with lost sheep, Peggy was my only company. His favorite story was about the mistake that ruined his life. Years before in Colorado Springs, he was working at a carpenter's bench with Winfield Scott Stratton. Said Stratton to him, "Come to Cripple Creek[3] with me, Macbeth. We'll make our fortune in the mines." But Macbeth, not "Peggy" then, decided to go to Salt Lake City, where there was plenty of work on new construction. Stratton went to Cripple Creek. His Independence gold mine made a million dollars. Macbeth, in Salt Lake City, fell from a scaffold and lost his leg. "Sure, if I'd had the second sight, it's a two legged millionaire I might 'a' bin."

Peggy still was able to saddle old Brownie and ride out with the .12-gauge shotgun. In an hour he brought back enough young sage chickens for dinner. A far from clean flour sack tied about his lower middle, he fried chicken and poached eggs to perfection; he turned a fine flapjack and baked good bread. Outside the bunkhouse door on a chair, he set the large, round pan of bread dough to rise in the sun. He covered the dough with a flour sack. On this soft warm spot the mother cat enjoyed her naps. But I did not lose my appetite for bread until I saw him washing out the homemade wooden bread box, using dish water and the floor broom.

Before I came, the house was used by a family who had been hired to cook for the cowboys. With no idea of sanitation, they had used a corner of the master bedroom closet in place of the outhouse. Odors, referred to by our family as "the ghost," returned for years in damp weather as reminders of these former occupants. A visitor who ate with them offered a dollar for his meal. "Take it," he advised, "and buy fly paper."

My first glance inside the house showed it to be alive with bedbugs. Thousands were crawling by daylight over furniture, walls, lamps and ceilings. Without delay, John and I made preparations to fumigate. We blocked stovepipe holes, stuffed all openings and cracks about doors and windows with rags and papers. In the middle of each room we put a heavy pan, half full of rocks and sand; on this a smaller pan of burning coals. Over the coals we poured quantities of powdered sulphur, probably many times what we needed. Then coughing and choking, we hurried outside, and watched the fumes spread, the house darken, and flies fall dead on the sills. For a few days we left the house sealed. When I fearfully opened the door, not a bedbug was in sight. I never saw one again.

Then work could begin on the house. After experiments using an earth augur and sand point, John triumphantly installed a pitcher pump in the kitchen, a sink, and a drainpipe to a barrel, buried in the ground at some distance from the house. This was the best, the first, and at that time the only, water system in an area the size of Rhode Island.

Handsome Rollicky Dick Felton and Toby Leitch laid a new kitchen floor. They completed the ceiling, where a sizable gap was still left between lengths of wallboard. They recalled admiringly how the mother cat used to jump from the rafters to the table, piled high with dishes, and never break a cup.

"Goosie" Hastings had cleaned railroad engines, so John pitted him against the kitchen range for four days. The range won.

Peggy tried to promote his own ideas of elegance; for instance, red and blue glass squares around the front door. When diverted to bookshelves, he designed what he importantly, but erroneously, called "show cases." There was, truly, an ample show of molding, and expert carpentry, but the six small glass doors revealed only about half of the books on the shelves.

David's oral history added details about the family's reading material:

Our family's ever-growing library ranged from Plutarch to Proust. We also subscribed to the Sunday New York Times, and such magazines as the Reader's Digest and Saturday Evening Post, which often arrived a month late. When we had read them cover to cover, they were passed to others, as there was always a shortage of reading material on the range.

Ethel's description of the house in "Rome Was Not Built in A Day" continued:

The bookcases, three on a side, flanked the fireplace. This was to have a chimney behind it. John predicted cheerfully, "Someone will come along who can do stone work." So he and I drove a team hitched to what he dubbed a "stone boat"4 to haul loads of red conglomerate rock to be ready for the hoped-for, unknown stone mason. Eventually he arrived. He only thought he could do stone work, but his knowledge did not extend to making a foundation for the base of the heavy chimney, nor to building it above the eaves. It soon began to tip away from the walls. The fireplace did nothing but smoke, until someone had the inspiration to top the chimney with two lengths of cement tiling. Then a fire in the small grate raised the temperature of the large living room, but no more than ten degrees.

In "A Part of Your Heritage," David reflected on other adjustments Ethel faced in the early days of ranch life:

Although Mother had spent six months at the Mills' Ranch, she was ill-prepared for the isolation of the ranch on Muskrat Creek. The closest neighbors were 13 miles away. Moneta was a 30-mile round trip by buggy. Lander, site of the Fremont county seat and the nearest doctor, was 70 miles across country from the ranch, 100 miles by road. The trip took two days, and we usually spent the night with friends.

Shoshoni, with the Union Pacific and a spur of the Chicago, Burlington & Quincy Railroad, was a departure point from which livestock and copper, gold, and silver ore were shipped out of the state. Its transient population supported 26 saloons, a doctor, and the only blacksmith shop in the area. The trip was 26 miles across country each way, so Dad usually went alone.

It was a happy summer. Mother and Dad, when he could spare the time, rode to all the places of interest within 30 miles of the ranch. They visited Delfelder's Buck Camp, 18 miles from the Love ranch, a rendezvous point for the sheepherders and campmovers in the region, and culling place where male sheep, or bucks, were kept separate from the ewes and lambs. They delighted in the Indian petroglyphs in the yellow and white sandstone cliffs of Castle Gardens. They found arrowheads, war clubs, and occasional human bones at sites of Indian battlegrounds and camps near waterholes. They probed the buffalo wallows in the wild hay meadow for the bones of bison, prehistoric and modern, and visited the Tar Springs[5] at the base of the Beaver Divide, where an oil well was drilled and abandoned years before.

Ethel described her early exploration of the ranch environs in "Rome Was Not Built in a Day":

John showed me the pool of tar, the incentive for the drilling. On the black surface were the bodies of birds and small animals, so encased in tar as to be almost unrecognizable, possible fossils of future ages.

A mile from our house, beside the meadow fence, were the ruts of an old freight road. It led about 150 miles from the Big Horn Basin, down Bridger Creek and on beyond our ranch into Rawlins. John had found rusty ox shoes upon it, from ox teams hauling wool over the road.

Sebastian Pfalzar, who herded for John, picked up an assortment of buffalo horns which had lain half-buried in the ground around the range. They were weathered and rough. He filed off the frayed exterior and spent his evenings shaving and smoothing the horns with pieces of broken glass until they shone like ebony. He paired and mounted them on heart-shaped varnished boards, connecting the bases of the horns with dark red, blue, or green velvet.[6] He mounted one, two, or three pairs on each heart and gave us several sets for a wedding present. They made a handsome showing on our living room walls. "Old Buffalo Horns," as Sebastian was nicknamed, when asked to sell his work, inquired, "What I do with the money?" then answered himself, "Get drunk. Better I give them away."

Remembering her days as a newly married woman, Ethel later wrote "The Old Indestructible":

"Don't you need a new hat?" I asked John as I watched him in the living room toss upon the mounted black buffalo horns his sweat-stained, battered Stetson with a 3-inch hole in the crown. He looked at me in pained surprise. "When a hat gets like this, it is Indestructible. Nothing can damage it."

"Like a cracked plate."

"Anyway I can always wear another to town. Come and see." He took me to his trunk in our bedroom. He removed the tray. Stetsons, wide-brimmed, new and expensive, filled the whole trunk. Several were black, the others varied in shape and shades of tan. All were size 7¾.

Living room at the Love ranch in the 1920s. The statue of Venus on the mantle was always a matter of conjecture for the children. A pair of Sebastian Pfalzar's buffalo horns is on the wall at the left end of the mantle.
Love Family Archives

I gasped at the thought that this might have been his idea of preparation for marriage. The actual fact came to light not long afterwards, when a horse roundup stopped overnight at the ranch.

"The saddle string is gone! Not a darn cayuse[7] in sight," exclaimed Omar Kanson, boss of the roundup, coming to the door. "They must have broke down the meadow fence."

"They are in the meadow, all right," John assured him. "I'll find them for you."

"What'll you bet?"

"A hat." A hat was always a Stetson.

Picking up a short length of lead rope, John went to the meadow, followed by the cowboys. "Beyond this rise is a low swale. You can't see into it from the hill by the house. We'll find the horses there." Standing quietly were the dozen horses, head to tail, swishing away the flies from each other.

Omar gave John another new hat to add to the supply that was to last for thirty years.

While John's gambling was limited to occasional stakes of a hat, he habitually risked life, limb, and labor on uncertainties of weather, markets, sheep, horses, and undependable men. He disregarded the advice of Lem who moved camp and played cribbage with him: "Never bet, except on a sure thing."

Lem was the son of "Tricky" Harold, who lived by his wits.

"Sure would like to go to that island, Monte Carlo." Lem told John, "where they have that big time gambling."

"Island?" John asked. "Mainland, near France."

"My dad went by boat to get there. Bet you a hat."

"Done."

The next day, uneasily, Lem asked to go to Shoshoni.

Back in his sheepwagon, he said to John. "I'll call off that bet we had about Monte Carlo. Been thinking it over, might not be an island after all, just a point o' land."

Without his "Old Indestructible," as other hats became in turn, and his cotton gloves, or well-worn roping gloves of the best leather, John never left the house. Even in the middle of the night when the bunkhouse was burning, he rushed about calling, "Where's my hat? Where's my gloves?"

The second large flood on Muskrat [in 1937] caught him in bed. When the Rat was on the rampage, I always stayed up, reading, between trips outdoors to measure the rise of the water. Usually the crest came about 2 A.M. That night the sudden surge of the flood had his boots bobbing in the water by the time I wakened him—but he saved hat and gloves before the boots.

"When St. Peter blows his horn," I predicted, "You'll be hin'most, looking for the Old Indestructible and your gloves."

Time changes all things. Years later when our boys were married and our daughter was in college, John was irrigating trees and flowers, carrots and chard about the house. He was sweating in the heat, but faithfully wearing his Stetson. Omar rode to the gate. In his hand was a straw hat, high crowned and ventilated.

"Cool," he remarked at John's astonished glance. "Big enough to keep wet leaves at the top."

On our next trip to Riverton John bought for himself a straw hat like the one Omar wore. We saw in the store two Arapaho Indians outfitting themselves for a rodeo. Above their working overalls shone satin shirts; above them on their short black hair were felt hats of cerise and orange. I realized then with a pang of regret that the Old West was gone.

One of the stock phrases on the range was: "Let's go to Loves and have something good to eat." Visitors brought news of the Outside World, and were always welcomed with food, lodging and hospitality. One visit was never forgotten either by hosts or guests. Late one hot evening that summer of 1910, a wagon rolled in from the south. The Reverend Theodore Sedgwick and several students had come from Boston to spread the Gospel. In Rawlins, joined by Bishop Nathaniel Thomas of the Episcopal diocese of Wyoming, they had rented a spring wagon and driven north. Capturing Rev. Sedgwick's eastern accent with her pen, Ethel wrote of their visit in "Gospel Wagon":

The Gospel Wagon was a light rig, loaded with camp equipment, several clergymen and students. One evening they pulled their team to a stop by the long building where Peggy Macbeth went out to meet them. (He later declared that if he'd known they were preachers, he'd have locked everything up!)

Bishop Thomas had planned the trip, and started the men from Rawlins to spread the Gospel among isolated ranches. After holding services at several places, they had become lost in the maze of little-used tracks across the Sweetwater Divide. Finally they had reached Muskrat Creek and the Love ranch. They wanted water, food, and a place to sleep. For a day and a half, Mr. Sedgwick said, they had been without bread and water, "and crackers, you know, without woetah go whoo!" They had found a herder camped by what they considered a stagnant pool and asked him for a drink. "'Help yourself,' he said, 'It's good water.' And to prove his assertion, he filled a rusty tin can, and drank before our very eyes. We thought he looked healthy, and if he could drink the water, we might manage a day or two by boiling it." But Mr. Sedgwick had seen enough of the empty country. "I have a wife and babies at home and a good bed, and I'm going back to them." Before they left for Moneta, he took a picture of John and myself beside the windmill. Later he sent us a copy of *The Spirit of Missions* containing his story of the expedition, which concluded:

> On one occasion we had lost our way. It was toward the second day of wandering without much food and no water. We had traveled fifty miles, when, to our great satisfaction, we saw a distant building. It meant water. At this lonely ranch, in the midst of a sandy desert we found a young woman. Her husband had gone for the day over the range. Around her neck hung a gold chain with a Phi Beta Kappa key. She was a graduate of Wellesley College, and was now a Wyoming bride. She knew her Greek and Latin, and loved her horse on the care-free prairie."[8]

By the end of August, Ethel discovered that she was expecting a baby. Delighted, she and John hastened to finish the ranch house before winter, while the hired men worked primarily with the livestock. The only income came from livestock; therefore, stock had first priority. She suffered a miscarriage about the end of September.

Mr. and Mrs. John G. Love at the Love ranch in the summer of 1910. The caption in the Spirit of Missions (November 1910) reads: "Around the bride's neck hung a Phi Beta Kappa Key."

Photograph and excerpts from "A Church Wagon in Southern Wyoming," published in *The Spirit of Missions*, Vol. 75, no. 11, 1910.

Ethel continued her description of finishing the house in "Rome Was Not Built in a Day":

To speed the work, John and I—inept as I was at tools—began to make the opening between the living room-to-be and the dining room. A window on the side wall made the start easier. He in one room and I in the other, labored at the handles of the six-foot saw to cut the wide doorway.

"We'll be a long time getting into the house at this rate," I ventured.

"Rome was not built in a day," John answered easily. It was the first of the many times this philosophical remark backfired.

Eventually, our big ranch house was shaped like an inverted "T" with stem pointing north, but with additions sprouting off in various directions. It was about 55 feet long and 40 feet wide, and was split up into 11 rooms. When I arrived, the dining room was partly attached to the house in a casual way, left without a floor, with a huge gap in the side, for future reference. The largest gambling table, with its slot on the dealer's side, a left-over from the Joe Lacey Saloon at Old Muskrat, I painted brown, covered with a bright, block-printed cloth from India to hold books and magazines. The smaller one was used on the porch. Later my children used it to study their lessons. The gambling stool saw service in the kitchen.

Peggy finished the doorframe before the thirst caught up with him. His paycheck in his pocket, he left for the lure of Shoshoni. There, drunk, he fell from a wagon, as he had from the scaffold in Salt Lake City. This time he was killed.

By Thanksgiving Day John and I moved into the house; one bedroom was clean and ready. Rolls of green-figured wallpaper had arrived from a mail order company. What to do with them no one quite knew, but there were directions. I made dishpans full of paste. In the evening John called in the half-dozen cowboys from the bunkhouse. They carried planks and benches. They put all the leaves in the wobbly dinner table. I measured and cut, pasted and trimmed lengths of wallpaper. Then in chaps and jingling spurs the cow punchers strode along the benches, slapping paste brushes and dangling strips of torn wall paper over the dining room ceiling. We were all surprised and tremendously pleased with the results and celebrated over a ten-gallon keg of cider.

Through the years, many a Jack, Slim, Red, or Chuck who stopped over-night, delayed by the weather, found himself nailing a quarter round along the top of a wall, making a shelf, or cutting another window opening. Toby Leitch consulted a list I kept in the kitchen for stormy day jobs. When he left, at various times, the gates opened, shut, and latched, the weaning pen was repaired, the fifth of our outside doors was removed, and a solid wall replaced the opening. The sixteen-foot square kitchen was diminished by

Dining room at the Love ranch, 1919. Note the wallpaper.
Love Family Archives

a pantry and a washing alcove along one side. A small table was hinged to the wall.

David added in "A Part of Your Heritage":

Gradually the house was furnished and decorated. A brass door-knocker, a replica of a gargoyle from the Cathedral de Notre Dame de Paris in France, came from Ethel's Wellesley friend, Florence Risley, affectionately known as Big Bear. Two soft, spotted bobcat rugs, a tanned brown pinto hide, a gray horsehide and that of a giant wolf, killed by my father some years before, decorated the floors.

Although on a seemingly isolated ranch, Ethel kept a record of some of their visitors in "Wagon Wheels":

Whether the house was finished or not, the guests continued to come. Three stockmen, state representatives, were familiar figures at the ranch. Sheep owners stopped, campmovers, herders. "Goosie" Hastings, who became a national champion bronco buster, returned from time to time to help with the dishes or bounce our boys on his knee. Trappers related stories of animals; freighters spoke of ox-team days. Occasionally there were silent Indians at our table.

There were few women on the Wyoming range in 1910, but their presence influenced the behavior of cowhands and ranch bosses alike. Hats were always tipped or doffed when the wearer encountered a lady, and removed when entering a house or church. Hats and spurs were never worn to the table. Strong language was modified. Ethel noted in "Someone Will Come Along":

I saw few women in the first years, none perhaps for a month; once it was six months.

When I walked through the shearing shed to see how shearing was done, to my puzzlement a man near the door called loudly, "Church time!" The sudden silence was appalling.

Washing was always a problem, with no conveniences, but different solutions. Said the thrifty Mormon owner of 2,000 sheep to his herder, who had asked him for a washtub:

"What do you want of a washtub? I've lived 20 years in a wagon and never needed no tub. If you ain't able to climb in over the wagon tongue, I'll get you a box. You'd ruin a tub. Do you know what them tubs cost? You kin wash your clothes without no tub."

"A fella likes a bath sometimes. Don't you?"

"Sure, I bathe reg'lar."

"What in?"

"Why, the dish pan, o'course."

The men, after some treatment of their clothes in a galvanized iron tub on the ground, draped their garments over greasewood bushes to dry. John used to accumulate laundry in a seamless sack, which, when full, he took to some town for semi-professional aid. After trying that method which returned my crêpe dress stiffly starched and ironed, the napkins bright blue, I heard of a colored woman named Hattie, who lived in Shoshoni and did washing. I sent a sack of clothes to her. A month passed and much more before they came back. Hattie had been arrested on a vagrancy charge, I think it was called. In court, rumor said, the judge asked her where she lived.

"Why you knows, Jedge, you-all bin there lots o' times." (Laughter in the court.) Hattie was sent to jail. I feared what was no doubt impossible, for I was small (5'2", less than 100 lbs.) and Hattie was not, but I had the horrid thought that she wore my clothes during her sentence. In shame, thereafter I struggled with my own washing. The next year added the difficulty of a baby's washing, so I bought the tools of the trade, clothes lines, pins, a basket, wringer, and hand washing machine.

As the family grew, so did the house, with an entry here, and a bathroom there, though minus a water supply; more bedrooms, a wall of closets, French doors between dining room and living room, kitchen cupboards, a cement[9] walk to the gate; after many years a wind charger and electric lights; periodical papering, painting, and roof repair. The house was never finished, but for thirty-seven years Rome was a-building.

Notes

1. William Cowper, "The Solitude of Alexander Selkirk." In F. T. Palgrave's *The Golden Treasury of English Songs and Lyrics*, ed. Oscar Williams. New York: Mentor Books, 1961.

2. A horse with a gait where it lifts up and then places each foot separately instead of moving two feet at the same time.

3. Colorado.

4. A heavy, sled-like conveyance.

5. Later known as Oil Mountain.

6. Salvaged from a brothel in Hudson.

7. Horse.

8. The Reverend Theodore Sedgwick, "A Church Wagon in Southern Wyoming," *The Spirit of Missions*, Vol. 2, No. 11, Nov. 1910, pp. 924–925. Used by permission of the Episcopal Church Archives.

9. Concrete.

CHAPTER TWO

~

1911

"The Customs of the Country"

Winter came early. Wind crusted the snowdrifts so that the sheep could not paw through to the grass and cattle also suffered, consuming more cottonseed cake and hay. Losses were high; so were costs for feed and manpower. John and his men were often out on the range to drive the stock to sheltered places. Alone, Ethel labored to reach an understanding with the cast iron cookstove. And she wrote, relaying the customs of the country in "Someone Will Come Along":

"It's a penitentiary offense not to bring the mail," John informed everyone who came for the first time. A rider on horseback brought a heavy flour sack of letters, packages, and papers wrapped in his coat or tied to the back of his saddle, or hanging from his saddle horn. A campmover driving a team lifted the mail down from among the sacks of oats, kerosene tins, cases of canned goods, slabs of bacon.

"Didn't remember Johnny Love's mail until I was four miles out of town," said one cowboy, "and had to go back for it."

Knowledgeable about delivering calves and lambs, John had been doubly solicitous after the loss of their baby, but he sensed that Ethel needed to talk to another woman. In December he took her to the Red Bluff Ranch. Perhaps Mrs. Mills, who had borne three children without medical assistance, would have answers to her questions.

Upon her return, Ethel discovered that keeping her house in order required her continued presence. She noted in "Someone Will Come Along":

Bishop Lyman, after whom a town was later named, came while I was away for several days visiting at the Mills' ranch.

"Was it like *this* when he came?" I asked John, dismayed at the sight after my short first absence. It must have been, for Bishop Lyman had inserted neatly under "M" on my kitchen reminder of our wants: "The Missus."

After the visit of another bishop, Ethel continued in "Someone Will Come Along":

While the range was little fenced, Mormon sheep men sometimes used to drive through, bringing their flocks from Utah. They traveled light, moving camp every day and topping off the feed.[1] John used to relate a conversation with a Mormon bishop who came by wagon. "What do you think of our people?" the bishop asked.

"Good workers," answered forthright John, "but great liars."

"How is that?" asked the shocked bishop.

"Well, I've always wanted to read the *Book of Mormon*. Every Mormon who has come along said he would send me a copy, but no one ever did. What do you call that?"

"I'll send you a copy," said the bishop.

"See that you do, Bishop, or I'll add your name to the others in my little black book." John had no little black book, but a copy of the *Book of Mormon* arrived and was read.

Ever alert for new subjects within her limited sphere, in 1910 Ethel scribbled notes about family pets in "Tom the Cat":

Two tiny kittens used to sit upon the kitchen stool, side by side, watching the absorbing kitchen processes. More yet they liked to perch upon my shoulders for a better view. "Yes," said one man to whom I was introduced much later, "I have met Mrs. Love before. She was taking a pie out of the oven, and she had a kitten on each shoulder." They preferred John's broad shoulders to mine at mealtime, and would sit quietly through a whole meal, never offering to stir.

In contrast, it was always a wonder to me that Tom, the cat with his glossy black coat, lived to complete a natural end, with bacon at fifty-five cents a pound. Never a wagon stopped for the night—and we on the main road from nowhere to nowhere—that Tom did not go over the camp supplies for bacon. It could not be hidden beyond his reach under bed, tarpaulin or sacks, or so well wrapped that he could not get at it, or even carry it off.

Tom's coming was in late summer. I stood at the kitchen door, bride of a few months, looking at the view. There was a near hill covered with a scraggly growth of greasewood, and a far hill as barren as the usual sheep range. Over the near hill came a large black cat, lone, confident; Tom had arrived. The closest inhabited dwelling in that direction was seventeen miles away. "Must be Mrs. Harrison's Tom," said my husband. "He was here once for a while, until Delfelder's men came along. They needed a cat, so they took him to Buck Camp, according to the customs of the country." We found out later that, according to the customs of the country, they were taking him to another camp where a cat was wanted, when, in his characteristic way, he showed himself the master of his fate, escaped from the wagon, and cut across country to our ranch. Here he stayed except for several months every summer. His head, chest, and shoulders were broad and powerful. His low build was somewhat on the style of a bulldog. I saw him bring in full-grown rabbits, and ground squirrels and gophers were his common prey. He returned from the dam in time for the duck season.

When Tom saw a gun, he followed the man who carried it, reasonably sure of a feast on wild duck. When the crack of a gun sounded, he and the other cats ran from every direction to the shore of the small lake in front of the house. There they waited for the wind to bring the ducks to the shore. At one time, my husband shot half a dozen ducks. He let Tom go into the shallow water and bring the first to land, and made after him with gun and rocks, but Tom refused to drop his booty. By the time John returned from the chase, the other cats had taken all the ducks.

Nor did Tom hesitate to stoop to petit larceny. I had put a dressed duck in an icebox on the north side of the house, because one duck was so ridiculously inadequate to set before the number of men who had stopped for food and shelter and news of the range. When I had the lid raised in one hand and the heavy duck in the other, Tom made a quick leap, seized the duck and was off, beyond my power to hinder him. I wonder how long he had been watching the ice box. Another time he sprang the latch of the kitchen door during the night, and stole a duck from the sink. Our company had salted codfish!

He nearly met his death on a duck hunt. The lake was covered with thin ice. Tom went out to bring in a duck which had been shot. While the ice bore his weight, it did not bear the combined weight of him and the duck. He broke through. For a long time I watched him struggle in the icy water, unwilling to let go of his catch. He broke the thin edge of ice time after time, until to my relief, he decided that life without the duck was after all preferable to staying in the water with it.

Tom clearly felt himself master at the ranch and even stood up once against the master of the house. My husband offered to show me how to put him and the other cats out one cold night. John began with a honeyed "kitty, kitty" to which none of them paid any attention. Then, with the front door open, he began the chase. The cats, disregarding the door, were fleeing from room to room, taking cover under the bed, or dodging behind the stove, or jumping over tables and under chairs, John pursuing them with the broom, and terrifying sounds. Bets were even on the cats or the man. One cat clawed up the bare wall to make a record leap across the dining room, then escaped through John's feet, up the living room fireplace chimney and through the cement tiling on top. The cats were out.

As Ethel got to know her new environment, she described "A Visit to a Sheep Camp" in a story by the same name:

Dawn glowed against the dark earth, the sky changing from deep fire shot gray to an incandescent opal. Broken bird songs sounded from unseen birds; sage chickens whistled softly to their mates, walking to water among the brush. They were not afraid. John never let anything be killed in the field. A bunch of horses, swinging in single file, galloped along the trail. At the water hole, antelope lifted their heads to sniff the air before scattering. The wind wafted gently, bringing the damp smell of rain to the nostrils of the horses and sheep.

Sometimes I went with John to visit the sheep camps. Below the top of the Beaver Divide was the bed ground—a broad hollow where the grass was worn away by the hooves of many sheep. The sheep wagon on the edge was silhouetted against the sky. A horse ate the rice pudding set out to cool. A collie lay beside the door.

As we approached, we overheard the Scottish herder. "Find yourself a sheady spot, Little Jackie, it's like to be all summer we'll stay at Monayta before the shearers will let us off to the mountains," advised lanky Two-fingered Bill to the short black lamb which had doubled up at his feet. He reached an arm inside the sheep wagon, rinsed the empty bottle from which he had fed Jackie, and thriftily poured the foggy water into the hand basin.

"Hey, Bill," John called. "How's everything this spring?" A much mustachioed sunburnt face atop a clumsy overalled figure appeared from behind the wagon. "Oh. It's you, John. Well, we wintered, and most of us can stay. But these severe summers on top of 'em will be the death of me yet. Last time I went to Lander old Grimmet [Lander's undertaker] was standing at the Fremont hotel, with his eye on me, but I told him, 'Maybe you'll get me underground some day, but not yet, no sir, not this year.'"

"Got a bum there, Bill?"

"Aye. Do you mind that old ewe that was a pet of the Delfelders and came into camp six year ago with a blue ribbon on her neck? The Wanderin' Jewess we called her. First with one bunch, then another. She was with me a summer and two dandy black lambs I got from her. Next winter she drifted with Scotty's bunch and he got her two blacks. Every year she had two, and the man she was with in the spring branded them. But nobody shipped her. She did lead a bunch around by the nose, but we all think she brought good luck.

"This here lamb is the Wanderin' Jewess' sole survivor. I lost a bunch in greasewood comin' from Poison Creek to Monayta. Generally she leaves the stuff alone, but there waren't much feed. The greasewood was wet and the sheep was hot and she ate it like a sheep from outside. I give her sody, but she died. Jacketed the other twin by wrapping it in the dead lamb's fleece, but the ewe I give it to wouldn't own it. I'm bringin' this one up on the bottle," he ended with a defiant glance at John. But John was oblivious to any implications. A lamb brought up on canned milk eats ten times what you can get for it, he meditated.

"Shearers struck, they tell me."

"Aye. Now they want 8 cents. Say the wool's full of reservation grit. Feed's all grubbed into the ground around here but I got to wait till . . ."

"Delfelder pays his 8 cents, but it's sweatin' blood for him to do it."

After another visit, she wrote:

The inside of the sheep wagon was dark and reeking with the wetness and odor of lambs. The heavy downpour of rain trickled slowly through the old canvas top in several places. Newspapers had been spread over the bed, gunny sacks over that, and drenched lambs lay about inert, apparently lifeless. They lay on the side boards of the wagon, ears or legs sometimes falling over the edge. A dozen dark lambs had the small floor space. Occasionally one lifted a wobbly head and opened a stiff mouth in an effort to emit a m-a-a that was very much of a failure. One lamb had lurched to unsteady feet and stood braced in a corner in an attempt to hold those uncertain legs upright. On the warmest place, the oven door, opened flat, lay a still, yellowish lamb, tiniest of all. At dark, Bill half opened the wagon's door and looked inside. At that three lambs raised their heads, and the one standing in the corner tried to take a step and collapsed. "Ah! Doin' fine, ain't you?" he said and taking the liveliest looking of the lambs by a leg each like a bunch of radishes, he reached into the dark. Carefully he mixed a half cup each of canned milk and water from a hot bottle on the stove, and put in a few drops of whiskey. Then he pried apart the stiff, cold mouth of the lamb on the oven door and forced a spoonful of hot milk down its throat. One after another he fed the same way. He threw four more limp bodies by the stove to warm.

"Looks like the lambs got my wagon tonight."

"Sheep look good," John commented.

"Sure, for their age and the winter they do," was Bill's reply. "But what kind of a business is it, I ask myself. Everything's agin you. The critters is agin you. The men is agin you. The shearers is agin you. The varmints is agin you. The market's agin you, and the weather's agin you."

"A true word. But those of us that's had the association with the woolies for years would find it hard to do anything else."

Ethel took over the bookkeeping. The expenditures from September 1910 to September 1911 for everything but manpower were $16,397.60. Her inventory of April 1, 1911, listed 3,000 sheep, 125 horses, 150 cattle, 6 dogs, 15 geese, 56 chickens, 6 sheep wagons, 5 supply wagons, 2 riding plows, 1 disk harrow, 1 hay mower, 1 cultivator, 3 plows, 5 fresnos, 4 buck scrapers, several sleighs, 1 stoneboat, 1 buggy, 20 sets of harness, 8 saddles, and miscellaneous wheel hoes, shovels, blacksmith tools, forge, and carpenters' tools, with a combined estimated value of the day of about $30,400. John paid a salary of $50 a month to the men working for him that spring, minus deductions for tobacco and the clothes they ordered from the Montgomery Ward Company. A surviving page of the family ledger shows the costs of items deducted: overalls: $.90; socks: $.20; suspenders: $.80; gloves: $1.25; overshoes: $3.50. Room and board were included in the wages.

The winter had taken a toll, as indicated by the reduced numbers of his livestock. Against his wishes, John had to borrow money from the bank in Lander to meet his payroll and expenses for the coming year. Ethel described her first spring roundup in "Roundup Time":

Wagon wheels in the spring or fall brought the equipment for a horse roundup. The wrangler drove a wagon piled high with oats, bed rolls, branding irons; or it might be a chuck wagon, the high end-gate hinged to let down for a table. At the back were shelves and drawers for cooking pots, plates, cups, and cutlery. Large outfits often brought a quarter or half a beef to feed their cowboys. The wranglers would throw down the bedrolls on the hill or among the ranch buildings. Horses were turned loose in the field, except for the wrangle horse to bring in the others. If there were only half a dozen riders, they usually ate at the house. Breakfast was at sunrise, or after the wrangler brought in the saddle horses for the morning ride. The cowboys started out slowly, to save their horses for the chase and the run back with range bunches.[2] It was a sight to see the boys trying to corral a dozen or two wild horses, the sleek, many-colored bodies glistening with sweat, panting and snorting as they tried to escape. When the horses were shut into the large dusty corral, the men looked them over, studying the brands and the condition and ages of the animals. I used to climb onto the sod roof of the log granary and watch the men separating the colts from their mothers and hazing them into the round log corral. There each colt was roped, tied, and branded. One man kept the fire going to heat the branding irons, and carried the proper iron to the workers in the corral. Sometimes there would be a "slick," a grown horse which had never been brought in for branding, but had run loose for one, two, or three years. He would race around the corral, dodging the rope, crowding between other horses, rearing, fighting the rope when it caught him. He had to be snubbed tight to the center post until the rope closed his windpipe. His kicking and breathing ceased. Then they tied a rope about his feet and quickly eased the one around his neck. They branded him fairly low on the right hip and cut the end hair of his tail. Then there was a scatterment of men from the corral at the final untying.

David's oral history elaborated on the same event from his own later experience:

Often the slick was also gelded. The shorter tails immediately showed which horses had been "treated," and served as more effective fly-swatters to keep the flies away from the wound.

In early summer, loudly protesting calves were put into this corral to be roped, hog-tied with one hind leg drawn high on the flank, branded, and castrated. The testicles, or "Rocky Mountain oysters," were immediately washed, rolled in seasoned flour and fried for a gourmet lunch. The fire to heat the branding irons was always outside the corral fence to keep the red-hot coals from igniting the dry manure and spreading.

My father's first brand was a star, but when the residents of Star Valley in western Wyoming protested his right to use it, he chose the outline of a flatiron. His sheep wore their flatiron brands high on their backs, so that herders could quickly see which animals had already been branded. After shearing, the sheep were branded again. Dad's horses wore a smaller flatiron on their right hind quarter; his cattle wore a Lazy G Quarter Circle brand on their left thigh, their right ear notched with a swallow-tail "V." Colts were

George Porteous holding the Loves' flatiron brand, Love ranch, 1930.
Love Family Archives

handled more carefully because their long, thin legs could easily be broken or dislocated. They were not castrated until they were about two years old and their testicles had dropped down from their body cavity.

Indians from the Wind River Reservation always seemed to know when there would be a horse roundup, and were welcome. Invariably a horse was accidentally killed. A horse carcass provided at least 1,000 pounds of meat, and they used it all, cutting it into strips and curing it to make jerky on the barbed wire fences—½ mile of fence per horse. The hide was tanned, beautifully, and the hair braided into ropes, belts, or hatbands.

Included in "Roundup Time," Ethel described an event a few years later, probably in 1920:

The Freese roundup which camped across the creek one spring years later was the roughest roundup I ever saw. The men came from nearly 100 miles away, and could not have had many horses, if any, at Muskrat Creek. Perhaps because John was away part of the time, they were particularly heedless of what they did. They left gates open, bummed[3] colts, ran horses through the barbed wire fences. There was quarreling and even fighting in their camp.

A butcher bird or Northern Shrike[4] was the cause of a change in their behavior. Black and white and elegant, he sat on a high greasewood bush near the house, uttering his raucous notes. Since butcher birds killed or drove away the smaller song birds, we had no mercy for them. My older son, then about nine years old, saw the bird and got his .22 rifle. His shot rang out. The bird fell. There was an immediate silence across the creek. This was a language they knew and respected.

Years afterward we had the best roundup. Young Doug Fuller, born and brought up by a water-hole, he said, was in charge. His wife, neatly and suitably dressed, was the cook. She fed the dozen riders four or five times a day around the camp fire, even making doughnuts for them in one of her Dutch ovens. The cowboys rode early and late, bringing in sixty or more horses a day.

In July 1911, John took Ethel to visit the Mills family again. She was expecting another baby and wanted to take no chances of losing it. Leaving her, John returned to the ranch to continue his work on the Big Dam. Ethel wrote of the trip and range chivalry in "Hats and Gloves":

A pair of white buckskin gauntlet gloves I treasured for riding. I wore brown corduroy divided skirts and jacket, and high-buckled light tan boots. My felt hat, not a Stetson, was soft and white. Around the broad rim was a deep edge of grayish-tan. Expecting to ride, I was quite unsuitably dressed for a sixty mile, cross-country summer drive with John in the buggy. It was as hot as the range can be in late July. About half way to the Mills ranch, as Santo and Blucher were slowly pulling the buggy up the sandy slope of Government Draw, unsheltered from the direct rays of the noonday sun, I remembered the cold water in the leather encased thermos bottle. The quart bottle, a recent novelty, had been a wedding present. I stood up beside the closely packed, narrow seat of the buggy to locate the thermos bottle. I took off my gloves to unscrew the cap and pour water for each of us. We stopped briefly at Delfelder's Buck Camp for a word with Shorty and a look at the wolf hounds in their pen. Otherwise we saw no one and passed no inhabited shack all day. Not until we reached the Mills' ranch at sunset did I discover that my right glove was missing. It must have fallen out when I was searching for the thermos bottle, twenty miles away.

We returned some days later by the same rutty seldom-used road, but saw no glove. The loss was a serious matter to me, for gloves were hard to replace. What was my amazement on reaching our house to see on the kitchen cabinet my missing glove! What rider could have seen it, probably attempted to try it on, knew its value to someone, asked at Delfelder's Buck camp, the only inhabited spot on our long drive, about who had been on the road, and left the glove at our empty house? We never knew.

Ethel wrote to John from the Mills' ranch.

1 Aug., 1911

Dear John,

I hope to hear soon that you had a good trip back to Conant Creek, and are making the most of my absence in many ways. Mr. Hudson came out from Lander in his auto machine on Sunday with his wife, her sister, and the boys. He asked me if his man had come to the ranch to get the fresnos. He really is to build a dam, although he will not be there to oversee the work. It is to be of good size, in the bed of the creek[. . .][5]

This is wonderful country! Currants and gooseberries grow wild, besides fish and sage chickens. Guns have been popping all morning over toward Skull Gulch—people out from town, I suppose. Mrs. Mills says that I am to take back some currants for jelly.

Quite often I sleep until nine in the morning, or later, in spite of early retiring. Mr. Mills always talks about it, but I do it again.[6]

It will really be a disappointment if I do not hear from you soon. Don't like the thought of you taking such long drives without me along to protect you, or to hammer on the buggy tire if it should become loose.

Ethel

Ethel's sister Faith, now a school teacher in Denver, wrote August 9 to let Ethel know Dr. Waxham had recently suffered a stroke:

Vera wanted me to write to you today to tell you about Father's condition[. . .] The past few days he has been much worse[. . .] Vera feels that if you care to see him alive you ought to come down very soon[. . .]Wire me and I will meet you at the depot if John can't come down with you. Lots of love. Write soon. Faith

It is likely that neither Faith nor Vera knew of Ethel's pregnancy. No explanation of why she did not go to Denver has been found, but it is possible Ethel was still at the Mills' ranch when the news came. The Love family Bible recorded that Dr. Waxham died September 4, 1911, of apoplexy. Ethel's stepmother, Helen, sent Ethel her condolences. Then, after putting six-year-old Ruth in a boarding school, Helen departed from Denver. Ethel never mentioned Helen again.

The winter of 1911 was the worst to strike the Wyoming range since the 1880s, yet the guest book showed that John's sister Georgia and her young ward Elma Robbins arrived from Tuttle, Colorado on November 18. In early December Ethel took the train alone from Moneta to Denver to await the birth of her baby. Only her letters to John have been found, none from him to her. She wrote from Faith's address, 1300 Birch Street, Denver, Colorado, December 9, 1911:

John dear—

Who is better than a—well it begins with an "s." You are in good care I know, and I haven't worried about you yet! When I get tired I just pretend to snuggle my head under your chin and have a little rest.

Ethel

21 Dec., Denver, Colo.

Dear John,

Your letter and that of Georgia reached me several days ago, so that already I am looking for another[. . .]

Since arriving here I have been busy going to and from town to Dr. Lawrey, Mr. Deardorf,[7] and doing a tiny bit of Christmas buying[. . .]

Dr. Lawrey has said that I shall have a Christmas party of my own—perhaps any day between now and then. She has secured the services of a special attendant for the party, as she thinks it necessary, who has been to see me and is awaiting a telephone call at any time. Arrangements have been made for a room at the Park Avenue hospital which is smaller and more quiet than St. Joseph's, and now the sooner the party, the better.

I hope that Georgia will not be so overwhelmed with loneliness while you are away on ranch business that she will want to leave. A little package is starting to you at the same time as this letter for a Christmas reminder.

It is late. I hope that you will have a good Christmas at the ranch, and let me hear from you at every opportunity.

Dec. 22

Mr. Deardorf has the petition for clearing the title of Pater's Chicago property ready for the court there. He says that the matter should be settled within six weeks or two months. My father's estate cannot be settled until next fall.

You have, I trust, sent me money before this. Some of mine I have already fallen back upon, but the reserve will have to be kept for Uncle Ernest[8] probably, and the work of the lawyers. This party for Christmas, as I warned you, is no light expense. Nurse, twenty-five a week; her board, seven; hospital room from twelve to eighteen a week, payable in advance—mark that!

There is much more which I would tell you but hardly care to write. Trusting that your trip to Riverton was pleasant and successful, and that I shall hear from you soon.

With one kiss for Christmas, Ethel

Faith wrote to John, December 31, 1911:

Dear brother John, Sister Georgia and Little Elma,

Hurrah! Hurrah! At last the good news. A beautiful bouncing boy. He came last night between 9 & 10 and what think: he weighs 8½ pounds!

Ethel poor child had a hard time but was a little brick. They had to take several stitches. But this morning she is doing nicely, they say. She is sleeping now so I have not yet seen her.

The boy is a dear—such lungs! He can quite put his father in the background if he keeps it up and improves at such a rate.

The first thing he did was to put his little fist in his mouth. I will write more later.

Hastily, Faith

Notes

1. Allowing livestock to feed off the top tender shoots of grass without grazing down to the roots.
2. Domestic horses which had been running free on the range.
3. Orphaned.
4. *Lanius excubitor*.
5. [. . .] indicates letters have been abridged to focus on the subject of the chapter.
6. He may not have recognized his former schoolmarm's delicate condition.
7. The solicitor handling Dr. Waxham's estate.
8. Another of Frank Waxham's brothers.

CHAPTER THREE

~

1912

"Roll, Jordan, Roll"

The year began with great optimism and joy, but the new family would be tested by separation, blizzards, fire, flood, and financial ruin in the months to come. Initially, though, all attention was focused on the safe arrival of the new baby. Faith wrote to John New Year's Day, 1912:

Monday and all is well. Ethel is still almost too exhausted to speak, but perfect rest is all she needs. [. . .] The boy is doing splendidly and almost has two teeth. School begins tomorrow and I shall be very busy, so remember that no news is good news.

January 5, 1912, Ethel wrote to John:

Dear John,

Son and I have been beginning the New Year together in a room full of flowers, wishing that you were here with us. You would be very proud of the little fellow, for as a baby he is a great success[. . .] If he always does as well as these first few days he will be the "prop and stay of our declining years." Dr. Lawrey says that he looks like Pater, Vera that he looks like you, Faith, like me, and I think he is more like Georgia. Anyway he is clear skinned, blue-eyed, and has long fair hair, mostly on the back of his head.

Perhaps because he is so big we impose upon him; they say it is because he is too lazy that he won't eat, but I think there must be some other reason. He won't work for his living; prefers to be fed with a spoon, or else frets for popcorn or roast beef.

The last week has been bitter cold here, and I have hoped that you would not suffer, or the sheep. You can write to me directly at "Park Avenue Hospital;" let me hear from you when you can.

I am able to turn over in bed by myself, but not to blow my nose yet. Haven't seen anyone yet but Vera once and Faith a little every day. Son and myself send love to you all.

Ethel

Ethel was slow to recover from a difficult breech birth, and the baby lost weight for several weeks. Her next letter, written January 11, was forwarded from Moneta to Shoshoni, where John was on business:

[. . .]Babe seems a wee bit better today, more like the bright-eyed, rosy-cheeked boy who came ten days ago. I have hardly had a good look at him yet, hardly held him in my arms, and have no intention of letting him go[. . .]

January 12

I am doing nicely, and would feel quite like myself but for the nerve-wracking strain of these days and nights. There is a man below who has just had an operation, and spends his time groaning and moaning, and some woman down the hall who wails and wails, and someone else who seems delirious every evening. Tomorrow or next day I'll write more, but tonight I'm quite tired and must feed the baby now. Love to all. Ethel

Meanwhile in Wyoming, the winter was vicious. Just as Ethel was struggling to regain her strength and get her baby well, John was fighting to save his ranch empire. Each, not wishing to worry the other, minimized the difficulties. Ethel's letter of January 24 was again forwarded to Shoshoni.

Dear John,

Your letter reached me yesterday, and you would know, if you stopped to think of the few lines you have written during the last month, that I was very glad to get just a word. Why not tell me a little more, whether you are keeping all the men, what you are doing in Shoshoni, whom you have seen, where the sheep are, and so on.

The boy and I left the hospital at the end of our fourth week, and you may be sure that I was glad to get away, where I can take care of him myself, and not have to trust to nurses. We took a taxicab, for it was a cold day. You would have been amused at the luggage—two suitcases, two plants, a basket, Faith, the baby and myself. Faith is going to stay with babe and me for a while[. . .]

Since coming to Mr. & Mrs. Kellogg's house,[1] the boy has had a hard night and day or so. He has not gained in weight at all during the last ten days, which is quite discouraging. I have not had more than one whole night's sleep since he came, and am beginning to feel the lack of it badly. Every two hours, day and night, he has to be fed. There are many things about the apartment which Dr. Lawrey has positively forbidden my doing, unless I want to be a permanent invalid, so we have engaged a woman to work here two hours every morning for a week or so. In three weeks Dr. Lawrey will examine me again.

If you don't write me more, I shall believe that you don't read my letters. Wish you were here to get up during the night and boil bottles, mix milk, heat hot water bags, and help take care of son; would let you do it, if you promised to do things exactly right[. . .]

Hoping that all is well with you, I remain your dutiful and affectionate wife. E

She wrote again January 30:

Dear John,

Your letter enclosing the one from the bank has just reached me. Son is lying on the table in front of me, while I answer. He likes company in the middle of the afternoon[. . .] Have you heard anything yet from the wool, or the steers shipped last fall? If a few hundred dollars would really be such a great help, I've just two practical suggestions, which will probably not appeal to you! Advertise the pinto stallion for sale[. . .] The account book shows how many times he was used last season, about a dozen, I think, and even if twice as many times, it would not pay for keeping him, even if there were no "interest or money invested" to consider. Also diamonds. While I don't like the idea of disposing of your gifts to me, I'd much rather be without and have one or two little debts paid. You may give me all the jewels you wish when you can afford it. Until then I'll be satisfied to be decently clad, though unadorned. If this seems best to you, ask Georgia to send down my pair of your rings, and I'll see what I can do with them. Let me know what they should bring.

Mr. Deardorf told me that he sent you a paper to be signed before a notary, a matter of form called putting in an appearance, as he sent them to all the heirs in Pater's will. You are included because under the Illinois law—and the matter comes up in a Chicago court—a husband has a share in his wife's property (children too, I suspect). It refers of course to my lots there. Mr. Deardorf has made out a petition to be placed before the court of equity that the title be restored to me, subject to the mortgage. If you sign at once, it will hasten matters. Seems impossible to get anything done before March, and the mortgage and taxes are due in February[. . .]

It's late and I get little sleep, so I will write no more now, but send my best wishes for yourself and the sheep.

February 9

This is just to be an excuse for an answer to your letter, for I really have very much to say! It is to ask you about Georgia. She spoke when I left as if she wished to go home in time to plant her flowers in spring, and I should like to have her stay if you can persuade her[. . .] My coming back will depend upon having some strong back and arms in the house for I shall not be able to fill stoves and do such things for a while[. . .] We could not ask her to stay for nothing, and would have to pay anyone else for help.

Son has been craving only one feeding between eleven and six for two nights now. If he will only keep it up! During the day he does his crying; has been losing his food again, and seems distressed after eating[. . .] He is longer, larger in chest measurement and has a head nearly two inches larger around than the average boy. He weighed a pound more than the average when he was born, but has not yet gained back what he lost. I give him a rubbing with olive oil every day after washing him.

Write when you have an opportunity and let me know what Georgia says about staying. Ethel

February 18

Dear John,

It is evening, and the first time today that I have had a chance to write. Baby cried all morning when I was not bathing him. Vera and the boys were here all afternoon, and now we are waiting for the regular Sunday call of "Uncle" Mr. Irwin. He came last night and brought Son a box of candy which we ate[. . .]

Yesterday I went downtown and had Dr. Chase examine my eyes. He says that they are just about the same. I'll have to go to the dentist's, for since coming to Denver I have suffered a great deal from my teeth. Mrs. Kellogg says that the average child costs its mother two teeth, and I feel as if half of mine at least were going. Pleasant prospect[. . .]

I was sorry to hear that the debt has been made so much larger this winter, and that you do not care for my methods of reducing it. The diamonds would not make much difference, but the other suggestion I think is good enough to bring up twice[. . .] An advertisement would cost only a dollar or two, and might save much anxiety[. . .] Do as you wish of course, but don't let a dislike for selling anything stand in the way of your own advantage[. . .]

I hope that you have the icehouse filled, and a cow ready to be treated like a lady. Dr. Lawrey insisted upon cow's milk. You see, I will know whether you really want me to come back by what you do to make it possible. I'd like to have the bedroom floor finished please, kind sir!

Hugh and Robert Shattuc, Ethel and Allan G. Love in Denver, March 1912.
Love Family Archives

Babe is doing fairly well. His weight seems stuck at seven and three quarters. The days have been so pleasant that he has been sleeping out ever since the first of the month, sometimes as long as five hours. You should see him smile[. . .]

It is a long while since I have heard from you, and I hope to receive a letter soon. Mrs. Kellogg has a wholesaler's catalogue (Vaughn's) of flower and vegetable seeds. By sending with her order, I can save about half on garden seeds. If you wish, send a list of what you want, and the garden record of last year from our file under G. And I'll send for what they have. Please don't have any more disasters. Ethel

With no letters from John or Georgia surviving, the nature of his "disaster" is not known, or whether John explained why he did not come to see his wife and son.

Ethel wrote again March 4:

[. . .]Your letter of February twenty-seventh came last week, the first for a long while.

You may expect us any time after March fifteenth, provided that the weather has moderated, you have a cow and a supply of Borden's milk, and Son continues to gain a little. If you do not come all or part way—or you'd better anyway, remember to bring clean blankets to wrap the baby, for I can't carry enough, and the foot warmer, thermos bottle, and an extra coat for me.

As to Son's name, didn't Faith tell you that I christened him "Nebuchadnezzar" before he was half an hour old? If you dare call him "Pete" again, I won't ever bring him back, and I'm going to write Georgia and tell her to spy upon you. I'd name him exactly for you if we lived anywhere else, but can't bear the thought of all the Johns in the county, and Jacks, who might take pride in having the same name[. . .] Dr. Lawrey wants him named for my father, saying that the name might be of service to him some time in the future. I can't think of any name good enough, that will suit him when he is little and when he is big! That is the "reason why"[. . .]

Georgia wrote me that she would like to stay, but needed money and ought to be at work[. . .] If you cannot persuade her to stay, I'd like to know, so as to get someone to come up with me from Denver, and it would be nicer, wouldn't it, to have Georgia?

I get so tired, especially at night that I don't care much about anything in the heavens above or on the earth beneath or the waters under the earth[. . .]

There has been an unusual amount of snow here[. . .]and the days are raw and cold. Snow was over fourteen inches on the level according to the government authorities at the beginning of this storm. I hope that the snow will not make lambing bad this year, and will still be good for the crops which you are going to put on your desert claim. Georgia writes that the icehouse is full, which is surely good news.

Shall I telegraph you from Denver or Cheyenne when I start or will you get mail often enough for me only to write? There are a number of things which make me wish to cut my stay here as short as possible.

E.

Years later David checked official accounts about the winter of 1912 and wrote in "A Part of Your Heritage":

In Wyoming, the weather continued severe. Sheets of snow driven by winds of 50 to 100 miles per hour caught the sheep and piled them up in draws, then drifted more snow over them and they suffocated by the hundreds. From one bunch of 3,000, all the men available working desperately for two days, shoveled out 500 living sheep. Storm followed storm. Day and night the men rode, red-eyed, frostbitten, and bone-weary, collecting and feeding what remnants of the herds they could find. Small wonder that Dad's letters were few, and that he did not come to Denver. From her letters,

Mother appeared to have had no idea of what he was enduring. When the winter broke at last, in March, my father's ranch empire was in ruins.

Ethel wrote March 10:

Dear John,

[. . .]A letter from the Chicago attorney states that affairs there will not come to court until the twenty-fifth of March. It seems best to wait here until the final arrangements regarding the Chicago property are made. Several offers are under consideration, though they are not what we wish, provided that the title to the lots is restored by the court of equity. If I leave, and the property is sold, the deed, not to mention other papers, like the mortgage, etc. will have to be signed by me before a notary, which means at least one trip to Moneta and considerable delay. At any rate, it will give you more time to get the cow, and for me to find out about Georgia's staying. Could you, or not, meet me about the twenty-eighth of March, or the first of April? I am desolated by these inexact and laggard arrangements.

Today I completed the order for seeds, which Mrs. Kellogg will send at once. She gave me, you might tell Georgia who is to have a share of the spoils, seeds of cypress vine, balsam, sweet marjoram, fennel, thyme, summer savory, gourds and some garden seeds, corn, radishes, peas, etc., in small packages[. . .] The saving on the seed is not so much as it would be on plants—however it amounts to seventy-five cents on an order of $4.50, which is worth saving.

Weather has been cold, windy, and snowy[. . .] It is probably well that I'm not on the way today, though I am disappointed, and hope you share my disappointment over postponing the trip. Remember me to Georgia and Elma, as usual. E.

In the margin she added: Allan Galloway Love weighs nearly nine pounds.

March 11

[. . .]I am fortunate in having several letters of yours to answer, and thanks to send[. . .]for the box of chickens and eggs which came the last of the week. Faith and I roasted two chickens immediately and the large bird, she said to tell you, was as large as her Thanksgiving turkey. If it had been about an inch larger, it would not have gone into the oven.

Brr, says Little Bear, you have changed, for when we were courting you used to torment me all the time to come to Wyoming, and now you don't, which is somewhat of a relief, although tremendously unflattering. And why, if I am to take for granted what it takes two pages to explain, didn't you guess why my little lad isn't named yet? Brr at you!

There has been more snow almost every day for the last week. In weather like this the baby can't take such a long drive. Reason I want the water analyzed at once is to see about getting a distilling apparatus if it is not good. You are used to it, and I am grown up, but baby's insides are very delicate [. . .] Freezing I don't believe will change the make up of the constituents of the water, so if you have an opportunity do send it[. . .]

Uncle Ernest has written requesting me urgently not to leave Denver until after his arrival, for he hopes to do something about the Chicago lots. I want to get that mortgage paid off before I leave. As things are now, it seems impossible to get off before the twentieth. I will take a train which will get me into Cheyenne about six in the evening instead of eleven. That will bring me to Moneta on the twenty-first. I don't want Mr. Kanson to take me to the ranch, I want you, and if you can't meet me so late in March, let me know, and I'll not come.

Isn't that sweet corn which we saved good for seed? You might test it and see. Georgia probably knows the usual methods of testing the ears. Will she stay?

I was very glad to hear that the bedroom floor is nearly finished, and hope that it will be ready soon. You know probably that the stain is on the closet shelf.

Son is fretting, and I must get this letter ready to send by Dr. Bayley. The house is so far out that there is no mailbox near, and letters have to be taken nearer town. Son weighs nearly nine pounds now. He is quite an armful[. . .] Au revoir until the twenty-first, dear man. Let me hear from you. E.

Further delays prevented her departure, and she wrote to John March 19:

Your letter of the sixteenth has just been received—postmarked "Chadron" [Nebraska] so that I thought you were there though you wrote "Moneta" and said that you were in Shoshoni! I am making plans now to leave here the twenty-eighth, reaching Moneta the twenty-ninth. It will be fine to have the wagon or buggy, and especially fine to have you there. But let me know if you cannot meet me[. . .] I am going to try to get the baby's basket and my cot off by freight the day after tomorrow. I am also going to send a few kitchen conveniences, mop wringer, etc., perhaps a washing machine, for they would be of more use to me than the money represented. They will be prepaid so that any one can take them out to the ranch who happens to be going by.

Snow is falling again. A blizzard is predicted, followed by cold. One gets tired of continually shivering[. . .]

Mar. 22, 1912

Your letter of the nineteenth was just received. Twice I have written you that I will leave here on the twenty-eighth, reaching Moneta the next evening, and battle, murder, and sudden death combined shall not change my plans. Hoping that you will have received one of my letters in time to meet me. Ethel

Armed with little more than good judgment and a sense of irony, Ethel and her baby returned to the ranch.[2] Forty years later, she wrote of their arrival in "Roll, Jordan, Roll":

Early one morning in December of 1911, John drove me from the ranch to the railroad in Moneta. The team trotted quietly over the nearly bare earth as starlight brightened to sunrise. The fifteen uninhabited miles made the first part of what was then, including an over-night stop in Cheyenne, almost a two-day trip to Denver. There my baby, Allan, was born on the thirtieth of December. Complications kept me in Denver until the end of March.

During the long return, Allan cried continually. The train reached Moneta about dark. No one was there to meet me. I picked up my own letters saying when I was coming.

There had been months of heavy storms while I was away. Melting snow over the half-frozen ground caused a flash flood.

A wagon was backed up to the platform. I walked onto it, and standing with the baby in my arms, was driven through the water to the corrugated iron hotel.

When Omar Kanson offered to drive me to the ranch in his buggy, the lower flats and the roads were still water-logged. He chose a longer, roundabout route, following the sandy ridges as much as possible. The sun shone. Allan slept, well-bundled in his blue blankets. Among them, to be sure that he would stay warm, I had tucked a hot water bottle. Somewhere along the way, it jolted out of the buggy; gone for good, I supposed, when I missed it.

The sheepherder who found this unusual article in the sage brush must have been surprised. No doubt he examined the wheel and horse tracks near, and reasoned in the way of the range, where news travels on the wind, that the only baby for twenty miles in any direction should have that hot water bottle. Soon a man on horseback relayed it to the ranch.

Allan's first drive continued all day. We saw no one. Toward sundown on a side-hill slope of gumbo, both horses slipped in the mud. While they struggled frantically, I jumped out of the buggy with Allan. Omar managed to disentangle the team, and finally we reached the house.

John, his sister Georgia, and nine-year-old Elma were busily replacing books on the lower shelves of the book cases. They had just finished cleaning the floors, which were not yet dry. For the only time in the ten years John had held his homestead, Muskrat Creek had spread over its banks, fed by swollen gulches and draws, and flowed through the house. Freezing nights cut down the supply of water, so soon all would be well again.

Georgia and young Elma were delighted with the baby. John accepted his son with interest, but the effects of winter storms and spring floods on the sheep made it necessary for him to be more often than not away from home.

Georgia's quiet, humorous efficiency and Elma's play made the following weeks pass quickly. Since Elma was missing school, Georgia saw that she went on with her reading. Once at the word "Pope," Georgia asked,

"Do you know who the Pope is?"

"Yes," answered Elma, "He's Uncle John."

"Oh? What makes you think so?"

"Aunt Ethel says that everyone has to empty his own wash water except the Pope, and Uncle John doesn't."

When Georgia and Elma planned to leave, in early June, John was to drive them to Moneta. Their bags were packed for the three o'clock start in the morning.

Black clouds, thunder and lightning showed heavy rains up the creek, although we had only showers about the house. All that afternoon John had been chanting happily, "Roll, Jordan, Roll," in anticipation of water to fill the small reservoir, already nearly empty, in front of the house, and partly fill the large one down the creek, on which he had had men working for many months. I fed the baby, and went to bed about nine o'clock.

Then Jordan rolled. I heard John shout, "The creek's coming down." A suddenly increasing roar of water charged the air, while I pulled my bathrobe around me, stepped into my sandals, and picked up the baby, asleep in his blankets. When I reached the back door, water was up to my knees. John lifted the baby and myself in his arms and, water swirling about us, carried us up the slippery hill behind the house. Already on top were Georgia and Elma, the little girl jumping up and down, screaming with fright. Even in the dark we could glimpse as well as hear the tremendous volume of the water. Together we waited, standing on the hill, while the crest of the flood came, passed, and seemed to be diminishing. Then we moved wetly to the long building, then the bunkhouse. The creek had circled, but not entered it. We sat there for the rest of the night, the chill of the great body of water, the smell and sound of it all around us.

At daylight we returned to the house. Stench, wreckage, and debris met us. The flood had gone. Its force had burst open the front door and swept a tub full of rain water into the dining room. Chairs and other furniture were overturned in deep mud. Mattresses had floated. Doors and drawers were already too much swollen for us to open or shut. The large wardrobe trunk of baby clothes was upset. Everything in it was soaked and stained. Around all the rooms at the height of the table tops was a water mark, fringed with dirt, on the new wall paper. Mud crusted the stove. Kitchenware, groceries, and silverware were filthy.

I found the thermos bottle, which I had filled for Allan's late feeding. The only other bright spot in life was the fireless cooker.[3] It had sailed from room to room. But inside was the oatmeal which I had started at dinnertime. Under the clamped lid it was clean, cooked and hot. That was our breakfast.

Some of John's men rode in on horseback to see what had happened at the house. Down the creek they had watched the flood take out their work on the Big Dam. Muskrat Creek, they said, full to its age-old banks, looked like the Mississippi River. The men began the long, slow, clean-up by shoveling mud out of the bedroom windows. It was hard to tell an overcoat from a table-cloth, so covered were they with mud. Georgia and I brought anything and everything to the kitchen sink. John pumped water over all, until things were recognizable. Then we hung them outside on clotheslines, in the vain hope that they would dry. It rained every day for a week. My shoes, first soaked, then dried stiff on the stove, I could not wear for days. Chairs began to fall apart as the glue dissolved. Later, when John's office desk could be opened, we found the largest drawer full of a tangled mass of roots and sprouts a foot or two long. The envelopes of garden seeds had disintegrated. Hundred pound sacks of sugar and flour in the store house were spoiled. Most of our cats had drowned. One of the first things the men did after our flood of 1912 was to hitch a team to our sheep wagon and pull it up the hill beside the woodpile. It was a comfort to have a clean and dry retreat after working in the house, to have a little fire in the small, pot-bellied stove, and above all, to be away from the creek. John, the baby, and I slept in the wagon until fall. The fresh air agreed with Allan. He forgot his night feeding, and his cheeks grew rosy.

In June Georgia and Elma returned to their home with our thanks and re-grets. By day I went to the house to continue salvage operations, which never seemed to be done. Even years later, when the kitchen range was moved, scallops of dried mud fell from the under side.

In "A Part of Your Heritage," David added from his parents' reminiscences and Ethel's "Roll, Jordan, Roll":

Among the most disheartening effects of the flood was the loss of many of Mother's treasured books. Gone also were most of the diaries, poems and short stories she had written through the years, and photo albums of family and friends. Photo negatives were reduced to gelatinous masses before they could be liberated from drawers swollen shut. The sense of loss grew with each new discovery. With the fear of another flood weighing on her mind, at the end of one long frustrating day, she stormed up to Dad and issued an ultimatum, recorded in her story "Roll, Jordan, Roll":

"This house moves or I move," said I, sure that never again I could sleep so near the treacherous, ruinous Rat. I should have known better than to fling any ultimatum into the teeth of fate—or a Scotsman.

"There won't be another flood. This was a cloudburst." John defended Muskrat. "The Little Dam backed up the water. Now that it has gone out, I'll make a dike along the bank of the creek."

We were both mistaken. From water running over the porch, sliding into the corners of closets, seeping up through the floors, to a double performance twenty years later, Jordan continued to roll.

An effort to find a house mover was desultory and unsuccessful. Someone came along who said he could do it, but we should have to supply beams fifty-five feet long, square, railroad irons, and dozens of hydraulic jacks—probably only a beginning of needs. Meanwhile, I tried to live as near the ceiling as possible.

We considered moving to the long building briefly, or putting up a house on the hill. There were always deterring considerations. The house remained where it was.

From then on each March to November I watched the Rat. If the creek rose over the low dike it was sure to reach the house. When the men were gone, I went out in rubber boots with shovel or hoe to deflect the stream of water. From time to time, during nights when the creek was high, I would light a lantern for a look at the stakes which measured the rise of the water.

That spring of 1912, in addition to being occupied with the baby, house-keeping, and the effort to restore the house to a livable condition, I shared the distraction of the arrival and stay of the bankers, with whom John had done business for at least ten years. They conferred with him for several days before leaving. Then two others came, inspected and counted the sheep, studied the wool returns, store bills, account of wages due. At last at the dinner table, the vice-president rubbed his hands together. "Mr. Love," he explained politely (not "John," as usual), "We need more collateral. You know the sheep business is in a bad way just now, what with high feed prices, winter losses, poor lambings, and low wool market. We can get our money out of you, Mr. Love. We can't out of others. Delfelder owes us three times what his sheep are worth. We have to carry him. It's our depositors' money, you realize. You must understand our position. We are obliged to cash in on your sheep, much as we dislike to do so. But we will let you keep your cattle, on one condition. Just sign a mortgage on your ranch."

To John, signing a mortgage was a sure preliminary to losing his land, and love of the land ran strong in his blood. This offer, to him an insult, aroused his wrath as nothing else had ever done. "I'll have that land when your bones are rotting in the grave!" he exploded. "Come outside, where I can tell you what I think of you!"

What this was, I never knew. He told our sons when they were grown, and the bitterness he had felt toward the dead was past.

David said his father's remarks to the bankers were "colorful, awesome, with word combinations never heard before or since":

The tongue-lashing he gave the bankers they never forgot. Years later when Allan and I were in high school in Lander, these pillars of the community crossed to the opposite side of the street when they saw Dad approaching.

Ethel concluded in "Roll, Jordan, Roll":

The aftermath came quickly. Buyers arrived to take the sheep, sheep wagons, dogs and equipment. Cowboys rode to collect the string of saddle horses, Punch, Bug, Kentucky, Snooks, Essie, Flirt, Snip and the others. Gauvion St. Cyr, and Sybil, his mate, were led away. The boys gathered the hundred and fifty head of cattle. John paid his own cowboys, and they departed. Ranch work stopped. Before he left, the childless banker asked, "What will you do with the baby?"

"I think I'll keep him," I said.

In later years, David learned what happened next and recorded it in "A Part of Your Heritage":

Only the honeymoon sheep wagon was spared, and a few large wagons, whose queen bolts[4] had mysteriously vanished.

As the last dust cloud from the departing visitors and their loot dwindled and disappeared over the horizon to the north, a deathly quiet seemed to hang over the ranch. The bustle and noise and industry that had involved each day for the last two years, the sounds of the stock, the wagons, the pounding of hoofs, the shouts of men, all had ceased almost abruptly. Dad and mother were very much alone. They stood, side by side, on the hill looking out across the ranch, across a quarter-mile flood-devastated empty creek bottom, across the rolling hills with no moving specks on them, and close at hand the sodden ranch house. Years later, in brief, sentimental, reflective moments, we learned bit by bit what they thought and what they said during this crisis in their lives.

Dad put his big arm gently around mother's thin shoulders and, in a soft voice with the Scottish burr more pronounced than usual, said, "Lass, you were not born for this kind of a life. You can make your way better in the world you knew in the past. It might be better for Allan, too. I don't want you to leave me, but I won't blame you if you do."

Mother knew the effort it must have cost him to say this. She knew also something of the agony he had just gone through, because to her had come the realization that all these things and these emotions were very important to her, too. With complete honesty she looked him straight in the eyes and said slowly and distinctly in little more than a whisper: "I've thought a lot about leaving you and leaving the ranch. I didn't know if I could bear to live here any more. Now I think I can. My place is here with you and with our son. We're not quitters. We still have the land, we owe no money, and we can still have our dream. Remember, only two years—two almost lifetime years—ago, we vowed to each other, and we meant each word . . . for richer, for poorer . . . in sickness and in health . . . until death us do part."

Notes

1. Long-time family friends.

2. In years to come, she also had a copy of Mary L. Read's *The Mothercraft Manual* (1916) to reference as her children were growing.

3. An insulated wooden box in which heated soapstone discs would cook food slowly.

4. Queen bolts tie together the running gears, single-trees, and double trees, which hook to harnesses, tongue, and bolsters. Without them, the wagons were useless.

CHAPTER FOUR

~

1912–1913

"Love's Labor Lost and the 3 D's"

One loyal hand, George Rushton, returned to help the Loves rebuild their lives. He and John soon discovered that the equipment left at the site of the Big Dam had been overlooked by the bankers. Likewise, because of the spring flood, there had been no spring roundup, so a few of the Loves' horses and cattle still wandered free on the range. John, the stubborn Scot, revived his dream of completing the Big Dam. With water to irrigate hay and alfalfa fields, a large garden and fruit orchard, his ranch empire would be more extensive than before.

Ethel used Rushton and his kindness as a focal point in the Loves' recovery in "Our George":[1]

Omar, one of the other cowboys in camp, handed George a cup of his black coffee, brewed all day, the kind said to float a horseshoe. "This here'll grow hair on your brrist."

"It's on the top of my head I need it," answered George mildly.

He had worked for John some years before and after we were married, in sheep camp, on the Big Dam, or at the ranch. Our first baby, Allan, recognized George as soon as he did his own father. Whenever George entered the house, he picked up the baby, jumped Allan to make him crow, and held him during meals. Before long he had Allan with him on the saddle of Old Mollie or on the seat of the hay rake.

George had had a wife and boy of his own; "a good looker, but a bad lot," was the man's estimate of Maggy. She had taken their little boy from the ranch on Muskrat Creek to one on the Sweetwater River for a prolonged stay. George continued to send her his paycheck, when he had one. Rumors that she was living there with another man were slow to reach him. When they did, he went south and found out for himself. After brooding indecisively over the situation when he returned, he asked John to let him have a horse and a gun.

"Sure," said John, "I'll give them to you. You want Maggy back?"

"No. No."

John waited before saying more. "Well, you needn't be afraid. Any jury will turn you loose." Then he continued, "But you'd be the loser. You'd always have to remember that you'd killed a man. What would folks tell your boy about you? Any good come of killing? Think it over."

George thought it over. He never made that ride.

He stayed with John after the sheep had been seized, and the flood on the Muskrat had cut out a section of the Big Dam across the creek.

The dam was about 700 feet long, 100 feet across the base. It had a core of clay, but the rest was of earth, tamped down only by the teams working to raise it. At the headgate the planned height of 25 feet was incomplete when the flood came.

The other men who had been working on the dam were paid off and left.

"It oughta bin a guvment job; too big for one person to swing," was their comment.

They had already finished making, laying and covering the long concrete tiling; put in place the tall steel headgate; dug the ditch, graded and laid out by a surveyor, to take the water to the fields. On a number of our desert acres they had grubbed off the sagebrush, plowed, harrowed and leveled the ground, then seeded them with rye and winter wheat.

Only John and George were left to face that tremendous gap in the dam. They kept the work teams busy all day, hitched to fresnos or scrapers, moving dirt into the break.

They fed the horses in the corrugated iron barn by the creek bank. Wearily at night they rode the two miles back to the house. I spent the days alone, except for my baby, Allan, just learning to walk.

"If the dam holds, I can pay you," said John to George, who had been working for little more than the cost of his clothes and tobacco.

"If it don't hold, you don't need to pay me," answered George.

Month by month the work proceeded, while the dam grew slowly higher, with little interruption from the generally favorable weather.

One day, there was a noisy clatter of wagons, five of them, all swarming with Indians, rattling across the creek. Children were jumping off and racing about, dogs barking, Indian women in bright blankets following with the men, whose black braids were bound with red cloth. They streamed around

George Rushton working on the Big Dam at the Love ranch, 1910. The horses are John Love's Percherons, Gauvion St. Cyr and his mate Sybil. There is no record of how many men and horses were used, or equipment, such as fresnos and scrapers, to build the dam. A rough estimate of the volume of earth and rock used in the first version of the Big Dam is about a million cubic feet, or 37,000 cubic yards.
Love Family Archives

the buildings. I took my baby in my arms, shut all the house doors and, trying to hide my uneasiness, walked out to them. It was my first encounter with Indians, and I was alone on the ranch. One thing after another the men brought to me and asked for, while I continued to shake my head each time. Their clothing reeked with the odor of outdoor cooking over sage brush fires. It was not reassuring to watch them sharpening their many long skinning knives on our grindstone. The women did not talk. Only one word was spoken by any of them. She had a papoose wrapped closely on her backboard. She came to look at my baby. "Nice," she said.

On another visit, an Indian woman was at the well when John and I drove into the yard. She was straining water into a pail through a flour sack as white as any of mine. An unfamiliar white-topped wagon stood beyond the corral. "Lone Bear and his family," said John. The Reservation line was only about fifteen miles from our lower fence. Lone Bear was an Arapaho chief, and his wife had been to the Mission school in Fort Washakie.[2]

While her husband worked with John, she and her little boy came to the house and spent the day with me. It was a strange, nearly silent visit. Like most Indian women educated at the mission school, she understood English, and probably could speak it, but would not, for shyness. To amuse the four-year-old, I brought him Allan's toy train, and set up the small circular track. His mother would not let him wind the engine. She did this herself, very carefully, making pleased, but wordless sounds, then handed it to him. He attached the cars, and as much as any little boy, enjoyed making the train whiz around the track.

I showed her a palm-sized rock found in our field, and asked her how the Indians used it. She lifted the edge of our pinto horsehide rug, and began scraping the underside.

In the kitchen where I was baking bread, she touched or pointed at utensils, looking her questions. I named and explained them to her. She laughed at my cast iron frying pan, probably like her own. By the pitcher pump in a cup of water she discovered John's false teeth. She raised both hands, at the same time uttering sounds of horror. With words and amateur signs, I tried to make her understand what the teeth were. She picked up her little boy to show this wonder to him, and told him about the teeth in their own language.

I put a stiff feather in his hair. I clapped my hands for him to dance, but he retreated bashfully behind his mother. My bread was ready to take from the oven. I offered him one of the rolls, fragrant and hot from the pan. Still he would not dance. Then I remembered my last bright red tomato, and held it toward him. He came with a leap out from behind his mother's chair, bending over and stamping his little moccasined feet on the kitchen floor in a lively Indian dance.

An exceptionally sudden, heavy snow fell about the eleventh of September. On the night of the first day of the storm three Mexicans drew in with a light wagon. They had been "pulling wool," collecting tufts of wool caught on the brush or barbed wire, or taking it from dead sheep. The four men had separated in the early morning before the storm began, and planned to meet at our ranch that night, but the fourth man did not come. Snow continued to fall. Next morning, George and John rode out with the others on horseback in the blinding storm to look for the lost Mexican. As I fed Allan in his high chair and spent the day alone, I wondered how many would be lost by nightfall. At least they were warmly dressed. The Mexican had left camp the day before in his shirt sleeves, without coat or matches, when the sun was still shining. He was not a man likely to disappear. He had a good reputation and a bank account. The storm and the search for him lasted for three days. They found no trace of him. Years afterward, pieces of clothing and scattered bones, which may have been those of the storm victim, were discovered among some rocks.

On one of the coldest evenings that winter, when snow was on the ground and the well outside was frozen, two "riders of the grub line" asked to stay overnight in our bunkhouse. They built a rousing fire in the large round stove. When it was red hot, they poured in more coal, and leaving the damper wide open, they went to sleep.

The crackle and flare of flames awoke me. "The bunkhouse is on fire," I cried to John. While he pulled on his clothes, I went to the kitchen, and began to pump pailfuls of water which he carried to the fire. The riders ran out of the bunkhouse just before the roof fell in. All they took with them was the nearly empty coal hod.

It was impossible to approach the burning log building. The intense heat melted the glass in the windows. John and George pulled the buggy from the buggy shed next to the fire. George threw snow on the near-by roofs. They poured water by the pailful on the spreading sparks. While the flames continued to rise, I continued to pump water and the men to carry the full pails. Fortunately, the little wind was from the north, or all the buildings would have gone. By daylight the fire was almost burned out. The yard gate was charred, and the side of the buggy shed. The men rode on, to tell of the "big bonfire" they had escaped from at Loves'. They would not stay to snake the still smoldering logs away from the ruins.

"I should have thrown their worthless carcasses back into the fire," said John, in wrath at the total loss not only of the bunkhouse, but its contents, including tools, canvas tops for the sheep wagons, pack saddles, all of the new machinery, pump, windmill wheel and fan for the well in front of the house.

Fewer wayfarers stopped over night after the comfortable bunkhouse had burned. John gave George the stove and dishes from the cook room for use at his homestead cabin near Horseshoe Creek, west of our ranch. Men could still "bed down" in the long building, but no more was it a center of independent sociability for all comers, where they could eat, smoke and linger at their will. Louis Guinard[3] penciled his loneliness on the doorway of the long building:

"All Alone by a Stormy Night"

Je pense à toi	I think of you
Je pense aux beaux jours	I think of the beautiful days
que j'avais vus couler	Which I saw flow away
au foyer paternelle.	At my paternal home.
A qu'il ne serait	Never to see again
Jamais de revoir ce beau	This beautiful country.
pays natale.	of my birth.

The house, with our private sheep wagon on the hill as a possible annex, became the only source of winter warmth and food.

There was then little to distinguish day from day, week from week, or month from month, except for the birth in Riverton April 17, 1913 of my second son, John David. "Blessed," was what I called him, until some years later the name, shouted loudly in all affection by his older brother, gave promise of future embarrassment.

David later explained more about the circumstances surrounding his birth in "We'll Rebuild Again":

Mother took the train from Moneta, where she stayed with close family friends, Dr. and Mrs. Albert B. Tonkin, during her confinement and for several weeks afterward.[4] None of the correspondence between my parents about my birth has been found. I do not know who cared for Allan while Mother was confined, or how long she was away from the ranch.

Ethel reflected on some of her new challenges in "Our George":

Beside the pleasure of watching the two babies' development, I had the contrasting daily struggle with what I thought to myself as the three damned d's—dirt, dishes, and diapers.

David added more details about their daily life in "Dreams, Dams, and Disasters":

My parents' days began at dawn. While Dad did the ranch chores, Mother cooked breakfast and packed lunches for him and George: sandwiches of homemade bread and "bottled" beef (preserved in glass jars), sometimes cheese, rarely fruit, occasionally cake or cookies, and a gallon or more of water.

Then four, six, or eight horses, depending on the job for the day, were harnessed, and a saddle horse saddled. The two miles to the dam, or three to five miles to the far fields or end of the ditches, took one to two hours each way. At the end of the work day, back at the ranch, the horses were watered, grained, rubbed down and checked for fistulas, collar sores, or other injuries. The cow was milked again, wood chopped, and coal scuttles filled. The warm days of summer were so precious that only rarely could time be spared for a picnic to Castle Gardens or a trip to town.

Ethel wrote of that summer's work in "Our George":

Meanwhile the years' accomplishment on the dam showed plainly. As the dam rose, it backed up the water coming down the Rat. The lake spread for half a mile behind the dam. It made a shining mirror, visible, riders said, from the top of the Sweetwater Divide, twenty and more miles away. I took a snapshot of water, headgate and dam. What looked like a fly speck was George with a four-horse team, doing the final leveling.

John brought surveyor Ed Crabb to check the height and width of the dam, and to measure the capacity of the spillway. To keep wind-driven waves from washing the top, John and George set posts and nailed sheets of cor-

John G. Love holding Allan Love, Ethel P. Love, George Rushton holding David Love. Picnic at Castle Gardens, summer 1914.
Love Family Archives

rugated iron between them, so firmly that some were still in place forty years later. They hauled loads of rock for the further protection of riprap.

While Ethel described the process of building the dam, David provided an account of his later experience with the building materials in "Dreams, Dams, and Disasters":

The riprap was blasted from nearby sandstone ledges along the west abutment of the dam. Fifteen years later, while poking around the ruins of the dam, Allan and I discovered a rusted iron box containing copper cylinders about two inches long, sealed at one end, open at the other. We were using them for whistles when Dad saw them. Shaken, he asked sharply, "Where did you lads get those?" When we answered, he said, "Take them out away from the ranch house, and bury them at least two feet deep. Handle them carefully. They are dynamite caps and they could blow your hands off or your eyes out." Chastened, we did as we were told.

As the dam reached the newly allowed height of 25 feet, the weight of the earth fill collapsed the oval concrete pipe running from the headgate to the main irrigation ditch. Repairs which consisted of building wooden molds, ordering cement to be brought by train to Moneta, and by wagon to the dam, took weeks to complete.

One day in mid-summer, 1913, Dad announced to Mother they had gotten water all the way to the farthest ditches. The fields were cleared and planted and the crops were growing well.

However, Ethel recounted the problems associated with the water in "Our George":

With irrigation came also gnats and mosquitoes. With my treadle sewing machine, I sewed cloth sacks for John and George to wear to protect their heads and necks, with holes for their eyes—much like those worn by the Ku Klux Klan. We called them "gnat sacks."

The Big Dam along Muskrat Creek at Love ranch, 1913. John Love and George Rushton, entirely without benefit of state or federal funds or mechanized machinery, had created one of the largest irrigation projects in the young state of Wyoming.
Love Family Archives

The rye and winter wheat had been irrigated and were growing tall for the harvest. John had bought and planted along a ditch, hundreds of young trees with berry bushes beside them for a windbreak. That summer we had a lulling interval of satisfaction and anticipation, with an undercurrent of uneasy suspense, awaiting a real test of the dam's strength.

One day the sky in the west was blackened by a hailstorm. Accompanied by a high wind, it pounded down upon our small trees and tore them to shreds. Only bare fibers were left of the berry bushes. The wind blew the hail into deep, white drifts over the range. On warm hillsides and draws they melted to feed the creek.

Water filled the dam, overflowing into the spillway. Under the pressure, the dam burst. The pent up water rushed along the Rat to endanger the railroad bridge thirty miles down stream.

"Looked like the water came first from a badger hole near the top," reported a man who saw the break. "Then the whole dam melted away, and was gone,"—an exaggeration.

The hailstorm inundated the southwestern half of the Muskrat Creek watershed, so the largest torrents, thick with sand, poured into the creek from the south, downstream from the ranch buildings. The flood water spread out northward, covering the planted field west of the Little Dam with sand,

The Love ranch after the hailstorm, 1913.
Love Family Archives

ruining the soil for further cultivation. The hail, flood, and sand destroyed the fruit orchard and the crops—corn, grain, potatoes, and hay. The sandy floodwater filled the windmill well near the Little Dam, and the gail force wind rendered the windmill useless. The hail was less on the planted fields below the dam. John salvaged five loads of rye, three of alfalfa and more of winter wheat, enough to prove up on our two desert claims. From his meadows above and below the dam, he cut 26 loads of wild hay. This was all he had to show for his years of expensive effort on the dam. "Love's Labor Lost," was his summary.

Ethel recorded her thoughts on this event in verse:

"Dark Dawn"

> Earth and sky are Mother and Sire.
>> Of them are the mountain, the wold and the sea.
> Living in each is One, other than I,
>> Eating and mating and like unto me.
> Stronger than I are the sun and the storm,
>> The thunder that rends the tree in the glen,
> Savage the roar of night-prowling beasts,
>> Fearsome am I in forest and fen.
> Gifts I must give Them, lest They take all . . .
>> Their anger is swift as wind or flame.
> I beseech the Mighty Makers of Things,
>> Call Them, call Them, call Them by name.

Ethel concluded in "Our George":

George eventually left. He never had trouble finding work, but he did not go far. "There's our George come home," Allan would cry out joyfully, seeing George get off his horse at Thanksgiving time or Christmas.

George returned at intervals for a few days or weeks. His visits, strangely enough, coincided with John's need for extra help. He might be sharpening the small sickles for the old mowing machine, or oiling harness when George appeared. They rode the range to bring in horses, unused now during most of the year. Of those they had worked so steadily on the dam, some had been sold, two were struck by lightning along the fence, Sam, "big handsome fool—maybe they can make him pull," went to the army.

One by one the remaining farm implements were borrowed and never returned; the walking and the riding plows, the harrow, the evener, the seeder, finally most of the fresnos and the last of the scrapers. Only the "Mormon

Ann"[5] remained, used occasionally to reinforce a low dike along the bank of the creek or to clean out the barn.

David wrote of those disheartening years in "Dreams, Dams, and Disasters":

My father's dream of an irrigation system ended when the Big Dam was destroyed. Only several years later, at my insistence, did he begin to plant flowers again, a few trees, and a tiny vegetable garden next to the house.

Dad was 45 years old, and he was exhausted. He had done everything to the best of his ability to bring happiness, wealth, and an easy life to his bride in their three years together, only to be thwarted by acts of Nature. All that remained were his wife and babies and the ranch property.

No longer a "muttonaire," and expecting no help from either the state or federal government, he swallowed his pride and went to work as a sheep-herder for Jacob Delfelder for about $50 a month, spending most of his time away from home for the next two years.

Dad never again gambled with Nature, having gained a profound respect for her forces. For Mother, these first years of marriage were training for future challenges. Allan was later fascinated with construction of all types, especially the type of dams and ditches our father had attempted to build. He graduated from the University of Wyoming in civil engineering, each day for five years passing under the motto: "The control of Nature is won, not given," and for the next ten years worked on dams and ditches for the Bureau of Reclamation at Alcova and Cody, Wyoming. I, in turn, grew interested in the relation of land to vegetation patterns and their connection to people. Our sister Phoebe spent her professional life working on land reclamation and poisonous plants.

Notes

1. In her original writing, Ethel frequently changed the names of people to protect their identity. The initial title of this work was "Our Chet."

2. Formerly the Camp Brown military post.

3. Father of one of John Love's former partners, Jack Guinard.

4. Dr. Tonkin had been a pupil of Dr. Frank Waxham at the medical school in Denver, as well as an All-American football player at the University of Colorado. His practice in Riverton also extended to the Reservation, where he was much loved by the Indians. When he died in 1934, his was the largest funeral gathering ever witnessed in the state of Wyoming. J. D. Love, personal communication.

5. A shallow, flat-bottomed scraper pulled by two horses.

CHAPTER FIVE

~

1913–1915

"Raw Material"

With two young children and a ranch to run, Ethel had little time to write during the next few years. The Wellesley Record *published the following note from her in its 1915 issue for the graduates of 1905:*

I have been busy trying to get some raw material in shape for you teachers, and this report is late because the raw material has been teething.

Few family records of the next several years remain. Two entries in her journals of the late 1940s, when she and John were preparing to leave the ranch for good, may explain why:

Saturday, November 2, 1946: I've been living in the past, remembering college friends, Vera in Oregon, Faith in various places, Robert and Hugh at college, Allan and David in Sherwood.[1]

Letters were nearly all flooded, and most of the rest of them I burned.

Tuesday, July 22, 1947: Looked over all account books—more revealing than any diary. Destroyed statements etc. through 1940. It is a matter of pride to minimize one's losses.

Rather than dwelling on mundane and difficult daily life, in hindsight Ethel chose to situate her family's place in the growth of the state. She recounted some of the events which shaped Wyoming's short history in her essay "Panorama":

No one at our ranch was scalped by Indians, or raced, his body bristling with arrows, to the house for safety. No horse thieves were hanged there; no buffalo skinners in our time; no band of rustlers shot it out with the sheriff's posse and a thousand rounds of ammunition, as one may see any day in the movies; we had no sheep and cattle war.

Yet such events were so close to our present that we heard the stories from people who had seen or taken part in them. A nurse told me that her first memory, after coming as a little girl to the mining camp at South Pass, was seeing her mother with other women, sewing shrouds for a party of men killed by the Indians.

At South Pass, Esther Morris, called the Mother of Women's Suffrage, held her famous tea party, at which she persuaded two of the attending candidates, Col. W.H. Bright and Captain H.G. Nickerson, to present, if elected, a bill for women's suffrage in the newly organized Wyoming Territory. This was passed in 1869. She was an intimate friend later in Cheyenne (where she lived with her twin sons) of Mrs. Mary Bellamy, the first Wyoming woman elected to the State Legislature, who much later was a friend and neighbor of mine in Laramie.[2]

A boy, Bob Hall, who helped string the first "talking wires" across the state, became a rancher and a State Representative. (He and his family were friends of my husband.) He told how the buffalo scratched their itching backs on the telegraph poles. Indians shot arrows at the glass insulators to see them shatter; then wooden caps were designed to protect the glass. One of these I saw at the Tom Sun ranch museum at Devil's Gate, near Independence Rock. Bob Hall also had a large iron strong-box, fitted with a lock, such as the Wells Fargo Express Co. used to transport gold dust by stage from the mines at South Pass and Atlantic City. The box was too heavy to be carried away on horseback by bandits robbing the stage. The owner had found it in his field, near Devil's Gate south of Casper.

An eastern bride, Mrs. Kirk, lived for a while with her husband at the road house at Lost Soldier[3] on the stage line to Casper. Years afterwards she told me of seeing Cattle Kate ride by on the stage road, a handsome, well-dressed young woman, astride a fine high-spirited horse.

Cattle Kate, with her supposed confederate Jim Averell, was hanged in 1889 for cattle stealing—her history almost contemporary. While the coroner's verdict was that this was done by "persons unknown," Jim and Kate's moccasins and locks of her hair were long preserved at certain ranch houses, mementos of what happened that summer night, by a scrub pine.

Among the people I have met who remember the 1892 Johnson County range war near Buffalo was a friend who, as a child, heard of the April 9 killing of Nate Champion and Nick Ray. She ran so fast across a field to warn her father, that she lost her shoes. People in the Hole-in-the-Wall country brought her hair ribbons.

A little old man, withered and bent, who stopped overnight at the ranch, said that he used to cook on buffalo hunts. He had been the last cook on the last buffalo drive which the government held to collect and ship the buffalo remaining on the plains. That could not have been later than the 1880s. I asked him about something which had always puzzled me. Did he make "light or raised bread" in camp at that time? He said he did. He boiled young willow twigs to start his yeast.

An old bull whacker,[4] Cal Lemon, worked on the Union Pacific long before there were fences or other railroads nearer. He was driving horses when he would stop overnight at the ranch. After the drive, he freighted only a few sacks of wool at a time over that same road. He was a powerful white-haired man of tremendous proportions. "Time to stop freighting," he said, "when a man can't wrassle a 400 lb. wool sack alone."

I might have learned more of his early experiences, except for his pipe, strong enough to have dated back to ox team days. Dinner over, when he lit his pipe, I put my small boys to bed at once. The smoke was too much for their lungs and stomachs. I escaped, too, as soon as I could, trying to stifle my coughs.

David, with his eye on the family's own history, wrote of his parents' attempts to rebuild their finances during this period in "Dreams, Dams, and Disasters":

After the bank foreclosed on the ranch loans, my father continued to work as a sheep herder for Jacob A. Delfelder at day wages. Occasionally he brought home motherless or "bum" lambs for Mother to raise along with her two babies—the beginning of a small, new flock. However, despite his fondness for "the woolies," he never again attempted to raise sheep on a grand scale.

In January of 1913, Dr. Waxham's estate was settled. Mother's share after the lawyers and her Uncle Ernest were paid was $1,587.64. She and Dad used her inheritance to buy a small herd of "Arizona" cattle—a crossbreed of skinny, roan short-horns and Herefords, which, they discovered, were not well-suited to the cold winters of Wyoming.

My parents also tried raising poultry. Fertilized eggs were purchased for next to nothing in Moneta, then incubated in the sod cellar behind the main house. A kerosene lamp kept them warm until they hatched. When the lamp stopped working, hens that could be trusted were set on straw-lined nests of 6 to 12 eggs in wooden orange crates in the dusky hen house. Mother found a ready market at the sheep and cattle camps and the Moneta store, and was elated when the eggs from fifty chickens brought $35.24.

A surviving ledger page gives a partial account of her successes and failures.

April:	9 chickens hatched	2 hens died - sickness
	eggs 391	" " " - suicide
	2 roosters eaten	1 chick disappeared
		1 chick eaten by cat
		1 hen died
		5 chickens died (cold & wet)
		1 chick died (sick)

Her three-year effort to raise geese netted the sum of $12.00 and the down for a few feather pillows before the geese died. Yet, she had no choice but to continue. At times, eggs were the only cash crop.

Letters continued to be Mother's lifeline to the Outside World. Her friends and sisters accused her of not reading their letters, as she asked more questions about their lives than she answered about her own. Although we were little more than babies, our parents were already concerned about how to prepare us for life in the Outside World. They had had little experience with babies and small children, and Mrs. Mills was miles away. Although most of Mother's friends were teachers, Maud Thompson was the only one who was both an educator and a mother.

Maud was now teaching in the School of Organic Education in Fairhope, Alabama. In her letter of Feb. 3, 1914, she discusses the situation in the school where she teaches, her daughter Rhoda's growth and development, and she also sent her husband's, William E. Bohn, newly published book, First Steps in Verbal Expression, *along with* Natural Education *by Winifred S. Stoner,* Montessori Method & the American School *by Florence E. Ward, and* Letters of a Woman Homesteader *(1914) by Elinor Pruitt Stuart.*

The summer of 1915, Ethel's sisters Faith and Vera, and Vera's sons Robert, age 7 and Hugh, age 5½, came to visit. On an untitled scrap of paper, Ethel described their arrival:

My sisters from Denver in their Ford made a daring trip into the unknown wilds, where once they drove thirty miles in the wrong direction before realizing it. "Everything looked alike out there." Only one bridge, that near Moneta, spanned any gulch. Their car became stuck in the bottom of a sandy draw. One sister walked to Moneta for help, tying bits of cloth on the brush to guide herself back if necessary. Meanwhile, a rider, Brocky Jones, noticed the stalled car and rode over to see what the trouble was. He fastened his rope to the front axle. My sister started the engine, and with the horse pulling, the car crept up the bank. Her little boys enjoyed this exploit of horse and rider, and the strange outfit the cowboy wore, including the woolly chaps. They walked about him admiringly. One asked, "Do you have a blouse to that suit?"

During their visit, a letter came from Denver friend, Alice Storms. This was the first mention of the war fomenting in Europe, although it was surely a topic of discussion in Moneta's general store. This was also the only reference found to articles Ethel had been writing about life on a Wyoming ranch in an attempt to improve the family finances. Neither the articles nor their publications have been found.

Alice's letter reflected some of Ethel's concerns: educating her sons at such a distance from Wyoming's public schools, and the dangers of pigs. She enclosed a list of publications and catalogues of educational psychology, primary education, and kindergarten materials. Alice wrote:

What editor had the good sense to appreciate your "How to Live on Nothing a Year"? I want to read it. He must have had a bad disposition or be horribly impecunious. $10.00 indeed! Idiot! Must be the war—but that ought to make it even more valuable 'cause so many will have to live that way.

I'll look up the pig question and see if they eat little boys. I'd adopt a silent watchful waiting attitude till we can find out.

Here's hoping one of those magazines will be perspicacious enough to make not only bathtub but a trip to Denver possible.

Ethel may have sent Alice the following vignette "Pigs":

A rancher gave John two young pigs, "and the man really meant to do me a favor," mourned my husband. George Rushton fed the pigs—shut up in a cow shed—our surplus milk, vegetable scraps, and corn; but before long they escaped and were running at large, returning to the cow shed only for food. They followed, grunting, after John and George, like dogs. But unlike most dogs, they could not be ordered home. As they grew into hogs, I had months of worry, because my small boys also began to stray. Once when the men rode beyond the ruins of the Big Dam hunting sage chickens, the hogs went with them, but at the first unexpected crack of the gun, they scurried the two miles back to the cow shed.

A longer trip became their last. A sheep man who lived miles away sent his campmover Omar to borrow our sheep wagon. Omar came on horseback and led a team to drive the wagon to his ranch. When he left, George missed the hogs. We had seen them last at mid-day, taking a nap in the shade of the sheep wagon. Apparently when the shade began to move, so did the hogs. They traveled under the wagon, mile after mile. Omar, inside, did not notice them until he was nearly at the ranch house 20 miles away. There they rested a day. They did not have to walk back. He loaded them safely into a supply wagon on the third day, glad to be rid of them.

They met their predestined end, much to my relief, and that of John and George. Their meat was a welcome change from mutton and chicken. Much of it I canned in glass jars, processed in a steam cooker, four hours a day for three days. It made delicious pork pies. "Gather up the fragments that nothing be lost," was one of John's favorite exhortations, so after making sausage, I cooked the heads and feet of the animals in the copper wash boiler. We had many pans of jellied head cheese, or "potted heed," as John called it.

David wrote later in "First Memories":

By mid-1915, the family finances had improved somewhat, although I was too young to be aware of how. Mother took Allan and me to Denver, possibly to visit her sisters, possibly to have me checked at the free Better Babies' Clinic, and possibly because she'd had another miscarriage and wanted to see a doctor herself.

I remember nothing about my life for the first two years and four months. Until then, my brother Allan and I had lived almost exclusively on the ranch, completely shielded from the Outside World.

Our secure little world was abruptly expanded when Mother took us to Denver in September 1915. In our buggy, Dad drove Mother, Allan, and me to the Chicago & Northwestern Railroad station at Moneta, the train station and the town both only ten years old. Assuming that the train would be approximately on time, Dad left us and returned to the ranch to do his chores before dark. However, the train was not on time; it had been "indefinitely delayed." Mother had no choice but to spend the night at the Kansons' hotel-roadhouse-saloon.

My first memory was of waking in the darkness of the strange hotel room to hear Mother stirring around. The dark was startlingly shattered when Mother turned on the single electric light bulb hanging in the center of the room. At the ranch, our lights were the soft flame of kerosene lamps, lit in the sequence of removing the glass chimney, striking a wooden match on pants (men only), the stove, or under a chair or table, lighting the lamp wick, turning it up (not too high or it would smoke), replacing the chimney and adjusting the height of the flame. The sudden, brilliant light and later its abrupt extinction (without turning down the wick, putting a hand behind the top of the lamp chimney, and blowing out the flame—taking care to not blow spit on the hot chimney and crack the glass), was a new and disturbing experience.

We waited in Moneta all the next day for the laggard train. Finally in the evening it arrived, and we boarded. The next thing I remember was the train wreck in the middle of the night. With a crash our passenger car was turned on its side, metal screeching against metal. The screams of terrified passengers, the yelling of train crews, flashing torches, broken glass, the fire from the coal car attached to the engine filled my world. Clouds of steam shot from the punctured boiler; the great steel drive wheels of the engine were partly buried in mud. Allan and I clung tightly to Mother, whose quiet voice tried to calm our hysteria and that of other passengers. Eventually a rescue train arrived from Casper, and we continued on our trip.

We spent the night with friends in Casper before taking the Colorado & Southern Railroad to Denver. Mother had reserved sleeping car accommodations. As she struggled aboard with several suitcases and her two small boys, a Black conductor, resplendent in blue uniform and visored cap, kindly picked me up and carried me onto the train. Never having been held before by someone I didn't know, I reacted in terror with screams and struggles, to Mother's embarrassment and the amusement of the conductor and the other passengers. Mother wrote to my father:

1544 Lafayette, Denver, Colo.
September 9, 1915:

Dear John,

Mrs. Kingsland has spent the evening or I should have finished this note to you long ago. Now I am so sleepy that it is likely to be very stupid.

We had a horrid trip down, but not nearly as bad as it might have been. All trains were late. Mrs. Johnson met me in Casper, and I spent the night at her home, thinking that the train would be like the one the night before, which also was "indefinitely postponed," and did not go through for thirty-six hours. We reached Denver Sunday, about two hours late. Faith, Vera and Aunt Mary[5] were all at the station in the car and we have surely had a fine visit ever since[. . .] Everyone asks for you[. . .]

Of course you want to know how the boys liked the trip. Allan wanted to know if it was you in the engine making the train go. David missed the buggy, and asked, "Where's that barn with George in it?" He was badly frightened when a man picked him up and carried him into the sleeping car for me. Since coming here he will not leave me, even for an auto ride. Allan will. He likes the streetcars better than the auto.

Denver seems very different; the trees meet across nearly all the streets and the vacant lots are built up with fine new houses[. . .]

Vera's boys are fine, large and bright, but great to tease and romp. Our little ones are still somewhat timid with them. School opened two days after I came. Robert is in second grade, and Hugh the first. I went to Faith's school with her one afternoon when the boys were asleep and helped her get ready for the first day. She is in the same school, seven miles from here.

Aunt Mary is a dear as usual; she has begun "sewing me up" as she threatened. Needless to say they are all horrified at my lack of a wardrobe. Clothes went to the wet wash today, also returned. I'll tell you all about it later, for we may go down to see how it is done. The girls have been talking of it for some time[. . .] Next letter may tell about when I'll come home. Best regards to George.

Do you miss me? E.

David added in "First Memories":

My father must have wondered why the trip took so long, and what Mother hadn't told him. She wrote to him again September 23:

Your letter of the fourteenth with enclosures reached me some days ago. As to the ink, if it is not on the desk, it is in the small drawer at the right where I kept the other box—'lessin David removed it. I saw him with it before we left, but rescued it.

Evidently you are qualifying for a cook. I am sorry not to see Toby before he leaves[. . .]

Vera has been abed all day with severe cold and chills. The weather was damp and cold for many days after I came. Robert and Hugh and my boys all had slight colds. Faith too.

Today I went to the ΔT Alumnae meeting and saw many friends. Dr. Bayley and Mrs. Kingsland were here on Sunday for dinner.

Sunday was a fine day. We all piled into Faith's auto and rode all day, going to Golden, up Lookout Mountain to Genesee Park, and back by the dahlia farms, where there are seas of flowers.

There is a Dry Farm Congress here on the first of October and some interesting exhibitions in connection with it—poultry, cattle, home economics and even kindergarten things. I want to see that.

The girls are anxious to have me stay all winter, but I think by the middle of next month I'd better start back.

Will write more definitely by and by—it may be sooner!

Allan says he doesn't ever want to go back—He has learned to ride a velocipede and the Irish mail.[6]

Burton Seed Co. of Denver has fall rye at $3.00 per cwt.

Do you miss me? Ethel

David's "First Memories" continued:

Mother entered me in the Better Baby Clinic where babies up to age two-and-one-half years were eligible for a free and thorough physical examination. (I had not been seen by a doctor since my birth.)

I was taken from her, stripped, and sat on a rough wooden bench along with many other naked, terrified and screaming youngsters my age or less.

The splintery texture of the pine bench rasped against my bare bottom. Cold, impersonal hands thumped, pounded, twisted, and measured all parts of me, a bright light was shone in my eyes, ears, nose and mouth, despite my protesting in every way I knew. After an eternity I was put safely back into Mother's comforting arms.

Ethel wrote John of their activities during the visit to Denver and the boys' reactions to being away from home for the first time.

5 Oct., 1915

John dear,

Your letter came some days ago. It is nearly eleven now, but no one is yet leaving our circle for bed. Faith has been doing up our birthday package for Ruth, Vera cutting out a winter gown, Aunt Mary mending, and I have been working on a nightie for Allan. Several times lately I have been moved to write and wish that I had done so for your birthday [October 2]. I hope you will never have any less happy returns of the day.

Royal and Antoinette Gelder stopped in Denver last week, and came one evening to see the babies and me. Royal is an engineer, and we talked about dams for an hour. He had had some experience with a slippery blue clay fill that kept sliding out. I'll try to remember all his suggestions for your benefit. Faith says that there have been more men in the house since I have been here than they had for a year before. In spite of that, Allan asked shortly after we arrived, "Where are all the men in this house?" It was the one lack he noticed.

He had a scare—the boy next door threatened to knock his head off!

David is more loyal in his memory. He says that he wants to go back some time to the hay stack and the sheep wagon and you and George.

The days are growing cold, many are damp and threatening, but so far there has been no snow or killing frost. On Sunday we took a ride nearly to Littleton, but were so chilled, and the sky so black that we turned around and hustled home.

Just now I think I'll start back between the fifteenth and nineteenth of October.

I wish you had told me more of the ranch and how things are. Have you heard from Toby? Did you give him the picture of himself? Goodnight and best wishes. Ethel

David's "Memories" concluded:

I do not remember how long we stayed in Denver—time means little to a two-year-old—but by the time we started home, winter had come to the ranch. On the train, between Casper and Moneta, as I looked south through

Allan and David Love, Denver, September 1915, Ethel wrote to John: "Faith persuaded me to have pictures taken of the boys, saying they will never be so cunning again. I'll have a dozen pictures printed—good-bye three dollars!"
Love Family Archives

the window at the snow-covered, rolling, treeless hills, across the Poison Creek valley, a lone cottonwood tree, bare of leaves, came into view. The tree is still alive, after more than three-quarters of a century. It awoke in me a fascination for old trees and their heroic struggle for survival.

With few visitors and no radio, Ethel and John, George and Toby were practically the sole contributors to the children's growing vocabularies. As she did the

chores which filled her days, Ethel talked to her little boys, explained, and ques-
tioned. Prompted perhaps by William E. Bohn's book, she recorded their every
word. Small bundles of undated paper scraps, some pinned, some stitched together
on the sewing machine, documented the story of their development. Later Ethel
combined these scraps, polishing and presenting them to Allan and David, the tag
on this gift reading:

"Christmas Greetings, 1946. This has been a labor of love, and is my most important present! Mother"

"The Story of Allan and David"

My two young adventurers with words, Allan and David, arrived within fifteen and one-half months of each other. Allan already had his own crude bridge of articulate communication built of a dozen and a half words used independently.

Words were a source of fun, almost from the time the boys began to use them. While Allan knew and used correctly his own name and David's, he invented or imitated baby sounds using Baa and Gagoo for his brother and himself; so by name-calling began their first experiments and improvisations in speech. This amusement continued for years.

When speech began the boys were "Us," and Allan spoke of himself in the plural. For a while, though, Allan called himself "the boys." When he was aware of his separate identity, he mused, "This me wants it," and "David is a little Allan." David, considering the same idea, repeated over and over, "I'm not Allan, no. I'm David."

At thirteen months each boy had a vocabulary of thirteen words, used independently. This is about normal. Allan's included, "Look," "Oh, tut," and "Yes." David used only nouns, and he used 30 nouns before he made use of a verb.

David chattered rapidly and entertainingly at two years. Once I counted forty sentences in five minutes, not including parts of sentences or repetitions. He used 679 words. My record for Allan, who I nicknamed Thistletop because of his soft towhead hair, is not complete having been neglected when David was born.

A trip to Denver when the boys were three-and-a-half and two brought no acceleration in the number of words learned—but Christmas did! On that day, shortly before his fourth birthday, Allan spoke twelve new words, all names of toys. He was too old for the Better Baby contest in Denver, but David went through that ordeal. His defects were: underweight, over height, a high arch in his mouth and a delayed tooth; but his score was 98.8.

A drive to Castle Gardens to cut a Christmas tree was John's usual December treat for the boys. They went eight miles and back in the buggy, the team in fuzzy winter coats, breathing frostily, sometimes in zero degree weather, the boys bundled into numerous sweaters, coats and leggings. Before the early dark, they returned triumphantly with a fragrant pine tree, not too tall for our low ceiling. It was put in a pail of rocks and sand in one corner of our living room. When the boys were two and three years old, I trimmed the tree, while David walked around and around it chanting, "O tree, tree, tree."

But the next year when the shining ornaments were unpacked, tinsel, red balls, paper chains and cotton piled on chairs, I left the boys alone to trim the tree. Bits of their delighted dialogue reached me at my desk in the dining room.

"Which is better," asked Allan, "God or Santa Claus?"

About this time he began to wonder, "Where were we before there was any world? When we are dead there will still be a world, and houses with people in them, other people." Then he mused, "Potatoes can't feel a feeling, can they? If we were potatoes, we could go through a meat chopper. Where did the first person get whooping cough?" (This is the same question their sister Phoebe asked many years later, but with regard to chicken pox.) "You can't unscramble eggs, can you, Mother? You can't turn a blot back into ink?"

David was less philosophical, but ventured, "A coyote is the whole world to a flea, isn't it?"

By the next year David was finding dragons in the rubbish pile, and a horned monster by the creek. The devil's horn he discovered, Allan, our realist, declared was only a goose's wish bone. A germ was crawling on his neck, he announced. "I saw one going into its hole on a log, a white one. I saw another on a greasewood." He asked how long a germ lived. When he heard that one might become a grandfather in twenty minutes, he reflected, "Well, that's a long time to a germ, isn't it?"

Much later a dream-telling room was made in the boys' cave, but they told dreams only to each other.

Before sunrise one morning, John, hearing an alarm among the chickens, went outside in his nightshirt and shot a coyote. It was skinned and examined to see whether it had killed a chicken. It had. There were feathers in its stomach. David was wroth. He cried out, "That was a bad coyote! He disobeyed his mother. He didn't chew his food! He swallowed it whole!"

When David was five or six, we began hunting arrowheads and chippings. While the rest of us labored along scanning gulches and anthills, David rushed by chattering and picking up arrowheads right and left, which we had

David, Allan, Ethel Love, and dog at honeymoon sheep wagon at Love ranch, 1916.
Love Family Archives

missed. He explained to me, "There's a god of chippings, named Lars, that sends us ant hills. He lives up in the sky and tinkers with the clouds."

I asked him once where Allan was. "Oh, he's hunting flies, dear, old fashioned little things."

At five Allan looked back over his years. "We don't think as much as we used to."

David's reaction was, "The days just flash by."

Notes

1. Sherwood Hall was an orphanage/boarding school affiliated with the University High School in Laramie, Wyoming. Allan and David lived there in 1928–1929.

2. Lake Marie in the Snowy Range west of Laramie was named after her.

3. Now Crooks Gap.

4. Ox team driver.

5. Mary Works, a long-time Waxham family friend.

6. According to Merriam-Webster, "a 3- or 4-wheeled toy vehicle activated by a hand lever."

CHAPTER SIX

~

1916–1917

Growing Challenges

As the new year began, John was again able to hire a few men to help on the ranch. The boys, now going on 5 and 4 years old, were nurtured at home but also became more aware the outside environment. A special Christmas gift, representing wonders in the wider world, arrived from Denver friend Alice Storms: a Schoenhut Circus, whose jointed wooden clowns and animals with slotted hands and feet could balance and dangle from tiny ladders and carts, or later from more creative places. Ethel charted the children's growth on the kitchen door jam, and their growing vocabularies on her calendar. The family was also alert to the dangers inherent in ranch life.

In "Peace on Earth, Good Will to All," David wrote of the spring of 1916 which brought the last cattle drive of longhorn cattle, en route from Texas to Montana:

"Don't *ever* go outside, laddies, while they're here," ordered Dad, as dusty, bawling streams of cattle and hollering drovers swarmed through our ranch. It was the first time I ever thought I should be afraid of cattle.

One day a cowboy came to the door, cradling his bleeding hand as he tried to protect Mother's clean kitchen floor. His forefinger, caught between his lariat and the saddle horn as he roped a wild steer, was hanging by two tendons. Calmly Mother had me dip her surgical scissors in the water boiling on the stove and hand them to her. Deftly, she snipped the tendons, dropped the finger into the hot coals of the fire box of the stove, and with a needle and thread, sewed the flap of skin over the stump. With a sweet smile to the dazed cowboy, she said: "Joe, in a month you'll never know the difference."

Spring brought new worries for Ethel: her young sons were no longer content to remain in the house. She wrote about one unanticipated danger in her essay "Red and Blue":

A pack of a dozen wolf hounds was kept at Delfelder's Buck Camp to chase and kill coyotes. They killed rattlesnakes, too, shaking and biting them to death. "They ain't happy in the spring till they've been bit," said Shorty, who took care of the hounds. "They're used to it now, and their heads don't swell up no more." Every day he cooked for the dogs a five-gallon can of mush, enriched with a pailful of lard. Almost weekly he killed a horse for them, besides. Still the hounds were always hungry. Dangerous creatures, they were kept in a high, wire enclosed pen, so that they were eager for the chase. There was an ugly rumor about a baby whose mother had stopped at Buck Camp when the hounds were loose.

After a run, two of them were left at our ranch. Perhaps they were not found when Shorty loaded the others into the wire cage on the wagon for their return to Buck Camp. In the morning I fed Blue and Red along with our own dogs.

That hot afternoon I was working in the kitchen. Allan and David were playing outside, when John, from the woodpile on the hill, shouted, "Laddies! Run! Run to the house! Here come the hounds!" Down to the creek and across, Red and Blue were tearing toward the children, almost upon them when they reached the door and slammed it shut. The hounds, not to be thwarted so easily, leaped furiously at the kitchen windows, high above the ground. They shattered the glass of the small panes, and tried to struggle through, their front feet catching over the inside ledge of the window frame, and their heads with slavering mouths, reaching through the broken glass. I had only time to snatch a heavy iron frying pan from the stove and face them, beating at those clutching paws and snarling heads, while the terrified boys cowered behind me. The window sashes held against the onslaught of the hounds, and my blows must have daunted them. They dropped back to the ground and raced away.

The next morning, John hitched up a team and took Red and Blue the eighteen miles to Buck Camp and the strong wire pen where they belonged.

Both boys grew up fond of dogs, but the younger said many years later, that whenever he sees a hound, cold chills run up and down his spine.

Not long after this, a collie puppy named Dumpling joined the family, perhaps because John always needed a good dog, perhaps as an antidote to the children's fears.

As the little boys thrived and grew, so did the region, and growth meant change. In notes for "Panorama," Ethel wrote:

John, David, Allan, and Ethel Love on the porch of the Love ranch house, 1916.
Love Family Archives

Our "early days" were the pre-Ford era. They merged slowly into an easier time. Cars brought change: sage chickens and antelope almost disappeared.[1]

People drove by instead of stopping. A Kissel or Cole car, bright blue and shiny, driven by Adolph Kanson, came to the ranch in 1917 over what was considered an impossible road. It brought our gasoline powered washing machine.

David rejoiced in "First Memories":

No longer would we boys have to stand beside the old washer by the hour, pushing and pulling the polished hardwood stick which drove the gears that rotated the dolly that agitated the clothes!

A cowboy named Charlie Chittim, his pretty, brown-eyed, citified wife and son, like me four years old, had homesteaded at a poor water seep three miles northeast of our ranch. They lived in a one-room frame shack and were frequent visitors that summer because Mrs. Chittim was very lonesome. She confided to Mother: "I can't cook a thing, but I do make delightful fudge." My father grumped: "If all she's got to offer are fudge and brown eyes, the marriage won't last." It didn't.

Ethel Love, washday at the Love ranch, 1917. David wrote: "The laundry was done about once a week, depending on the weather and the ranch activities. Water was heated in large copper boilers on the cookstove and carried to the wash and rinse tubs, in warm weather in the yard. Mother did the washing by hand, using a hand agitator and a hand-cranked wringer. The clothes were washed—sheets first, socks last—pressed through the wringer, whose chrome reflected GAT YAM, into two galvanized rinse tubs, then rinsed and hung to dry. In winter, often the clothes froze on the lines. Stiff as boards, they were stacked near the stove until they softened and dried. The next day, Mother ironed. Flat-irons were heated on the stove, then clamped onto a wooden handle. As they cooled, they were replaced with others which had been heating. Scottish economy dictated that the stove be cooking something as well—often several loaves of bread and a kettle of soup or stew—to relieve Mother from having to cook supper after a full day's work."
Love Family Archives

Their boy was named Noyes. I understood it to be "Noise," and found it appropriate. One day he took the polished hardwood stick from the abandoned washing machine and hit me violently on the skull. Dazed and sick, I retaliated with as much savagery as I could muster. I was carried to my room, checked for permanent damage, and admonished that we didn't attack guests, no matter what they did. The logic of this was unclear to me.

Allan and I did, however, enjoy Charlie's later visits. An excellent trick shot, he always came armed with a .38 pistol. In anticipation of his visits, Allan and I saved rotten, unhatched eggs. We would take a bucketful of them up on the hill behind the ranch house, and throw them as high or as far as we could. With a single shot, Charlie broke each one in the air. The yellow and green splashes when the eggs were shattered compensated for the foul odors that permeated the scene.

In the Outside World, the talk of war continued. A Denver friend of Ethel's joined the American Army Nurse Corps. Faith wrote to ask if John felt he must enlist, adding: "What are you doing about it—anything?" She reported that Vera and her boys had gone to the west coast, hoping that a change of climate would improve Robert's health.

Ethel's notes for June 1917 said: "John injured in fall from horse." David wrote of what lay behind that notation in "Ride a Cock Horse":

> Ride a cock horse
> To Banbury Cross
> To see a fair lady
> Ride on a white horse
> With rings on her fingers
> And bells on her toes
> Sheshallhavemusicwherevershegoes![2]

With a four-year-old boy on one knee and a five-year-old boy on the other, Dad recited this verse with ever-quickening cadence, his knees and feet jumping higher and higher, faster and faster, jiggling from one side to another. Clinging desperately with our legs, waving our arms to retain our balance, Allan and I squealed with delight as we rode our "bucking bronco." When Dad reached the last line, his arm ready to steady us, the ride would accelerate to a climax.

These nightly rides after supper were, Dad maintained, "to settle our stomachs." Mother feared that such a joggling after a full meal might cause indigestion, and the excitement could keep us from going to sleep afterward, but said nothing. Dad was nearly 49 years old, and after a lifetime of wishing, now had two sons of his own to enjoy. It was well that he had the supper interval to rest from the day's work before the roughhousing began.

To us, Dad was a giant, the invincible hub around whom our lives revolved. We were not aware that he was leading a rough and sometimes dangerous life. Mother we took for granted, having yet to learn what courage, intellect, and resourcefulness lay beneath her gentle smile.

In June 1917, a group of seemingly hard and reckless riders came to the ranch. Their saddle horses were lean and fast, with a good cavvy[3] of extra horses, and a nighthawk to watch them at night, to bring them in at daylight, keep them shod, and care for their afflictions. They also brought a roundup wagon and a cook. As always, our corrals were the drawing card.

One day, while out reconnoitering for the forthcoming roundup, these riders spotted the magnificent wild mare, locally called Old Essie, and her band of wild horses. Many times, Dad had tried to corral her and each time she had escaped. By now she was probably about 20 years old—too old to break, but not too old to produce superb saddle stock. He proposed to the riders that in exchange for helping him bring in the band, he would get "Old Essie," half her herd, and they could have the rest. They could also have free use of his corrals for any other bands they might capture.

Certain that Old Essie would travel in a large circle, they plotted a relay pattern. After she and her band had been worn down, riders on fresh horses could almost certainly bring them in. Starry-eyed, we listened as the plans were made.

Dad told us that we could watch the dangerous process of corralling wild horses from the dirt roof of the granary. Here we would be out of harm's way. The only stipulation, he spelled out firmly, was that when the horses got within half a mile of the corrals, we must lie down and just barely peek over the top of the granary roof. If the wild horses saw us, they might wheel and bolt over the riders forcing them into the corral wings. The riders could be injured, and the horses would escape. Solemnly, we promised to obey.

The riders started out about four o'clock in the morning, when the air was cool and the landscape and sky were turning from gray to pink. "Looks like a scorcher coming up today," commented one of the riders laconically, gathering his reins in a gloved hand and easing into his saddle. Then they were gone, and the long day of waiting began for us. Occasionally streamers of dust rose off to the north, where Old Essie led her group along the near edge of her great circle.

From time to time, a dust-covered rider would appear over the horizon and ride to the ranch. Allan and I would rush to the corrals with a bucket of freshly-pumped water and a dipper, and be rewarded with an appreciative grin which cracked the gray mud caked on the rider's face. While the night-hawk saddled a fresh horse for him, the rider would move into the shade of the barn. Each man drank slowly, sloshed water on his head and hands, and drank slowly again. Then he would remount and gallop away, our wishful spirits riding with him.

The hours dragged. We made a hundred trips to the hill above the house to scan the northern horizon. Finally, as the shadows began to lengthen and the blazing heat to diminish, at last they were coming! A man on a fresh, very fast horse was "riding point," that is, riding just ahead of them. Even wild horses will follow a leader, especially if they are tired and there are riders pursuing them. Through the pasture gate they streamed, racing like the wind, the point rider low on his horse's neck. Running south, the wild horses could not see the buildings or corrals below the brim of the hill.

As the horses topped the horizon, Mother, George Rushton—too old to ride fast any more—Allan, and I hurried to the granary and scrambled up the logs. We were flat on the roof when the band thundered down the hill east of the corrals. As the man riding point swung around the pole wings to lead the band into the corral, Old Essie, sensing the trap, suddenly bolted south-ward and across Muskrat Creek, 100 yards away. On his fastest horse, Dad raced after them, turning them in a big arc toward the east. The other riders, farther behind, would cut across the arc to divert them into the corral wings.

With a tremendous burst of speed, the beautiful wild mare tried to squeeze between Dad and the other riders converging on her. The wild herd, mostly sorrels like Essie, their manes and tails streaming silver in the wind they generated, appeared to flow along the ground. Parallel to Muskrat Creek lay a grassy strip not unlike the turf of a race track, but broken here and there by clumps of greasewood, the green thorny bush, where prairie birds nested for want of trees and sage chickens sought shade. Leaning far forward along his horse's neck, Dad urged him to greater effort, gaining at every jump. In our excitement, we forgot our promise, stood up, and cheered.

Suddenly, with a crash, Dad's horse stepped in a badger hole and cart-wheeled into a clump of greasewood. Stunned, we four stood rooted to the roof. Gradually the dust of the wildly flailing horse subsided, and for a few seconds there was no movement. Then, slowly, Dad's horse struggled to its feet, one front leg swinging loosely at an odd angle, and stood, sides heav-ing, with its head down. Beside it, Dad's body, black against the grease-wood, lay still.

My whole world burst into a scream. "Oh, Lordy, Johnny's a goner," George murmured in a choked voice, breaking the trance holding us immo-bile. As one we started toward the edge of the roof, but stopped as Mother's voice, strange, flat, cutting, ordered: "Boys, go to the house. Allan, build up the fire quickly. David, help Allan fill a big kettle of water and put it on the stove. Then stay there and don't get in the way. George, unbolt the hinges of a door in the long building and bring it for a stretcher. Run!" Her last word cracked like a rifle shot. George jumped off the roof as if he'd been lashed, moving as quickly as his odd shambling gait would permit. Gathering her skirts, Mother jumped off the roof, and with graceful strides ran through the corrals toward Dad. We also ran, terrified by Mother's voice, looking back frequently, as we scurried to the ranch house.

The riders converged, their horses sliding to a halt. Jumping down, they raced to where Mother was bending over Dad's motionless form. As Essie and her band hit the barbed wire fence on the south side of the pasture half a mile away, came the screech of wire ripped from staples and cedar posts, the whining crack as the wire snapped, the splintering of the posts, and the screams of the horses as the wire tore into their flesh.

Carefully, Allan built up the fire in the kitchen stove, while I pumped the large preserving kettle full of water. Together we dragged it to the hottest part of the stove, splashing only a moderate amount on the floor. Then we waited at the door while time stood still.

The men carried Dad in on the door. His normally ruddy face was ashen, dotted with beads of bright shiny blood, his eyes closed. One hand dangled loosely, blood dripping from two fingers. Mother, in her faded blue dress, walked at his side, and directed the men to put him on the guest room bed. Huddled out of the way against the west wall of the dining room, Allan and I waited—miserable, dry-eyed, mute.

The riders, exhausted, dust-caked and sweat-drenched, were no longer hard and loud, but solicitous and helpful. This could have happened to them today.

Carefully they removed Dad's boots and outer clothing, then scattered to chop wood, take care of the saddle horses, feed and water our chickens, milk the cow, help the roundup cook get supper, and draw straws to see who would shoot Dad's broken-legged saddle horse. Quickly Mother checked Dad for greasewood puncture wounds, found only small ones, then looked for obviously-broken bones. There seemed to be none. She diagnosed correctly that he was in deep shock, so with hot packs and massage worked to restore his circulation. The late afternoon turned to dusk and then to night. A kerosene lamp was brought. The food the men brought from the roundup wagon remained untouched. Finally, Dad began to groan and twitch, mumbling, "That damned horse! I never did trust him." We had not heard him swear before, but he was alive.

At some point, Allan and I crept off to bed. Much later, as we lay in the dark, fearing that our world had collapsed, Mother came into our bedroom, put her arms around us, and in her normal soft voice said not to worry, that Dad would be all right.

Next morning we discovered that Dad had been punctured by hundreds of greasewood spines and small twigs, some driven through his fingernails by the force of his fall. The chemicals in them stung like fury. The full extent of his injuries was not apparent for another 25 years, when he began to suffer severe pains in one shoulder and have only limited use of one arm. X-rays showed that his shoulder blade had been broken. Equally painful as the damage to his body was the damage to his pride. Again, Old Essie had escaped.

Dad's recovery seemed slow. Unused to sickness, he suffered loudly and was very demanding. Allan and I helped wait on him, enjoying man-to-man talks about riding, taking chances, care of horses, responsibility, admiration for Mother, and the necessity for all of us to help each other. Our father was not invincible after all.

Within a few days, Dad was up and walking around stiffly. Finally, one evening we begged again to "Ride a Cock Horse." Reluctantly, he complied, but after a few jumps, announced that the bronco had gone lame and couldn't buck any more. We really didn't mind. We now felt needed and useful, and soon we would ride real horses like men. Perhaps we would be the ones to capture Old Essie. (No one ever did corral her; she died of old age on the range.)

In contrast to such challenges, Ethel's friends provided a link to her former life. Among Ethel's papers was the following unmailed letter[4] from Ethel to Florence Risley, known by her friends as Big Bear. While at Wellesley College, Ethel, Caroline Holt, Florence Risley and Winifred Hawkridge, close friends, had called themselves the Bear Family. For years afterward they continued to use their own affected language. Ethel, the smallest, was Little Bear, blonde Caroline Holt was Goldylocks, Florence Risley, the tallest, was Big Bear, and Winifred Hawkridge was Middlesized Bear. John they called the White Elephant, because Ethel had been undecided for so long about marrying him. Ethel's expressions "made a new experience" and "realize the Germans" are translations from their German class at Wellesley:

23 July, 1917

Belovedest Big Bear,

Here is a peace offering of a moss agate for you, one of my prettiest, from the agate beds about forty miles away. You may want to make some more jewelry. If you do, I have a beauty, just the size and shape for the end of a hat pin, if you'd like to make one for Goldylocks for Xmas.

Win is in Wyoming as you probably know, at Wolf, near the northern border. She wrote that she had a nervous breakdown, and is to recuperate for six months. Wish I could go see her before she leaves, but it hardly seems likely. To get to Wolf, one has to go via some other state. Railroads don't go across Wyoming in that direction!

My sister Vera has been spending the winter in California with her two boys, and she too has had a nervous collapse, being three weeks in a sanitarium. I don't wonder. She went because Robert's heart was weak. Then the dear boy broke his arm in two places and cracked another bone; had to have two or three Xrays taken before things were in proper places again. Then he indulged in an intestinal indigestion, and both boys were carried out to sea by an undertow. The rescuer was six hours under a doctor's care! After that, the sanitarium.

Somehow life on the range seems harmless and safe compared to her record. My boys have been doing only things like removing all the nuts from a wagon, riding the ridge pole of the house, playing with and spilling a can of gunpowder, and drawing crayon pictures on a clean bedspread. Simple sports of childhood.

I "made a new experience" this spring, raising lambs on a bottle. There are six, and the largest weighs more than either of my boys. It is a task to feed them. If they had to be bathed and dressed they would be harder to care for than babies; one overfeeds, and they turn back their heads and die. Thank fortune they grow faster than babies. I fed 'em every hour, then two hours, from early morning to dewless eve, four tablespoonfuls each of warm skim milk, until their capacity increased. Now all six follow me about like dogs. I am quite scornful of Mary with only one little lamb. They eat only twice a day now, unless we have enough milk for three feedings. They swell about the middle like balloons. You can tell at a glance which have eaten and which have not. I'd rather raise fifty chickens than one lamb. Have about a hundred and ten this year, not as many as usual.

It is surely hot this summer; ninety-nine in the "shade" is the highest so far, and there isn't any shade except house shade. At night the thermometer occasionally gets down to seventy. There aren't more than three or four months in the year out here that haven't zero weather or ninety "in the shade" in them, though the falls are fine. As one little girl not a hundred miles away said, "Spring, summer, winter. What's the other one, papa?" "Yes, fall—that is four kinds of winter, isn't it?" One of our cowboys remarked: "I've no fear of Hades after June in Moneta."

My husband saw thirty hawks yesterday in a bunch, and declared that they were gathering to go south. I looked at him. "They ought to go north, oughtn't they?"

The boys have forgotten every German word they ever learned, except to count, and that will soon be forgotten, so far as I am concerned. I can't *realize* the Germans, but I just about do hate them.

Sorry the boys don't know much French either, but Allan has 'compassed reading. He has read and reread three books, and read parts of three more in English. Writing is more difficult for him; numbers easy. David is the sweetest and most difficult little piece that ever spun picturesque yarns.

Please write me in due season, Big Bear. I hope things are pleasant for you in the college, and I love you very much. L.B.

Nearly forty years later Ethel wrote of another event of that summer: "The Wolf Drive"[5]:

In August of 1917, while World War I was raging abroad, the ranchers and trappers around Delfelder's Buck Camp decided that what they needed was a wolf drive, a scheme both grandiose and possibly unique in the history of the United States. Using the Buck Camp as a center, they would enlist a thousand men to start from fifteen miles out on all sides and drive all the wild beasts of plain and forest before them—even rattlesnakes—into a round pen in the center.

It was at Buck Camp that my husband first heard of the Wolf Drive and saw the official printed programs. Three cowboys were finishing the huge wire pen where the drive was to conclude.

"Dell said to make sure the corral was 'horse high, bull strong, and hog tight,'" said Cactus Jack.

Ben the trapper, pulled his team up beside John. "What's Dell planning to keep here?" he greeted them. The lank and grizzled dog which had followed him trotted off to nose around the cook shack.

"Look," Cactus Jack shoved a handbill toward him, "Dell and Farlow[6] are havin' themselves a really big turnout.

Shorty broke in, "Stores is goin' to close everywhere for this business. Lander, Hudson, Shoshoni, Riverton. Big Bugs is comin', bronc ridin'. And Espanita, the world champion rifle shot! A woman! They'll all be here next Monday."

"Jimmy Weisner[7] promised he'll rope all the bear they get," said Cactus Jack, "And Dave Shoening says he'll take care of the moose and the elk."

"Where you been, Ben? You ain't heard of this drive?"

"Hell, I only been gone three weeks! My trap line don't go near no towns," Ben asserted.

"Stick around," said Cactus Jack. "You'll see plenty of folks without goin' nowhere. Bet you'll be glad to take your dog and get out on your trap line again by the time we get through with this business."

"Paper says Ed Farlow's bringin' a hundred Shoshone and Arapahoe Indians."[8]

"Ben, you must have crossed a furrow plowed a mile around the camp, and another circle five miles back? There'll be another ten miles out and still another fifteen. That's the startin' line."

The trapper's dog returned, followed by an assortment of sheep dogs. They began to sniff curiously at a triangular shelter in the back of Ben's light rig. A sharp little bark came from the shelter.

"What's that you got there?" John asked the trapper easing himself stiffly from the seat to the ground.

"Young coyote. He's crippled. Caught this'n by the toes in a trap. I heard Shorty wanted one to gentle. You kin keep him, Shorty, if you got a strap and chain."

Shorty stepped up to look at the caged animal. It growled.

"I'll stake him out where the dogs can't get at him."

"City riders will be here, too," said Jack, "Hundreds of them."

"Huh! City fellers! They think they got all the brains. Don't give the wild critters no credit. If they tried to trap a coyote, they'd know. Snap one of their cheeks out!"

The pole and wire pen stood like a vague eye looking out over the slightly rolling plains.

John brought the story of the Wolf Drive back to me on the ranch. People we knew, or did not know, stopped to ask about the Wolf drive and secure directions on how to get there. Details accumulated:

"They'll shoot a cannon off at nine sharp to start the drive."

"There'll be a big red balloon in the air to show you the way to Buck Camp. Just make for the balloon, then stop on the one mile line and wait until noon. Get to the corral at 1 o'clock."

They had three hours to make the fourteen miles—a good stiff walking pace.

Some of them looked at our horses grazing around the ranch buildings. "Are you going to leave them out?"

"Not on your life," John told them. "Don't want them driven out of this country along with everything else. They're already broke, and I wouldn't want to have to do that all over again."

"You going to ride, Johnny?"

"No, I'm taking the missus and the two little boys in the buggy. Wouldn't do to let them miss this shindig."

Allan was five years old, David four. When I asked them in later years, they recalled only a few of the grimmest details.

That morning before dawn I fried chicken and made sandwiches and cookies for the eighteen-mile trip to Buck Camp. John hitched Slopey and Brown Molly to the white canvas-topped buggy, stowed the lunch in the back and tied on the gallon water bag.

I brushed the boys' hair until it shown like the sun, and before they were buttoned into their wash suits of brown and white and blue and white, I had answered a hundred questions about where we were going and why.

Off we went. The little cloud of dust pouring off our buggy wheels mirrored one which turned the distant horizon into a slight haze. From everywhere in what had often seemed like the middle of nowhere, we were four among thousands heading for that corral. Whatever else it might catch, it had caught the imagination of the country—Noah's Ark on a grander scale, and not a docile beast among them!

The cool of early morning soon changed to warmth, then to heat. The narrow buggy seat felt cramped with the four of us, and soon the boys had to be put on robes which covered the boxes in the back. Our pace was so slow that it was difficult to be patient, or quiet the boys. There was little to see in that vast open country, except an occasional, uninhabited homestead tarpaper shack. No fences lined the little-used road, rutty and rough, through sand, up and down short gulches, winding back and forth to avoid a long one. The mid-August grass was short and already cured, the sage brush stunted and sparse.

After two hours of travel, it was a relief to hear the "Hi-ya-ya" of the Indians in the distance, and to glimpse through the dust the figure of a horseman pursuing a running animal.

The farthest furrow had been left behind; the riders had passed it. But as we approached the one-mile furrow, the gathering was spectacular and tumultuous. As many as 700 cars were parked on the line, all resembling black Model T's, although in the mélée were Overlands, Dodges, and a scattering of Packards and Marmons with chauffeurs. A din of horns, and the shouting of cowboys added to the confusion. Antelope were escaping through breaks in the line; coyotes as well, followed by cowboys, swinging their ropes on galloping horses. Rabbits slipped under rocks, then rushed out again after the line had passed, only to find themselves in the following crowd, which by now may have numbered 2,000 people.

Keeping a tight rein on our horses, John drove us directly to the round corral for the grand finale.

People continued to arrive—an ex-governor with his wife and daughters, a United States senator and his wife, several state representatives. Among these, the tallest and most vigorous was the Honorable Jacob A. Delfelder. Coming penniless to Wyoming in the late 1880s, he had run up his holdings to fifty thousand head of sheep. The popular boss of Buck Camp, he was known to all as "Dell." There were others who were later to be in Cheyenne[9] and Washington—men of business, and men of no legitimate business whatsoever.

A cowboy in a fringed yellow jacket twirled a rope in the air, while cameras ground out pictures. We did not see Espanita anywhere. "At least," I said to the wife of a senator, "Dell has brought together more people than have ever been in this country since the Reservation opened."[10]

Amid the clamor of the line converging toward the wings of the pen, the remaining antelope and coyotes dodged desperately away. The cowboys were more successful in driving the range horses into the corral, their manes and long uncut tails flowing behind them in a dusty varicolored stream.

Where were the other animals? No bear had to be roped by Jimmy Weisner; none had been rounded up. The moose and elk were in the hills and mountains, safe from Dave Shoening. The mountain lions, if any really lived on the plains of the county, and the bobcats, plentiful enough everywhere, escaped capture.

Six movie companies, including Selznick, were taking films among the crowd. Rumors in the 1950s said that the films were shown once in Lander and then lost, with the possible exception of one locked away in some bank vault.

Coming to the buggy on that blistering day, a tall man in a white hat said to John, "Now that I've had a day at Dell's Buck Camp, I've no fear of the hereafter—none whatever!" Wiping his face with a damp white handkerchief he added, "I'll trade you a gallon of whiskey for a drink of water, if you've got one. Imagine that, Johnny? Me! Water!"

John left me holding the reins, while he joined the stockmen clustered about the wire pen, to identify their own brands on the milling horses. Our team, excited by this commotion, reared and would have bolted, but for two men, who seized the horses' bits and held them. John hurried back to the buggy. With a "thanks" to them, and "Lots of flatirons in there," to me, he climbed into the buggy. "Had enough of this? We won't be home before dark if we don't get on our way."

Gregarious, but mindful of his two small sons, he wanted to avoid the slaughter of the rabbits, which was just beginning. As we drove away we saw the trapper and Shorty dragging the lone, crippled coyote, meant for a pet, toward the pen, the closest thing to a wolf anyone in that vast crowd saw all day.

Dell's Buck Camp had barely recovered from the Wolf Drive when civic duty required its facilities once more. A primary election to sample the country's reaction to the Volstead Act[11] was held in August 1917. Ethel described the family's trip to the polls in "Election Day":

Our voting precinct was at Mr. Delfelder's Buck camp in a log structure of two rooms. John and I were officers of the election. Most of the two dozen voters were men working in sheep camps. To open the polls, we drove early, with the team and buggy, and stayed to spend the night. Our two small boys went with us, and we took, as a precaution, our own bedrolls. Someone sent out a case of beer, which served as an incentive to the men to come in and do their civic duty. I was the only woman voter. New bread boxes with slots in the top had been sent out for the ballots. Seeing the liquid refreshments being enjoyed so freely, Allan and David asked if they might have some—and were told that they might. But the first taste was enough and they were never tempted to try again. With importance they were able to remark casually that they did not care for beer.

After the votes were counted, we spread our bedrolls on the floor. We all spent a restless night, tossing and turning, and were glad to see the morning. After flapjacks and coffee, we started on the day's drive home. David was feverish and itchy, covered with red welts, though the rest of us had only a few. He had to stay abed for several days, poisoned by so many bed bug bites.

It was too high a cost to compensate for the voting privilege. Thereafter, John went by himself until the precinct was abandoned; then we voted in Moneta and could make the round trip in a day.

David recorded his less restrained version of this first trip to the polls in his vignette "Beer and Bedbugs":

Our parents were not aware of the whole story. The cowboys all voted in favor of the Volstead Act so that the price of bootleg would go up. I remember that Mother and Dad slept outside, while Allan and I slept in the bunkhouse with the cowboys. What Mother thought was a taste of beer for us, was more than enough to give Allan and me severe hangovers when we awoke, covered with bedbug bites, the next morning. We were truly miserable.

As the summer cooled into autumn, wispy mares' tail clouds began to appear, frozen feathers of ice crystals against the deepening blue of the sky, forerunners of change in the weather. On our last trip of the day to the outhouse, Mother would point out shooting stars in the darkening sky. If we could say, "Money, money, money!" before they disappeared, she said, untold riches would come to us. Dad chose, to Mother's disgust, to quote from James Whitcomb Riley's "The Passing of the Back House"[12]:

> . . . The torture of that icy seat would make a Spartan sob,
> For need must scrape the goose-flesh with a lacerating cob—
> That from a frost-encrusted nail, was suspended by a string—
> For father was a frugal man and wasted not a thing . . .

That fall, Ethel's calendar recorded that Toby Leitch bought himself a car, a novelty in the Loves' world of horse-drawn vehicles. David recounted a vivid memory of Toby in "The Action Corral":

One day Toby staggered blindly into the kitchen, a cowboy supporting him on either side, his face a mask of blood and bone splinters, after being kicked in the face by a horse. Sagging, he collapsed on the kitchen stool, then leaned over the sink, while I pumped cold water to clean him and stop the bleeding. Gently Mother opened what had been his mouth to ease out his shattered teeth, which rattled like pebbles as they hit the enamel sink. Carefully she stanched the bleeding and wrapped his face in light curtain material to keep it from sagging during the buggy trip to Moneta. From there he took the train to Riverton, where Dr. Tonkin patched his face so skillfully that it looked almost normal—though different.

From then on there was awe in Toby's eyes when he looked at Mother. He took many of the photos of our family.

David described the family's growing sense of the war in "Peace on Earth, Good Will to All":

Winter arrived with the first snow. With few visitors, those mostly un-informed, and only one weekly newspaper, news of the Outside World was sporadic, but we knew that the war continued. A change came at Christmas: Mother and Dad took a moment for silence, then wished quietly and seri-ously for "peace on earth, good will for all." Empty words with no explana-tion to two small boys, but because our parents were so serious, we felt that we should be, too.

Dad at 49 was too old to be called into service, but most of the cowboys volunteered and left us. One I remember especially well. His name was Willie, a bachelor with no great brain or education, but with all the exuberance of living. He was a special friend because he paid attention to Allan and me. He made his lariat come alive, spinning it all around his horse, over our heads, un-der our feet, back and forth as we jumped up and down, squealing with delight. As he sat on the step of the long building the day he went off to war, I begged him not to go because we needed him on the ranch. Grinning broadly, his gray eyes shining with excitement, his deep voice said, "Son there ain't nothin' new here. I'm goin' to where there's excitement and adventure. I'll see the world and come back to you a hero with lots of medals." So he went.

Both parents were deeply concerned about the war, especially about the exodus of these young men who were so much needed in this pioneer territory. Out of their hearing, in a troubled voice, Dad often quoted lines from Bartholomew Dowling's "The Revel"[13]:

> When the brightest are gone before us,
> And the dullest are most behind—
> Stand, stand to your glasses, steady!
> The world is a world of lies.

"What are Kaisers?" Allan was heard to ask. There is no record of the reply.

We boys became aware of Liberty Bonds, which patriotic duty made us buy with what little money we had, of slogans like "The war to end all wars," "Making the world safe for democracy," and the struggle to create the League of Nations which would outlaw all wars. With her background of world history, the awareness of 5,000 years of wars and their consequences, Mother became as active as circumstances permitted, collecting, knitting and sewing warm clothing for soldiers and civilians, and assembling first aid kits. She also began a letter campaign to encourage politicians to support the League of Nations as the best and perhaps the only hope for world peace.

"Tut, lassie!" said my father. "What good can one woman on a far away ranch do for world peace?" Mother flared back at him, her blue eyes flashing: "All through history you can see that the right man or the right woman who is in the right place at the right time, and who is willing to dare, can affect the whole world for good or for evil." Partly because of the way she said it, and partly because it is true, it has been ringing in my ears, loud and clear ever since.

Finally, the war ended. The League of Nations was crushed, but not Mother. She said, with conviction: "Its time will come. Our work was not in vain."

Notes

1. Killed by sport hunters from town.
2. Mother Goose. "Ride a Cock-Horse." *Fifty Favorite Rhymes of Mother Goose*, Racine, WI: Golden Press, Western Publishing Company, Inc., 1963.

3. String.

4. Perhaps some letters were unmailed due to the intermittent access to mail service at the ranch, or perhaps Ethel wrote drafts so she could use the same content for several recipients. In later years, Miss Risley returned some of Ethel's letters to her, knowing she was working on her memoirs.

5. Published in *Writing at Wyoming* (1958).

6. Ed Farlow, a Lander entrepreneur.

7. He owned a steam calliope and merry-go-round in Lander.

8. Farlow had toured the country and parts of Europe with his own Wild West show, see American Heritage Center archives.

9. The Wyoming state capitol.

10. The Wind River Reservation, government-imposed home to both Arapaho and Shoshone Indians, was officially opened August 15, 1906.

11. The Act, which provided for the enforcement of Prohibition, was enacted when Congress overrode President Wilson's veto.

12. Attributed to James Whitcomb Riley, but not in his published works, and may have been written by someone else. John's version blends lines from two stanzas in the original.

13. Bartholomew Dowling, "The Revel (East India)." In *Victorian Anthology 1837–1895*, ed. Edmund Clarence Stedman. Boston: Houghton Mifflin, 1895: 101–102.

~

CHAPTER SEVEN

1918

The Beginning of the Mirage

The coming of the new year revived the Loves' hopes of a more prosperous future. Just as their little boys were growing, so was the young state of Wyoming. Ethel wrote of its growth and changes in "Mirage":

Oil to us was once just a word recurring through the history of Wyoming. Indians and trappers told of curious oil seeps. Captain Bonneville in 1832 wrote of finding the "great tar springs" near what is now Lander. His party used the oil as a remedy for the cracked hooves and harness sores of their horses, and as a "balsam" for their own aches and pains. Jim Bridger, scout, Indian fighter, and fort builder, mixed tar with flour and sold it along the Oregon Trail to emigrants, who needed axle grease for their wagons. They found, too, that buffalo chips made a hotter fire when a little tar was added to them. These primitive usages began a hundred-year expansion into the manifold employment of today's oils, greases, medications, and fuels.

When sixteen-horse teams hauled Salt Creek's light oil about fifty miles to Casper in 1890, and the unrefined oil sold for ten dollars a barrel, exploration spread over the state. Facts and anecdotes about oil remained part of the conversational stock-in-trade of the range.

Into our locality came a woman and a man—some stories say her husband, some not—to speculate in oil lands. They drove into quicksand, where they lost one horse. They managed to get the buggy out with the other horse. Beside it the woman hitched the man to the buggy. With this team she continued her way to Oil Mountain, before returning safely to town. Any compensating rewards are not mentioned in the tale.

On the same Oil Mountain, thirty miles from the Love ranch, an oil well was drilled and deserted in 1883. When, in 1911, John took me to see it, only the tar spring, the incentive for drilling, was left. That area of nearly twenty square miles, filed on for oil, since it did not fit into a later section pattern, was ignored by the land survey.

Thirty miles in the opposite direction, on the Deer Creek Divide, a drilling crew from Colorado put down a well which proved dry. They were bitterly remembered by ranchers for robbing the country of all the scarce cedar wood. They burned it, to no benefit, under the boilers.

One man who owned a large ranch was "bitten by the oil bug." He made roads on miles of land by hauling a drag fastened behind his wagon over the brush. He was said to have done thousands of dollars' worth of assessment work in a single afternoon.

Then suddenly, beginning in 1917, oil became a dominating issue. Salt Creek's shallow wells at last had a market for all the oil they could produce. The demand for gasoline mounted with the numbers of cars and trucks on the roads. The Wyoming State Highway Department was created. It used more oil to make roads into highways for more cars. Fabulous amounts of oil flowed through pipelines to the Standard Oil Refinery in Casper. A foreign order, war-inspired, was for two million barrels of oil in a year.

The first refinery there had six workers. Fourteen hundred were employed by 1920, hundreds more in offices and at the fields. Instead of fifty barrels a day refined, the capacity had increased to fifty thousand barrels daily, said to be then the greatest in the world. Casper, our nearest big city, could not build fast enough to accommodate the people attracted by the oil boom. It grew from two thousand, to twenty, twenty-five, some estimates said thirty-five thousand. New refineries were built; one supplied Casper with natural gas. Oil companies were formed every day. So many companies had so many wells in operation that oil stocks flooded the market, auctioned daily by a new Oil Exchange. A million and a half dollars' worth of stocks changed hands in one riotous day, in the Exchange, in the offices and the lobby of the Midwest Hotel in Casper, even on the sidewalks where the crowds overflowed. For months brokers made from a hundred to a thousand dollars between breakfast and midnight, and there were more than a hundred of them. "How much is Jupiter today?" took the place of "good morning."

Wildcat ventures spread in the wake of more stable development at Lance Creek, Poison Spider, and Big Muddy. From four to twenty miles away from the Love ranch, six different companies started six different wells at six different times. They freighted out their heavy equipment, at first by horses, then by trucks. Bridges were built over draws. The county "did something" to the previously neglected roads. John nailed a box to a post at our fence corner about a mile from our house. For a while freighters left mail there for us every other day.

Such excitement was contagious. Into our repetitive talk of sheep, cattle, horses, weather, and markets, new words appeared: anticline, syncline, red beds, sump, casing, drill stem, bits, crow's nest, cat walk, headache beam. Almost every herder had his own oil dome. We took up oil claims.

First, a prospector chose a promising location and dug a hole sufficiently deep to show "oil indications." Then he staked the legal boundaries of the claim, and in the center posted a location notice—a tin can, containing a paper form. It gave section-division, township, range, the names of site locators, and the name of the claim, sometimes that of a favorite dog or horse, "Jim 3," "Blue 6." A duplicate notice he filed at the county seat. Under the mining law, he could hold the claim so long as he did a certain amount of assessment work yearly. Several lawyers and bankers in Casper drove to the ranch, or wrote John, seeking a lien on future prosperity. He added their names to ours on some of his location notices. The locator's share was a royalty of one eighth of any oil produced, divided among the eight of them.

Different locators, whose claims stretched here and there for twenty-five miles from the Gas Hills to Moneta, included John's name and mine in their lists. Certainly some of these miles of land on which we shared an interest in the oil rights, would, by the law of averages, contain oil.

While this was one of the lean years in the Love finances,[1] and I continued to raise a hundred young chickens every spring, we enjoyed pleasant anticipation, which rapidly swelled into the exhilaration of the *nouveaux riches*. Yet we had none of the problems and responsibilities attending the vast wealth which we confidently expected.

Geologists had stopped with us since the time I assured one, "I know there's oil here, because my younger son's initials are J.D." [as in J.D. Rockefeller]. Now David, at age 5, was saying, "I like these men. They are different." They talked lightly of adventures in Mexico, China, and Alaska and, a song and a joke on their lips, gave an expert hand in the dish washing.

Four miles up Muskrat Creek from our ranch, a fly-by-night company erected a rig. Their chief activity was stock selling. They hired a few roustabouts and a cook, spudded in a well. The group around the rig furnished pictures and material for a lurid prospectus and more stock selling.

Since this made the fifth well drilling south of Moneta, and since another derrick was in sight to the north, John Goodman, then the owner of the town, began to sell town lots. He filled the insignificant local demand, made many sales in Casper and as far east as New York City. His predictions of Moneta as an oil center, even the site of a future refinery, boosted sales. "Corner lots" brought a premium, although there was only one intersection in town. The population, including the Clark family of five at the station, and the railroad hands at the section house, may have been twenty.

Mrs. Goodman, home from New York, had a wonderful new wardrobe. She drove to see me at the ranch one afternoon. I was in house dress and apron as usual, washing the bread mixer and seven bread pans, when she appeared, a figure of unprecedented glamour in black satin and diamonds, an elaborate coiffure, the highest of French heels and expensive perfume.

The time had passed when I did not see a woman for months. There was usually a woman at an oil rig, wife of the driller, caretaker, or cook. One came to visit with me, wearing the first overalls I had seen on a girl, topped by a lacy, beribboned boudoir cap. Curtains at a sheep wagon window showed that the owner's wife was in camp.

An inventor named Roush, during those exciting days, made the rounds of the oil camps. He demonstrated what he said was a sure method of discovering oil. It saved the expense of drilling dry holes. To watch him test his contrivance, John, some other men, the little boys, and myself gathered in our yard, conveniently a few feet from the house. Mr. Roush held, by one end of a thin cord, a black bottle. The size of a pop bottle, it was weighted with secret ingredients having an affinity for oil. These contents were concealed by black friction tape wound around the bottle.

Mr. Roush stood on the spot to be tested. An enormous diamond on his middle finger sparkled in the sun. As we waited, breathless, the bottle began to vibrate. Slowly, it made a circle, then spun faster and faster. This indicated below ground a large, splendid pool of oil. Mr. Roush, his lips counting silently the number of turns made by the bottle before it stopped, told us the depth in hundreds of feet to be drilled to reach oil. We were unanimously impressed, although we regarded the results as purely theoretical, and later heard that they were the same wherever he went.

Another visitor was "Black Mike." He came inquiring the extent and kind of our oil holdings, both claims and mineral rights on patented lands. The last time he knocked on our door, he had printed forms already typed out for John and me to sign. They would have transferred to Mike our total oil rights. He offered for our signatures the bait of twenty-five dollars—having no conception of the dizzying heights of our expectations. He was called "Black Mike" we were told because he "did the dirty work" for a certain oil company.

A range ne'er-do-well, grizzled and tattered, caught a ride to our house. He inquired importantly whether he might stay with us a few days while he did some validating work on his oil claims. Then he asked John if he might borrow a shovel. But to get to his claims, he said, he needed a team and a wagon. Having succeeded so far, he demanded, "Now, where's your oil?"

Claim jumping, violence, stock flotation, and litigation accompanied early oil findings, as had discoveries of gold in the past, and later, uranium exploration in the 1950s.

"What will you do," I asked a woman at a drilling rig, "if your husband strikes oil?"

"I'll leave," she answered, "right away." She had experienced the riff-raff following an oil gusher.

The mirage of riches from oil continued to flicker for the next 60 years.

A blizzard in early April 1918 left between eighteen and thirty-six inches of snow on the plains of central Wyoming. One of Ethel's untitled notes recounted:

John fought the April blizzard, wearing his buffalo-hide coat and bear cap, between the ranch and the Fremont Hotel in Lander. From their unheated rooms at the hotel, the occupants congregated around the potbellied stove in the lobby, as much for company as for warmth. As John entered the lobby, icicles dripping from his moustache and eyebrows, a drummer[2] exclaimed, "My god, man, what room were *you* in?"[3]

David's memories included another event from that summer:

A cowboy, badly bleeding, staggered into the ranch house one day, during one of the only summer storms. Bucked off his horse when the hail started, he could neither catch the skittish animal nor retrieve the slicker tied to his saddle. His hat was hurtled away by the wind. The hail pelted down, pulverizing the skin on his head, his hands as well, where he'd tried to protect his face. By the time he stumbled to the house, the skin and muscles beneath his scalp had been destroyed and he could no longer hold his eyes open. John drove him to Moneta where he took the train to the hospital in Casper. From then on, he wore a skullcap to hold the skin of his face in place. Ironically, the remainder of the summer was scorching and dry.

Ethel's untitled notes for the summer mentioned:

The boys found the tracks of a wolf with a club foot. They began to watch for him, and dubbed him "Old Club Foot." The tracks reappeared like clockwork—every thirty days during the summer—but the wolf was never caught. When they asked their father why he didn't kill him, John answered, "He leaves our cattle alone, so we leave him alone."

As the summer came to an end, the family began to make preparations for winter. A ledger page in Ethel's writing recorded that each month from April to October two men with two wagons made the trip to the mountains to stock up on firewood. She also noted in "Our George":

The question, "Has Johnny Love opened up the coal mine yet?" was asked by some of our visitors, hoping to take advantage of John's hard work—but John never told where our coal came from.

Oct. 11	coal	14 sacks	several days
Nov. 11	"	1 small wagon	" "
Nov. 21	"	2 tons 2 wagons each day, 3 men	
Dec. 1	"	2 men, 2 wagons (no coal)	
Dec. 2	"	1 wagon	
Dec. 3	"	2 men, 2 wagons	

George Rushton went with John to dig the coal. They drove two horses with the supply wagon to Castle Gardens. They located a coal seam, then hitched the horses to the scraper brought on the wagon, and scraped the surface dirt from the coal vein. John insisted on doing his mining in full sunlight, for once he had been caught by a cave-in, knocked down and half-buried in coal. Using pick, scoop and coal fork, they took out enough coal for a load. The coal slacked badly, and we sometimes thought it more than 100 per cent ash, but it kept a longer and steadier fire than wood. We needed about twelve loads to keep the two stoves going night and day until warm weather.

David's memories from this time period included both the preparations for winter and details of daily life:

We brought wagon loads of staples from Moneta: grain and cottonseed cake for the livestock and chickens; for us, 100 lb. sacks of potatoes, onions, cabbage, beets, carrots, squash, sugar, salt, lard, flour, dried beans, dried fruit, corn meal, bacon, coffee, baking powder, and 50 lb. tins of honey and molasses, to store in the cellar behind the house.

Mother made flat panfuls of yeast, which she dried in the pantry on the north side of the house. As she cut the dull tan paste into 1-inch cubes, the fresh, clean fragrance filled the kitchen and remains one of the best memories of my childhood.

One of my worst memories, however, was baths, once a week, in the kitchen, the warmest room in the house. A washtub was filled with water heated during supper on the stove, and set on the chilly linoleum floor. As the youngest, and possibly the dirtiest member of the family, my turn to bathe was last. From the removal of my lace-up shoes, hated knickers and long underwear, the tub edge biting into my backside, to the murky and tepid water, I dreaded the whole process.

Then came bedtime, usually around 8:30, often earlier. On cold nights, Mother heated soapstones or flatirons minus their handles in the oven during dinner, then wrapped them in layers of newspaper to warm our beds. Beneath the beds were chamberpots, which my father emptied when we were small; Mother refused.

Often, when the supper dishes had been done, and Dad nearly always helped, our parents read to us. Seated in easy chairs near the brown enamel heater, they read of the Outside World and beyond, their pages illuminated by the kerosene angle lamp on the wall, whose lower glass canister fed the fuel to the wick in the porcelain globe above. Both parents read to us often. Mother would read anything, sometimes even in French. Big Bear sent a book with colored illustrations, entitled *Monsieur et Madame*, which we deliberately pronounced "Muncher aim a damn." Dad read, recited, or occasionally roared out Scottish ballads, of battles and valor, brave men and fair ladies, by Sir Walter Scott or Robert Burns. Books introduced us to heroes and heroines, and took us on adventures far beyond our own horizons. My imagination was piqued by tales of faery queens and buried treasure, and I resolved to find—or bury—a treasure of my own someday.

Ethel Love reading to Allan in the living room of the Love ranch, 1918.
Love Family Archives

One of my favorite pastimes was to lie on the window seat in the living room, a pillow embroidered with the Waxham family crest of three red crowns and the inscription "*Alla Corona Fidissimo*"[4] behind my back, the afternoon sun bathing the room in a golden glow, to savor my favorite books. One afternoon as I recreated in my mind the stories I couldn't yet read very well, a ray of sunlight struck the bookcase, and dust motes sparkled in a magical shaft. "Mother!" I screamed, snapping my book shut, clutching it to my chest. These minute sparks of light must be the characters in the stories I treasured—and they were escaping! Without them, the books would be merely empty pages. Rushing to comfort me, Mother took a book from the sun-lit shelf to show me that the words were still on the page, and read a quick story to reassure me that my heroes were safe.

Big Bear wrote from France where she was working with the Red Cross, October 4, 1918:

You ask about the women working in and about Paris. They carry the luggage at the station, conduct the trolleys, run what few, entirely safe elevators there are, push carts & keep store.

By now I am hoping you are wading in oil to your knees. If you only knew, L.B., how sadly we need gasoline in Roanne you would just make oil grow in your garden.

The little green scissors came yesterday—just in time, thank you dear L.B., because folks are dying to right and left with Spanish *grippe*.[5] B.B sewed scissors under the lapel of his coat at once, just where they could cut off evil spirits that keep trying to sit on his chest.

Ethel's unmailed reply read:

15 Nov., 1918

Belovedest Big Bear,

The letters of September and October have just come. Somehow L.B. hasn't written any letters last month or two, just keeping broom and mixing spoon out of mischief. Now at seven thirty all the family is safe abed, including White Elephant, and L.B. has nothing ahead except a bath, and cereal to start for breakfast. Isn't it heavenly to have such leisure?[. . .]

Rumors have been flying around that the war is *over*. We haven't had mail for ten days, so don't really know[. . .]

There isn't as much sign of oil on Muskrat as there was last June. Oil company failed to pay "boudoir caps," and drank up proceeds of stock sold, so "caps" and her husband and others attacked the rig; and nothing is or can be done until rig is sold or workers paid. So endeth the first chapter. One man representing a large company was here this week, interested in another field farther away, but he says they will do nothing this winter.

Spanish influenza (confidentially called "flu") has been making the rounds even here. Shoshoni, with its two or three hundred inhabitants, had over sixty cases for its one doctor[6] to look after. There were three cases at Buck Camp on Election day. John was judge of the election there as usual, and having to stay all day and two nights, was well exposed. They have only a two-room shack. The cook "Shorty" had the "flu," so John insisted upon staying in a sheep wagon and holding the election there. He boasted when he came home that he had not washed since he left! But he escaped. He said the air in the shack was the worst he ever saw, enough to make a well man sick. He said tonight that Shorty had died.

How glad I was that the boys and I did not go over[. . .] Prohibition was one of the issues, and I wanted to vote for it. Don't think me a rabid tee-totaler, for I like something in the pudding sauce. But out here I have seen so many of its effects upon the men who go to town and often *don't want* to drink, and upon the men who sell the stuff, that war or no war, I'm very much in favor of prohibition. And, do you know, even the drinking men voted for it. Now I have three fine scarlet ballot boxes for bread and cake. Can't quite decide what to put into the third ballot box.

The only news here lately is the slaughter of the innocents among the chickens. A bloodthirsty badger dug under the foundations of the chicken house and dragged out three to their death. Later when he was trapped, the others had their revenge and ate him. Then a coyote broke through a window and killed several. Next a visiting dog slew a few. Do you wonder I hate to sleep and leave them in their perilous house?

We have acquired two angora kittens, named by the boys, Dodo and Doodle. They look just alike except that Dodo is about two sizes the larger, and correspondingly older and tamer.

Dumpling, a year-old, part collie dog completes the household. Last Sunday we had a visit from a yellow hound which belongs twelve miles away. John thought he saw him chasing chickens and shouted at him. Then he saw a coyote turn and run from the chicken house, in full daylight. The innocent hound was asleep and never even had a run after the coyote. The wild creatures were never so bold before. John has been putting out some traps, hoping to stop their depredations.

The boys have each spirited up a friend, "my lady." "My lady" has wonderful ears, she goes hundreds of miles a minute, can climb any hills. She has horses and dogs. One morning when David awoke, he remarked, "Lady killed the crown Prince last night." Allan's lady one day made the beds to surprise me. But unfortunately these ladies are not at all domestic. They prefer the free life of adventure! David's lady has wonderful jewels hidden here; Allan was much put out because David would not give him a glimpse of them. He usually believes David's wild tales, tho' occasionally when truth and imagination cross paths, he tells me angrily, "David is telling *lies*!" . . .

Best love and best wishes [Two bear tracks]

In addition to the usual housework, Ethel described a few of the activities that filled her days in "Our George":

"What do you do with your spare time?" asked a college friend in a letter. This was my spare time: I cleaned the clocks, I oiled and regulated the sewing machine, I made pillows from wild duck feathers, and puffs from goose down. I stitched and tied covers for wool comforters. For two of them I washed and carded the wool from our bum lambs. There was always sewing and mending. Bundles of remnants were an exciting challenge. From ticking to curtaining, I found a use for every piece. I never answered her question.

A fragment of her poetry entitled "Jigsaw" added:

> She sits
> And knits
>> This moment is hers,
>> And not to be lost.
>> She fills each one,
>> Fits it into her day,
>> Like pieces of a puzzle—
>> What will she say,
>> When the jigsaw is done?

Ethel had mentioned their dog Dumpling in her letter to Big Bear and later wrote the story of "Dumpling, Wyoming Sheep Dog." This dog, in particular, illustrated his value to the family and the dangers dogs faced:

Roly-poly and soft, a nearly pure-bred collie pup, Dumpling curled up at night in a box among my motherless bum lambs, longer-legged, but not much larger than he. Dumpling drank beside them when they crowded kneeling around a large pan, their noses down in the warm milk, their tails waggling madly in a frenzy of hunger and satisfaction, their flat sides suddenly distended by the food. He played and scuffled with them. When the lambs chased back and forth on our porch, Dumpling chased alongside them, his small excited bark joining the clamor of their "maa's." He began to snatch and tear at their flapping ears as they ran. A saddle cinch ring tied over his nose for a muzzle quickly taught him not to use his sharp little teeth on the lambs.

From the first he padded to the kitchen door if he wanted to go outside. Soon he learned how to open the screen and in time managed to open it from without, prying with his nose until he could get a small paw between screen and door frame.

Before he could keep up with Allan and David, he tagged along behind them from yard to granary, corral and chicken house. He discovered that he could find a good meal in a hen's nest. I filled a blown egg shell with red pepper and left it on the chicken house floor. He sampled it, and wanted no more raw eggs.

In a few months the lambs outgrew him. Their ecstatic tails were docked. They ate grass, and were turned out in the field, sheep bells strapped tinkling about their necks to keep away coyotes.

Dumpling lost his baby roundness. For half a year he was lanky and loose-jointed. When fully matured, he was a beautiful dog. While he had the typical collie markings, a silky golden coat, deep white ruff and white tip to his tail, he was somewhat shorter and broader in build, wider across the forehead. He outstripped my boys in growth. When the little fellows, lost to sight in the head-high brush, roamed exploring, looking for birds' nests, or, along the shallow edges of the creek for frogs' eggs, Dumpling always with them,

Ethel and Allan Love feeding bum lambs. Dumpling, left foreground. Love ranch, 1918.
Love Family Archives

all intent on discovering whatever was exposed under the tall tough cover of grass—a nest of birds, field mice, or snakes. I had only to call Dumpling to find out where they were. He came leaping and bounding over the grease-wood, far ahead of them.

Infrequently, as he and my little boys roamed, they happened upon a rattlesnake. It coiled in the shelter of a bush, while Dumpling danced and circled about it, barking, until he attracted the attention of John or George to come and kill it.

David added his own memories of Dumpling:

One day as Allan, Dumpling, and I explored a low hill north of the ranch house, we encountered a huge rattlesnake sunning itself beside a grease-wood clump. As the dog bounded toward it, yelping and growling, it struck, firmly clamping its fangs into the soft flesh of Dumpling's nose. Screaming, we watched as the heavy body swung for an instant, before dropping to the ground. We ran down the hill to the house, where our dog, whose head had already begun to swell, collapsed, sticky froth bubbling from between his clenched teeth. His body stiffened, twitched, and lay still. His head swelled to grotesque proportions, and for a few days he lay as if dead, weak breaths the only indication that he was still alive. But he gradually recovered, and was just as fiercely protective as before.

Ethel's story of "Dumpling" resumed:

During the winter months the boys often romped exuberantly in our large dining room. Dumpling raced along the porch beside the window. He found his only plaything, a battered old shoe. He worried it, shook it, tossed it in the air and caught it, trying to take part in the hilarity indoors.

In the bustle of preparations for a picnic, Dumpling took his stand in the middle of the kitchen floor, alert and eager not to miss anything. Either we took him or tried to leave him, it made little difference. He went. If tied, or shut up, he worked loose, once even broke a window to escape and go. Then he tried strategy. When we looked for him to tie him up, he was nowhere to be found. A mile from the ranch we discovered him trotting quietly under the buggy, or he appeared frolicking happily out of reach before us. Since we wanted him anyway, we stopped trying to make him stay at home.

When John was away on horseback, Dumpling sat at dusk on the top of the outdoor cellar roof, watching. From far away, perhaps two miles, he sensed the direction of John's return, and was off to meet him.

In Moneta one day, I was sitting beside the dog, who was sleeping under a window. Suddenly he wakened. He gave a low, conversational bark. I looked out the window. At some distance across the railroad tracks, a wagon was approaching. It was not ours, not drawn by our horses, but on the seat beside the driver was John. Dumpling knew—but how?—and told me.

He, like John, never lost his fondness for sheep. Occasionally John took care of a small bunch of bucks in the fall, old ewes in the winter, or yearlings in the spring. He fed and corralled them at night. During the day he took them to graze on the range. Dumpling hardly needed to be taught the shouts and arm signals meant to start the sheep from the corral, to turn them one way or another. He understood the signals to "go 'round them," to keep them from scattering, to bring in the stragglers, to herd them into the corral. When a particular ewe was pointed out to him, and he was told to catch it—or even a lively, unpredictable lamb—he stalked it, until he could push it against a clump of brush to hold, unharmed, until John could reach it.

"A good sheep dog," John admitted grudgingly, with a Scottish parsimony of praise, "but fast, too fast."

It was a sight to see Dumpling box with a pet buck, three times his weight. Face to face they stood, a little apart. The buck charged, head down. Dumpling dodged the wide, curved horns, and rushed at him safely from the side. The buck swerved and attacked again. Dumpling leaped away to circle for another dash from the rear. They kept at the sport until they tired and walked away together.

Dumpling practiced his talents for herding even on the chickens. One morning, very early I found him quietly moving all the hens into a corner between two walls of the house. To stir up a little excitement, he was known to make a rapid dash around and around the hens, setting them to squawking and flying. When John appeared, Dumpling, although breathing hard, was the picture of innocence. He never caught nor hurt the birds. His attempts to drive range horses or cattle were without success. Instead of "heeling" them, he ran to their heads as he did with sheep. But if he could hear the cowbell at sunset, he went for the milk cow and brought her to the corral.

Working with sheep was his delight. During lambing time in May, if we had no sheep of our own, he left us for the nearest bunch of sheep, to help the herder, who, needless to say, had his own dogs. I suspected that Dumpling was encouraged in this, for different herders borrowed him. One made a vain offer for the dog of a sum that would have bought twenty sheep or a good horse.

Late one summer night Dumpling awakened me with sharp barks of distress. I slipped into my shoes, left the boys sleeping, and went out into the moonlight to look for him. He was standing at the yard gate, caught by a wire in his eye. Evidently he had been opening the gate as usual, when a loose end of wire hooked into his lower eyelid. The pull of the gate spring held him prisoner while he braced himself against it.

I told him that I must go for the wire cutters before I could help him. He waited, only whimpering a bit, until I came back and cut the heavy wire. Without a struggle he let me hold him to remove the wire from his eye. Fortunately the eyeball itself was not damaged. He followed me closely into the house and for some days would hardly leave my side.

Like the rest of us, he carried a mallet to the croquet ground in front of the house, when we played in summer, though he was loath to let go of it. He nosed the balls out of place, quite unfairly, but impartially. Still we, as well as Dumpling, felt that the game was never complete without him.

When my baby girl Phoebe arrived, Dumpling considered her his own charge. He began his nightly watches under her crib. The boys were more his contemporaries and playfellows.

"That dog will save the children's lives someday," predicted an admirer of Dumpling. The opposite happened; they saved his.

Twice in winter his curiosity led him to follow an enticing scent along a trail which brought him to a hidden coyote trap, staked down in the brush. He was caught by the leg. Each time the boys missed him. They searched, once for two days, until they found him and were able to spring the trap before he was crippled.

Some trapper dropped on the road near our ranch a strychnine pellet, a marble of hard fat rolled in sugar. Inside was a measured dose of strychnine sufficient to kill a coyote. Dumpling snapped it up. The poison acted quickly. He fled, foaming at the mouth, straight to the yard. The boys saw him and called John and me. We watched helplessly, while he made fast, dizzying runs in ever closing circles until he collapsed limply on the ground. We thought he was dead, and brought a tub to cover his body. Then the tub moved. John lifted it. A jerk of Dumpling's leg gave us hope. Quickly we warmed a cupful of lard and forced it down his throat. In a few moments, to our amazement, he staggered to his feet. Gradually his strength returned. In time he made a complete recovery, except that the long silky hair on his hindquarters was afterward rough and dry looking.

On Dumpling's last visit to a sheep camp near Moneta, someone, perhaps a herder, mistaking him in the dark for a coyote, emptied his shotgun at the dog. Even that did not kill him, although we heard that he was dead. Several days later he reached home, having somehow dragged himself fifteen miles. His face was festering, torn by shot, his jaw was broken, some teeth shattered. These wounds healed after months of care, but his adventurous days were past. He was content to live quietly in the house for the brief remainder of his long life. He lay with his nose against John's foot, or rested his head on my knee. Every night he still slept under Phoebe's crib.

After Dumpling, not one of the other dogs at the ranch could take his place. His death brought grieving and tears. He lies buried beside a low bank near the house.

After a year of hoping for an oil boom, but dealing with the mundane tasks of family life, Ethel's untitled notes at the end of 1918 reported that the year came to a close with an uproarious community gathering:

Against our better judgment, we went to Moneta for a Christmas celebration at the railroad station. There was a rival celebration at the hotel. A man named Pete had obtained a Santa Claus outfit, and was to do the honors at both places. Each had a trimmed tree. First he went to the station where there were several small children. At the hotel the few other women in town were invited. Pete bought the same suitable presents for them all—pink silk stockings. As the evening progressed, with plentiful drinks, the celebration grew riotous, until the housekeeper ran amuck and attacked the cook with a cleaver while the guests fled.

Notes

1. Ethel's egg sales earned $128.72, but there is no record of income from livestock.

2. Salesman.

3. A Mrs. Rate from Lysite later sold this story to the *Reader's Digest* (J.D. Love, personal communication).

4. The most faithful to the crown, honoring a physician relative of Ethel's who had cured three kings.

5. Spanish influenza.

6. Dr. Emory Lee Jewell, known for his pioneer research on Rocky Mountain spotted tick fever.

CHAPTER EIGHT

1919

"The Equalizer"

An unmailed letter from Ethel to Wellesley friend Caroline Holt began the chronicle of the next two years.

11 March, 1919

Dear Carrie,

Your good letters to the boys, and mine came only a few days ago, and "return mail" means sending an answer tomorrow, which I hope to do[. . .]

I was so sorry to hear that you had the flu, and so glad to hear that [your] grandmother was better[. . .] Vera's boys have the flu now in Denver. The younger one is up again, but Robert seemed quite sick. Allan is writing a letter to him now.

Everyone who has been here lately has had a cold, and the boys are just beginning to recover from the worst ones they ever had. David was sick for about a week, in bed part of the time, and lying on the davenport a number of days. I hope it won't be whooping cough, but if they could have caught it anywhere I should call it that. It began with a loose persistent cough in the chest, went on to fever, indigestion, headache, cold in the head, with the cough the worst feature, and it still continues. David was about his worst when Allan became sick; now David is free of fever and lively again with a good appetite, but occasional cough. Today is the first day Allan has been at all like himself. Yesterday David came in with news of a new hiding place he had found, but Allan answered, "I don't care about anything in the whole damn world," in a most miserable little voice.

Of course John and I have a touch of the same trouble, but he can eat square meals and go after coal, and I can be about and do the necessary things tho' very stupid and somewhat dizzy. We don't think it's the flu, because of the coughs. It's quite inconvenient not to have a doctor—or druggist, or dentist, or plumber or clock mender, or carpenter—within thirty-five miles. The nearest doctor refused to come out when Mr. Fraser, a Scottish friend, had the flu last fall, but we have always managed pretty well. I'm a firm believer in castor oil and camphorated oil, hot water and such things. When I took the mustard plaster off David's chest, Dodo, our angora cat, thought she would take a taste of it. Shows how good it was!

A large pot of narcissi is in blossom now. The hyacinths from you came up after all, and began to blossom down in their collars. I put cones of heavy paper over two of them, and set them in the sun. The flower stalks of one shot up nicely, and the other is growing taller but has not blossomed yet. I have a calla with a sad history: first leaf eaten by a kitten, second leaf frizzed by cold when plant was on window sill in the sun, third leaf wilted by frost at night (I thought whole plant was dead, and put it away, but still watered it), fourth leaf arrived but was broken off, fifth leaf is just unfolding. What next?

Is it true that rats and mice can't bear the smell of peppermint, and won't stay near it?

Your letter was too good to answer this way, so I'll have to try again soon. I hope you will soon discard the signs of old age, and any feelings of it which the flu may have left you. Give grandmother my love. She is a dear if she is like you.

Little Bear[1]

The boys recovered. Spring came, and Ethel wrote in "Our George" of one of the responsibilities of the season:

Our bum lambs had grown until they outweighed Allan and David, who thought it fun to ride them sitting on their broad, wooly backs, before their erratic jumping tipped the boys overboard. Before the hot weather, the sheep had to be shorn. Allan and David hunted for the rusty sheep shears and an oil stone to sharpen them. We had no pen suitable for holding a single animal. But in front of the granary, in the large corral, they began the task in the morning. It was hard for their short arms to hold the struggling sheep, for the small hands to manage the dull, unwieldy shears. The fleece was heavy and the day hot. Toward the end of it they came to get my scissors to finish cutting the last dirty tags, more weary, determined, and grim than triumphant. It was their first, last, and only shearing.

George and the boys filled sandbags to dam the creek in summer. The boys sailed a small, fully equipped battleship that someone had made and left in

David, Allan, Ethel Love, and Dumpling in front of the ranch house, 1919.
Love Family Archives

the blacksmith shop, and they tried to swim in the shallow water. George took soap and towels to bathe. He used a safety razor and let Allan and David shave him. The operation took hours. They did it over and over again.

David added from his writing of "First Memories":

The high alkaline content of the cold water in Muskrat Creek made our skin itch—yet baths in the creek in the sun were infinitely preferable to baths in a washtub on the chilly kitchen floor.

Toby Leitch, who now homesteaded some waterless land six miles down Muskrat Creek, brought his mother and sister, young niece and nephew, visiting from Scotland, to stay with us for a few weeks. About our ages, Margaret and Robert were the only children we had ever played with for more than a day or two, and we thoroughly enjoyed their company. Margaret hinted that she and her brother had wonderful secrets. If we gave her the toys she wanted and played the games she wanted to play, they would show us these secrets. Of course we were curious, so after much suspense, they took us into the draw next to the corrals, pulled down their underpants, and showed us their genitals. With the disdain of a seven-year old, Allan scoffed: "This isn't any secret. People and cows and horses all have them." The scene ended abruptly and nothing more was said, but for the first time, Allan and I became aware that sex was viewed differently by different people.

David Love on the hill behind the ranch house, 1919. Love ranch, Muskrat Creek in the background.
Love Family Archives

That summer was also the beginning of "formal education" for Allan and me. Our first schoolmarm arrived, a pleasant, competent young woman named Miss Evans, allotted to us for three months by the Fremont County school board. I don't remember at what age we learned to read, but it was long before Miss Evans came. School was a welcome diversion from what Allan and I considered to be a boring life, but I remember little of what she taught us.

Besides learning from occasional visitors and Miss Evans, the boys were also made aware of hard lessons in personal safety. In "The Action Corral," David reminisced:

I do remember that Allan and I had been taught to keep our distance from range cattle, who were unpredictable and unaccustomed to people on foot. We had been particularly warned about a roan cow called "Arizona." One day that summer I carelessly cut through the action corral, unaware that Arizona was there and watching me. Suddenly, George Rushton, from the adjacent corral, shouted: "Run, David! Run for the fence, son!" I dodged behind the snubbing post just as Arizona lowered her head and charged. As she whizzed past the post, I lept for the fence and scrambled up the side. In a split-second, her sharp, black-tipped horns were battering the rails just below my feet while my heart thundered in my throat.

A bull generally shuts his eyes when he charges; a cow does not, so is far more dangerous. Even as a grown man, I don't approach range cattle on foot.

While the boys studied with Miss Evans and observed the activities around the ranch, John and George worked on the range, and Ethel gathered and sold 7,871 eggs, by the dozen and by the case. She also recorded her interactions with an orphaned colt in her story of "Our George":

We had a small, brown colt, whose mother, a flatiron mare of ours, was accidentally killed in the corral at Moneta. A friend brought the little fellow to our ranch. I fed him milk, lifting the pail over the yard fence so that he could drink without crowding me. Impatient for his food, he once trotted clattering into the kitchen.

"What shall we name him?" asked John.

"He's a jolly little horse," answered David. "Let's call him Jolly."

When the colt was old enough to rustle his own feed, John turned him out with the bunch of range horses.

I did not see Jolly for several years. Then, one day when we were driving, we watched some horses trail to water at a draw. John said, "There's Jolly. Do you recognize him?"

I did not. Jolly was brown. John stepped out of the buggy and called. A large, beautiful iron-gray horse raised his head, listened and remembered. He came slowly to John. Of Percheron stock, gentled by hand-feeding, Jolly needed only the sight of a nosebag to be caught.

It was very different with big, white Dan, who, John said, "always had to have his fun" before settling down to work after running loose in the winter. Like the range horses, he resisted being corralled and harnessed. They were, or pretended to be, afraid of the wagon. It was a light, low supply wagon, with the seat removed. I used to watch from the yard, my boys safe behind me, while the men hitched up the horses.

When John took his place in the wagon, standing like a charioteer, keeping a tight grip on the reins, George held the horses' heads, ready to jump aside, catch the back of the wagon, and climb aboard before it whirled away. Dan was quivering and shaking with alarm. From his bent knees he started in great plunges, before breaking into a run. "Whoa, Dan! Whoa, Dan!" John shouted in what was meant to be a quieting command. The horse beside Dan, if not sharing his fright, was dragged along, regardless. The wagon rattled and careened about the open space; then, up the hill, full tilt, to disappear along the road out of my sight. After a hectic mile or two of running, the horses trotted back down the hill, somewhat ready for the fall work. But nearly every day the air was punctuated by cries of "Whoa, Dan!"

John always drove the heavy team on the mowing machine. He knew how close, over the hollow sounding earth, he could safely cut hay around the bog holes in which we had lost cattle and horses. George followed, driving the lighter rake team.

In the usually dry weather, they could begin loading and hauling soon after the raking was done. The meadow extended a mile from the hay corral, so from three to five loads made a day's work. About a week finished the hauling.

John liked to have me ride with them for the last load. Sometimes I held the reins and called, "Whoa, Dan!" while both men pitched up the hay. Then, as the wagon swayed slowly back over the uneven road, I lay nestled deeply beside Allan and David in the fragrant hay. The billowy white clouds, moving across the wide blue sky, were close, so close, it seemed there was nothing else in the universe but clouds and hay.

John used to cut more hay eight miles down the creek near Mud Springs before the land was filed upon by homesteaders. He and George or one of the men camped out there until the cutting and raking were done. Then they hauled about fourteen loads of hay to the ranch. The round trip took a full day for one load. The men finished and topped haystacks in the square hay corral, and behind the barn made other stacks which gave shelter from the north wind.

The small boys teased to go with John and George. Sometimes they rode down the creek on the empty wagon. They came back perched on the load of hay, or ran alongside with Dumpling.

David filled in details of their daily routine during this time:

As summer drew to a close, Miss Evans' term ended and she returned to town. The haying was completed, and the cellar stocked for the winter. Yet the days continued golden.

Allan and I were awakened as we were most mornings by the rattle of coal and wood stoking the stoves in the kitchen and dining room. Warm in our beds, we ignored the closing of the back door as Dad went to feed the chickens, milk the cow, and bring in the wood Mother needed for fuel each day.

Meanwhile, Mother was ladling rounds of sourdough batter onto the soapstone griddle to fry with bacon and eggs. She had fed our sourdough culture the night before with flour, water and a little sugar to make flapjacks, biscuits, or bread in the morning. Oatmeal had been cooking in the fireless cooker overnight. After filling the wood boxes, Dad ground coffee beans in the grinder on the wall. Then, to be sure we were stirring, he came to our bedroom on the pretext of checking the porcelain chamber pots beneath our beds. (We called the metal ones "thunder mugs.")

John Love at the woodpile behind the ranch house at Love ranch, 1919.
Love Family Archives

Throwing on our clothes, we raced to splash icy water on our faces at the basin beside the kitchen sink. (We only brushed our teeth at night, using flavorsome, minty Pebeco toothpaste. Later I learned it was full of lead!) Whether we felt like it or not, we always said "Good morning."

Unless there was company, breakfast was at a small table pulled down from the kitchen wall. Allan and I were setting out the Blue Willow china, milk and cream, and condiments one morning when Dad said, "The chokecherries at Indian Grove must be ripe now. It would not do to let them be wasted."

As we put saucers of stewed prunes at every place, Dad winked at us. We would be included in his plans for the day! Mother, whose part of the choke-cherry process would come later, chose to remain at home.

We set off in the buggy early that brisk, sunny morning. With the rumps of the two-horse team roiling lazily before us, Dad began to reminisce about his early days in the country. Occasionally an antelope or rabbit bolted away through the sagebrush, startled by our voices and the rattle of the buggy wheels along the dusty track.

In mid-afternoon we reached Indian Grove, a cluster of aspen and choke-cherry bushes on a source of good water, about 25 miles southwest of the ranch. Fire pits and artifacts showed that this had been a favorite place for contemporary as well as prehistoric Indians, who used the chokecherries in the preparation of pemmican.

Our horses were watered and tethered, our campsite readied. We unloaded our buckets and began to pick. Allan and I had never seen chokecherries before—translucent, dark red miniature cherries, hanging like clusters of garnets from thin twigs.

"Daddy?" The sticky juice was staining our hands purple and running down our arms as we stripped the berries we could reach into our buckets. "Why are they called chokecherries?"

"Taste one, laddies." Beautiful little fruit to see—but when we tasted them, they were mostly pit, and made the insides of our mouths pucker. "How can these awful berries make jelly?"

"Your mother will work magic on them with sugar," Dad replied, his eyes twinkling. Picking began to pall. We were hot, thirsty and hungry, our hands and shirts stained and sticky. The chokecherries attracted ladybugs, wasps, and flies. But at the end of the overnight stay, the back of the buggy was filled with buckets of chokecherries, which Mother transformed into flavorsome tart jelly and pancake syrup.

Ethel's October calendar recorded a rare visit from John's sister, Laura Love Henkle, who came for a short visit from her farm near Stratton, Colorado. Laura was the last guest before an early winter began. In the 1950s, Ethel wrote "The Equalizer" about the Hard Winter of 1919, an ordeal so difficult that Ethel's blond hair turned white:

The preceding summer in 1919 was without rain, the hottest and driest of all summers. The scanty grass dried in June. Our meadow hay was almost too short to cut. In the fall when the herds of sheep came down from the mountains many owners moved them by train or trail to areas where there was hay. Low market prices discouraged shipments to Omaha. Some stockmen, faced by the poor range conditions, tried wintering their livestock in other states. A few took their sheep to the cut-over Wisconsin lands. They found there was no food value in the high, lush, green grass that puffed out a sheep's sides like a balloon, but left them deflated by morning. A few shipped cattle to Texas. They had no calf crop the next year. Some loaded cattle, horses, and riders on freight cars for New Mexico. There the cattle scattered and disappeared in the thick brush. Some stockmen stayed on the home range with their sheep or cattle. That, too, was a mistake. It would have been kinder and less costly to market them at any price or to shoot them.

Winter began the first week in October. There was a storm that left deep mud, although the earth had been dry. We got out our rubber boots and overshoes. Whenever we left the house we needed them until June. Another storm covered the mud with snow. The animals, having to struggle through both mud and snow, weakened rapidly.

At the same time, the climax of our imagined prosperity came that fall. John leased our claims to a large oil company, which was to start drilling within three months. The agent was Mr. Beale, an Englishman, probably fifty years old, a bachelor, who sang in the choir of the Episcopal Church in

Casper. He wrote John many letters in his beautiful, distinctive handwriting, and made over-night visits at the ranch. Immediately on arrival he took out and smoked his pipe. It had an unforgettable fascination for Allan and David. The amber stem was unusually long and carved. The pipe itself had silver trimmings and a silver lid that snapped back for lighting, and holes to let the pipe draw.

Mr. Beale had negotiated the lease. To sign it, with powers of attorney from the other locators, was the business which took John to Casper in November.

Our hardest winter had already begun, and grew worse. John went to Casper at Thanksgiving, by train from Moneta, for a number of days, leaving to the little boys and myself the care of the cattle. We drove them every morning to the meadow, where standing hay still showed above the snow. As the long line of a hundred and more trailed slowly by, the boys called some by the names they had given them, "Coachman," the "Rattlesnake-bit-cow," "Adam," and "Eve."

John returned feverish. He soon became much worse, his fever very high, his nights delirious. David caught the fever, and I put him, too, to bed. Allan drooped about the house for a few days, but then recovered.

David guiltily remembered in his account of the same time period "The Broken Plank":

As he usually did, Dad had brought home some red and green sticks of hard candy. He said that perhaps the candy had been contaminated and had made him sick, so none of us should eat any—throw it out! Nobody did. They lay, dazzling in the sunshine, on his bureau. After struggling with temptation for a day or two, I ate a piece. Then I got sick. Had I not disobeyed, would I have stayed almost well like Allan? It has weighed on my conscience ever since.

Ethel's "Equilizer" resumed:

Another snow closed the roads and covered even the meadow grass. Cattle hurried past at night, the snow squeaking under their feet, as they tried to find a corner away from the wind that pounded like a battering ram against the walls of the house. I shut off all the rooms except the kitchen, dining room and one bedroom, with the double bed and two children's beds to save heat. Frost pictures grew thick on the windows. My hyacinth bulbs froze at night on top of the kitchen range, where there was a slow fire. Snow hissed around the buildings, wind blew some snow into every room of the closed house, down the chimney, between window sashes, even in a straight shaft through a keyhole. The woodpile was buried in snow. The small heap of coal was frozen into an almost solid chunk. In the numbing cold it took me five hours a day to bring in fuel, carry water and feed to the chickens, and to put out hay and cottonseed cake for the cattle and horses that came crowding about the corrals to be fed. Allan kept them from me with a stick while I made a row of small piles of cake in the trampled snow. When the barn door was frozen shut, his efforts with mine broke it loose.

Drifted snow, we learned later, had blocked train service from Casper a hundred miles away. Thousands of small birds, followed by hawks, had sought shelter there in the streets and among the houses.

For weeks no one came by the ranch. John began to complain, a favorable sign. Why was I outside so much? Why didn't I stay with him? To try to make up to him for being gone so long, I sat on the bed at night, wrapped in a blanket, reading to him by lamp light, while the boys slept. He wanted his clothes. He wanted to go to a doctor.

Feed and fuel were nearly gone when there was a slight, brief break in the weather. A man on horseback stopped. His face was nearly black from exposure, deeply seamed from cold. John insisted on dressing, and having the man harness the team to the buggy. Well wrapped in robes, he started alone through the snow to Moneta and the railroad.

In a day or two our friends the Frasers drove in with their light wagon, on the way to their sheep camp. They had seen John in town. They brought a small load of coal and food and letters wishing us a Merry Christmas. At an oil camp near their cabin, drilling had stopped. The Frasers brought one of the workers, who stayed for a week. He chopped a supply of firewood, and did the feeding of the stock.

David added in "The Broken Plank":

We had never met him previously. Most of the people we knew were so afraid of catching Spanish influenza that they stayed away from where it was known to be—but not this kind, great-hearted man!

That year we had no Christmas, no celebration of Allan's 8th birthday, no recognition of the New Year, 1920. Our energy was spent just surviving each day.

Ethel's perspective continued in "The Equilizer":

John arranged with Charlie Cunningham to give him the use of a four-horse team and our large bobsled, in return for hauling oil cake and baled hay from Moneta to the ranch. He did occasionally bring out a load. One tipped over, miles away, in the snow, the bales split open, scattered and broken. Charlie spent the rest of the winter hauling for other stockmen. When the snow finally melted, the hard-packed, frozen tracks of the bobsled stood a foot above the ground. We never saw the horses again.

John stayed at a hotel in Riverton, where there was then no hospital. After what may have been a week or two under Dr. Tonkin's care, nothing seemed to break his fever. The doctor said he might as well come home and wear it out.

David well remembered in "The Broken Plank" when his father came home and relayed to Ethel what Dr. Tonkin had said:

She responded with fierce intensity: "He might as well have said 'to come home to die,' but I won't let you die. Do you hear me?"

The train trip and the long, cold buggy ride to the ranch were nearly too much for him. His fever rose again, and his delirious struggles frightened us all. He began to chant the Scottish ballads he had learned as a boy. Suddenly in the middle of the night he would sit up and roar:

> Hurrah for Scotland's king and law
> Freedom's sword will strongly draw
> Freemen stand, or freemen fa',
> Let us do—or dee![2]

He and I began to cough great clots of mucous from our ravaged lungs. Mother would hold us, too weak to sit up, until the coughing fits passed. Then, we would lie back, gasping, barely conscious. Only when she was satisfied that our lungs had been cleared would she go into the fresh air outdoors to do the chores.

Ethel continued her experience in "The Equalizer":

Day after day the thermometer clung to zero. At night when the sky was clear, the aurora borealis was bright in the north. Cattle would no longer go to the meadow. Unlike horses and sheep, they would not paw through the snow for food, but waited around the corrals and buildings for hay and oil-cake. One long-horned tan steer, not ours, would take his stand on a pile of hay, using his horns to keep our own animals away, until he had finished eating the pile. The bull broke into the granary. Our only, and small, supply of horse and chicken feed was there. Foolishly I went in after him and drove him out down the steep step. Cows began to die, one here, one there. Every morning some were unable to rise. By day, one walking would fall suddenly, as if it had no more life than a paper animal, blown over by a gust of wind.

Every quick short thaw left a crust of ice over the snow. A herder looking for feed brought in a straggle of starving sheep. They rushed eagerly for the bare, thorny tops of the greasewood bushes above the snow. The tracks they made were marked with blood.

On a gray afternoon of silently falling snow, I saw the shadowy outlines of many sheep, without a herder, soundlessly sweep by, half seen, then gone. They had drifted, we heard, for a hundred miles.

Despite having been so ill, David later recalled his mother's desperation in "The Broken Plank":

February came. The storms continued. Dad's fever-driven ballads became more preoccupied with death:

> We hae met 'neath the sounding rafters
> But the walls around are bare
> They ring to our peals of laughter
> But we know that the dead are there
> So stand your glasses steady
> This world is a world of lies
> Here's a cup to the dead already
> And hurrah! for the next that dies.[3]

"Hush, John, you'll wake the boys," Mother soothed. But even these grim interruptions were a welcome break from the fever-induced monotony in my mind.

Dad and I did not learn until much later, one night the fever had racked us so badly that Mother, in desperation, resolved to take us the next day by team and buggy to the railroad at Moneta and from there to the hospital in Casper, 100 miles away.

Because there was so little hay, the horses had all been turned out to fend for themselves. Only one team was kept in the barn—Slopey (so named because his hips sloped peculiarly downward), old, short, and reliable, and Darky, tall, young, and frisky. In the morning, Mother and Allan went to the barn. Neither had ever harnessed a horse before, although they had seen it done many times. They managed to put the heavy, stiff harness on Slopey, but Darky refused to cooperate. In the dim light of the cold barn, they struggled for what seemed hours to harness the deliberately ornery horse. He was so tall they brought a bench to stand on, only to have him shy away and dump them in the wet manure. He stepped on their feet. He reared and snorted. Allan climbed into the rafters and tried to lower the harness from above, but Darky danced away and struck at them with his front feet. Finally, in despair, they gave up and unharnessed Slopey. The discovery was bitter that the horses, their last resort, were of no help. Neither could be ridden. Mother said later that this was the lowest moment in her life.

At the edge of exhaustion, Mother had wondered at times if she were losing her mind to the isolation, the sickness of her loved ones, the cattle dying, the vicious storms, and the cruelty of the land. Totally absent were laughter, encouraging words, and hope. Then there was her imagined inadequacy to cope with the situations that the men had previously handled, such as the harnessing of the team. She reminded herself that three other lives depended on her, and for their sakes she must persevere.

The morning had begun with the same driving snow and wind howling mournfully around the corners of the house. After the fires were replenished, the invalids cared for, and the breakfast of mush and dried apples finished, Mother went to feed the stock while Allan brought in wood and coal from behind the house. Reaching the corrals, she saw the open granary door and the huge red bull inside, gorging himself on the grain and bran. Driven by hunger and the smell of food so near, he had hooked one of his long, heavy horns into the gap between the door and sill, and with a twist of his head, had torn the door off.

Furious, Mother rushed into the granary, picked up an old broom, and gave the bull's rump a satisfying clout. Ignoring her, he continued to gobble the grain. Moving to his head, she began to beat on it with the broom. The bull raised his head, leveled his horns, and started toward her. Fifteen hundred pounds of angry bull advanced on the tiny, frightened woman.

Mother backed away. He was between her and the door. Quickly she looked for some way out or up. She could not dodge sideways and there were no pegs in this part of the wall to afford her purchase up the logs. Suddenly her back was against the wall. Slowly the bull advanced, a stringer of bran-covered saliva dripping from his mouth. His small red eyes were rimmed with an unhealthy yellow matter. Mother stared at the polished tips of his horns, shining like old ivory in the dim light. The horns became rougher, more scaly, and dirtier where they emerged from the curly yellow-white hair on his massive scarred head. (In those days, a bull's horns were not sawed off or bent down by weights, but grew out and up as weapons.) The points were more than two feet apart. Perhaps she could keep her body between them when the final rush came, a brief respite at best. Once before, she had seen him twist his head in a lightning-swift hook and tear his horns into the belly of a rival bull.

Five feet, four feet. She fought the urge to turn around, cower, and shut her eyes—but this would be fatal. She had secretly wished for death in recent months, but in the manner and time of her own choosing—not one forced on her by this monster.

She thought about Allan. If he found her dead or injured, he would set out on foot to get help 15 miles away. He would go without telling the invalids (his father would sternly forbid it), warmly dressed, with a small sack of food, a tiny figure trudging across the vast landscape through the snow. He would note the wind direction and take bearings from it. But grown men couldn't walk the distance in this weather, so how could a child of eight?

She thought about her husband and David. The fire would go out, then fever, cold, and starvation would take their toll, perhaps in two or three days, maybe a week.

The vision of all this stiffened her, making her strangely calm. "Dear God," she whispered, "Give me the courage to face him down. If I die, they all die." She flicked her broom across the bull's eyes, noticing with faint hope that he closed them briefly, then batted his eyelids before opening them again to glare at her. A rumbling moan came from deep within him. His shoulder muscles swelled under the sagging, scabby hide, as he surged toward her. Mother's stomach muscles knotted, but she continued to flick the broom across his eyes.

Suddenly there was a sharp crack, like a rifle shot, as the floor board broke beneath him. Thrown off balance, he stumbled, struggling to regain his footing. The flicking continued. Rage gave way to confusion, then to fear of the little creature who faced him. Faster and faster she flicked the broom. The bull twisted his head from side to side, trying to escape the pain, trying to see. Slowly he turned and lumbered toward the door. The last few feet he was speeded by Mother, pushing on his rump, fearing that he might turn on her again, yet not wanting him to lose his momentum. He dropped the three feet from the doorsill, slipped, and sprawled in the dirty snow and ice of the corral. Immediately, Mother felt sorry for him. He had not been mean before, merely desperate for food, and she had gotten in his way. Had she not, though, the chickens and other animals surely would have perished. Hauling himself to his feet, he gave her a backward look, and continued his retreat.

Reaction set in. Mother sat on the doorsill, trembling with relief, but no tears. The brilliant sun came out and warmed her. She knew, suddenly, that she and her family would survive this terrible winter. The sinister shadows receded from the back of her mind.

Now came curiosity and awe. Had she been involved in a miracle, perhaps like Johnny Nolan, a roistering, rough, but devout Irish Catholic who owned a ranch on the Sweetwater? He had been caught on foot in the middle of a corral by a killer steer. There was no escape, and as the steer charged, Johnny had made the sign of the cross. The steer slid to a stop directly in front of him, then wheeled and killed Johnny's horse. In telling of it, Johnny's face would light up with religious fervor and he would exclaim in his thick brogue: "I dinna care what you ___ think! 'Twas a goddam meracle!"

Although sincerely religious, Mother was not accustomed to calling on God to help her. Was the broken plank an answer to her prayer—or would it have broken anyway? In later years when we were having doubts about the existence of God, she would say with a smile: "You have a choice of beliefs. Would you rather think you are here because of Divine Intervention? Or because of some extrasensory force in me that willed a preventative event to happen? Or that you are just plain lucky and the breaking of the plank was a fortuitous but completely random happening?"

Carefully she secured the granary door with boards and bailing wire. Then, with a bounce to her step, she returned to the house and greeted her family with the first genuinely cheerful smile they had seen in the year 1920. We wondered what had happened.

Despite nursing the invalids and feeding the livestock, when the mail occasionally did come, Mother wrote her replies. Her friends and family would never know what lay behind her few well-chosen words, nor could she know with whom her letters would be shared.

Caroline Holt, recovering from surgery for an abscessed liver, wrote in February, 1920:

I was *so* sorry to read of all that trouble you have had. I just don't see how you and Allan did so much even for a day, let alone weeks. And with your constant pain,[4] how could you ever keep going?[. . .]

I am so glad David likes the clay. My students like it too. I have them mold all their Biology instead of drawing [. . .] for they must understand a thing before they can make it [. . .].

My hyacinths [. . .] have scarcely ventured above the ground. But when I think of your losing all those cattle I am ashamed to mourn my hyacinths. Oh L.B., I hope Nature will decide to make it up to you in oil this spring[. . .]

Ethel continued in "The Equalizer":

It was March when David was able to sit all day in the big, wide armed chair moved close to the heater in the dining room. He played with plasticene, paper, scissors, and crayons. Allan read him stories. John was free of fever, but weak.

David added from his story "The Foot Race":

Allan—my brother, my hero. After helping Mother with the chores, he would sit with me for hours, helping me build structures from his erector set. He read to me, too, selecting stories that would make me think. As I listened, my mind forced my long-idle fingers to mold dinosaurs from the clay Goldylocks[5] had sent, using the lithographs in Mother's Le Conte geology text as a guide.

As I had, Dad gradually returned to reality, but his once broad shoulders were now angular and sagging, his body, skin and bone. He stopped roaring battle and death chants, and began to whisper gentle love songs:

> I have heard the mavis singin'
> His love song to the moon
> And I've seen the dewdrops clingin'
> To the rose just newly born
> But I know a song that's sweeter
> At the evenin's gentle close
> And I know an eye still brighter
> Than the dewdrop on the rose
> 'Twas thy voice my gentle Mary
> And thine artless winning smile
> That hath made thee mine forever
> Bonnie Mary of Argyle.[6]

When I moved to the dining room, he struggled out to join me, hanging onto walls and furniture.

Gradually, Dad's sense of humor began to return. Somewhere he found a small green booklet of Scottish jokes. He practiced silently, then committed them to memory, and finally, in his rich brogue, he tried them out on us. Laughter returned to our family. Our father was getting well.

He and I began to challenge each other. Our most important goal was to walk outdoors, but first we had to take five unsupported steps, then ten, then fifteen, then twenty. We made plans for a foot race, but the weather interfered.

In April came another of our deepest snows. A calf born during the storm we named Easter and tried in vain to save by the kitchen range. Cows, heavy with calves, died or lost their calves. My seventh birthday[7] came and went with no celebration. Dad and I began to pester Mother: When could we go outdoors? She continued to forbid it until our bodies were stronger and our lungs more completely healed. We tried to cough less frequently. Dad paced endlessly from one window to another, marveling or complaining. In some of the giant snow drifts he could see partly exposed bodies of dead cattle. One cow particularly fascinated him. Seeking shelter, she had frozen standing against the red rocks of the fireplace chimney against the north wall of the living room. As the outside temperature moderated, the cow's legs began to thaw and slowly buckle. Each day, Dad would look through the kitchen window and comment on her slow collapse until finally her stomach rested on the snow.

April passed into May. The weather eased before winter's fury descended again bringing deep snow on top of a sea of mud. Killing time with dreams, Dad and I planned our foot race, step by step.

Ethel noted small signs of spring in "The Equalizer":

At last the ants were out; not only the small red ones, but the large black ones which make their hills of small sticks, a sure sign of spring. The range grew green. The familiar scent of innumerable tiny moss flowers floated over the hills in the evening. The small fly catchers returned to their nest in the buggy shed, the red-winged blackbirds to the corral, and meadowlarks trilled from the fence posts.

David described the next steps in their recovery in his "Foot Race":

Finally, on a warm sunny day in late May, Mother gave her consent for us go out on the porch. We might or might not decide to run our foot race.

She and Allan helped us into our overshoes and sheepskin coats, and we stepped outside for the first time since December, both of us taking deep, exultant breaths of the fresh outside air. What joy to be alive! Hand in hand, Dad and I walked the fifteen feet from the porch to the yard gate, held by a heavy spring to keep the wind from blowing it open and letting the cattle inside. How heavy and cumbersome my overshoes were! Dad was having trouble maneuvering his as well, but said nothing. I began to doubt whether I could run the race.

As Allan opened the gate for us, Dad gave me a weak smile of encouragement. "Laddie, we made it this far together; we can make it the rest of the way."

But neither of us had anticipated the devastation that stretched before our eyes. As far as we could see, emerging as their snow tombs melted, were cows, yearlings, and a few calves, all dead. Those in the sun were already beginning to bloat and emit the gaseous sounds and smells of decay.

Each leaning on the other, we began our foot race, step by muddy step, going first the 20 feet to the store house and its attached buggy shed. In its lee were three cows which had frozen as they sought shelter from the wind. Our overshoes were already so caked with mud that our legs, trembling with fatigue, could hardly drag them from one step to the next, but we did not stop.

At first, except for the birds, the panorama seemed lifeless. Gradually a spectral wraith of a cow, hocks and knees rattling, tottered toward us: Big Brockle Face, so named by me because of her red and white freckled visage, one of my favorite cows because she was so gentle! If I had had the strength, I would have put my arms around her neck. Several other cows in a similar emaciated condition slowly appeared, searching feebly for the grass beginning to sprout.

To avoid thinking of the pain in my legs and the burning in my lungs, I tried to identify the dead cows. There was Arizona, my nemesis. Good riddance! Beyond her lay The Coachman and the Rattlesnake-bit cow. I tried not to see Adam and Eve, together in life, now crowded together in death, against the buggy shed wall. Dad said nothing, but as the extent of the disaster became increasingly apparent, tears streamed quietly down his face—his hopes for a better future, gone. I had never thought a strong man could cry. All I could do was squeeze his hand as tightly as I could.

How long it took to go the next 100 feet, I do not know. Reaching our half-way point, the long building, we collapsed, gasping, on the door sill, our legs quivering in spasms.

I looked down at the 2×12-inch rough plank of the sill. What had it witnessed when it was part of the hotel at the Old Muskrat stage stop? It had survived the shootings that left bullet holes with radiating cracks in the windows above the door. Other triumphs, other tragedies. Now it was seating us while before us lay one of the greatest tragedies we could have imagined.

Our foot race was over; we could not have gone farther. Putting his arm around my thin shoulder, Dad said with great effort: "Laddie, we did make it. We both won the race. We're still alive, thanks to your wonderful mother and Allan, and that's all that really counts. We'll rebuild, again."

We sat silently in the bright sunshine, motionless except to breathe great gasps of air.

Slowly we returned to the house and were greeted with cheers by Mother and Allan. They had not tried to help us—we had run the race on our own. Now, for our family, the nightmare of the winter was over.

Ethel's account of "The Equalizer" concluded:

In the warm June sun, cows that had survived the winter lay down, looked at the sun and died. That fall we might have cut hay almost anywhere, but no stock to need it could be seen in a day's riding. Of our more than a hundred cattle, perhaps fifteen or twenty were left, with feed bills that took years to pay.

The winter was what one sheep man called an equalizer. Whatever men had, or did, or did not have or do, they were equal at the end of it. "Well, Johnny," said another, who had had 50,000 sheep, but was now as badly "broke" as the others, "we walked into this country, and we can walk out again."

Neither did. He, Jacob A. Delfelder, died that year. John spent another twenty-five years on the range.

Ethel wrote at the end of the year:

> The year has cast his cloak away
> > Of cold, of tempest and of rain
> And now the shining sun again
> > Clothes him in fresh embroidery gay.
> There is no bird nor beast to-day
> > But in his own tongue singeth plain

The year has thrown his cloak away
       Of cold, of tempest and of rain.
In silver lapping jeweled spray
       River, spring and fountains play
Each in a garment new and vain
       Waiting for the spring's glad train.
The year has thrown his cloak away
       Of cold, of tempest and of rain.

Notes

1. Ethel.

2. John's version of Robert Burns' "Scots Wha Hae." Not an exact quote. Original in *English Romantic Poetry & Prose*, ed. Russell Noyes. New York: Oxford University Press, 1956: 166.

3. John's version of Bartholomew Dowling's "The Revel (East India)." Original in *Victorian Anthology 1837–1895*, ed. Edmund Clarence Stedman. Boston: Houghton Mifflin, 1895: 101–102.

4. Ethel suffered from back pain at this time.

5. Caroline Holt.

6. John's version of Charles Jefferys' "Mary of Argyle." Philadelphia: A. Fiot, n.d. (circa 1850).

7. April 17.

CHAPTER NINE

~

1920

"We Will Rebuild, Again"

Ethel sent the following note to the Wellesley Record *of 1920 for the class reunion she could not attend:*

I have been vainly trying to dig some forgotten adventures or attainments or travels out of the last five years, but nothing comes to light. Yes! Four years and a half ago I spent six weeks in Denver with my two boys. There Allan declared that he had a thousand aunts. Ever since then I've been here, just living. We live the ranchiest kind of ranch life. Our virtues and vices date back to 400 B.C. We keep open house for all who pass, and they are always men, men of all kinds and conditions from murderers to geologists. "When did you eat last?" is the correct greeting. More than one man has come in who has been out all night in a winter storm without supper or breakfast, lost. The two boys are growing into the "puppy dogs' tails" age, pulling out their first teeth with gusto. But they are still young enough to be divided in opinion about a treasure David found. He thinks it a devil's horn, while Allan tries to convince him that it is a goose's wish bone. They have instituted a "god of chippings" named Lars, who sends them luck when they hunt for arrowheads. Best wishes for reunion!

The Hard Winter was over and there was work to be done. David wrote of it in "We'll Rebuild, Again":

Although my father may have wanted to move our family to town after the Hard Winter, he had little choice but to remain on the ranch and attempt a new beginning. There was no time to rest after our foot race; the thawing carcasses, especially those near our wells and corrals, had to be removed quickly before they contaminated our drinking water. The next day, with Allan's help, Dad put the harness on Slopey.

Attaching the horse's tugs to a singletree, Dad hooked one end of a logging chain through the hole in the center, wrapping the other end around the legs or neck of each carcass to be moved. The first had to be the cow which had frozen against the chimney, just ten feet from the shallow well below the kitchen floor. Surging, then resting, Slopey dragged the carcass 200 feet away from the house and nearby Muskrat Creek. Neither my father nor the horse could do more that day.

In the days that followed, Dad's strength and Slopey's were pitted against the rate of decay of the carcasses. A tragic complication developed. Although the harness tugs were lengthened to their fullest, the singletree banged against Slopey's hocks after dumping each carcass. In those days before antibiotics, we had only gentian violet to treat the dripping sores which developed along the poor animal's hips.

Finally, Slopey became too weak to work, so Dad, who was getting stronger, with Allan's help, began to use Darky, who violently resisted dragging the rotting carcasses behind him.

By now, some of the carcasses had begun to disintegrate. Allan's awful job was to cart the remains to the dumping ground east of the corrals. The stench pervaded our lives through the summer and fall. Coyotes and badgers feasted on the remains, as did our few surviving chickens. (Free-range chickens will eat practically anything.) With so much food so readily available, there were no normal depredations.

Food for us, however, other than eggs, was in short supply. For several weeks we had no fresh fruit or vegetables, and even our bottled meat was nearly gone. No wild game was left on the range, few rabbits, and young sage chickens only briefly in late August. (The old ones were as tough as boots.)

In late summer, the annual horse roundup came to the ranch. The cowboys brought in our remaining horses, but did not tarry; they had trouble herding the horses into our fragrant corrals. After a year on the range, most of our horses were so wild that they would have to be retrained. Dad simply did not have the strength.

To feed his cattle the preceding winter, Dad had bought many tons of cottonseed cake. But when the animals died anyway, he was left owing thousands of dollars to the feed company, as well as to the railroad which had freighted the cake to Moneta. Because he could no longer pay for food at the Moneta store our credit was gone. I don't know how Mother would have fed us without visits from the Frasers and other friends.

Our herd, now only cows, numbered about 15 or 20. Somehow, Dad acquired an old muley Hereford bull.[1] Despite the bull's advanced age and the weakened condition of our cows, our calf crop the following spring was nearly 100%.

The little cash we had came from the eggs Mother sold or traded, and "pulled wool," scavenged from rotting sheep carcasses and sold to an itinerant hide and fur buyer.

Ethel wrote in "Mirage" of another blow which struck in 1920:

Our mirage began to flicker once more, welcome hopes a relief from the travails of the winter. However, the dream of riches from oil which had sustained us was not to be. The deep snows of the Hard Winter made impossible the hauling and building of an oil rig. Three months passed, six months, nine months, and nothing had been done.

During the winter Congress had passed a bill changing the method for proving up on oil claims. The Oil and Gas Leasing Act withdrew western mineral land from oil entry. Confusion about the interpretation of the law lasted many months. Gradually, it transpired that the original locators of claims inherited no rights or preferences unless a well had been begun during the six-month period after filing. Our leases, like others, were dropped. Oil companies could now lease directly from the government, what and when they pleased at a stipulated price. Locators were eliminated. The cost for a well in our area meant a capital outlay of at least fifty thousand dollars. It was the general opinion on the range that if a man had that kind of money, he did not need an oil well.

Bill Grace, on parole from the Pen, was interested in drilling on the "Bill Grace" anticline, six miles south of the Love ranch. "Bill Grace. He's good," someone told me. "A good geologizer. He can remember them long names," referring probably to Mowry shale, Morrison chugwater, red beds. Bill stayed with us for weeks, borrowed horses and tools to do assessment work on his oil claims near an oil derrick where work had stopped for the winter. Then to make sure of his rights, he took up a homestead there.

With him was another Bill, as stout a man as ever finished a long and hearty meal with a whole pan of gingerbread and a potful of tea, or ever buttered his pie. They were together at the table when we talked of the leasing bill just passed in Washington. "This here bill is the best thing ever happened," said Bill B. virtuously. "Stops all this jumping of oil claims"—the very thing he himself was trying to do. He left soon for the new oil fields being exploited in Louisiana. But Bill Grace with his flashing smile, said to be grub-staked by a banker, was still looking for the black gold when last we saw him on the post office steps still wearing patched overalls.

The oil boom simmered down. Workers had been discharged months before at the rig up Muskrat Creek. The hole was till-bottomed at twenty feet. The stock was worthless. The promoter, stout and seldom seen, was rumored to have gone to Mexico. Other wells struck hot water, or were dry and abandoned. Only the one in Dutton Basin continued drilling. Many Moneta town lots were sold for taxes. The barn there burned. Lance Creek wells were sealed. By the mid-twenties Casper's population began to dwindle, until the loss reached ten thousand or more. The number of refinery workers was reduced. Later, scrap iron from a dismantled section of the refinery was shipped overseas.

Our mirage faded. It left us only the memory of how we thought it felt to be, roughly, millionaires. But our disappointed hopes, and the loss of nearly all the cattle that winter, were insignificant beside our thankfulness that John and David had recovered, and we were all together again about our table.

In "We Will Rebuild, Again," David wrote of other developments during the summer of 1920:

Because of the unusually large amount of snow and rain during the preceding winter, grass and flowers now grew on the range in lovely profusion. Old timers reported that hay was now growing where none had ever grown before. Once-dry stream beds now flowed where before water had only flowed after storms.

The early 1920s were times of social and economic change in central Wyoming, as well as in the rest of the country. Congress passed the 19th Amendment, giving to women all over the country the same right that Wyoming women had had for 30 years: the right to vote. Waves of returning veterans began to flood the once-barren range land. The government, benevolent and appreciative now that the war was over, offered them free homestead land parcels of 150–320 acres, pontificating: "Nothing is too good for our heroes!"

Families with accumulated soldier's pay, savings, and hopes for a new and wonderful life, left the security of their former homes to establish new ones in this unfamiliar land, belied by the transitory and deceptive verdancy of the range.

Ethel described the plight of the newcomers in an uncompleted draft of "Wagon Wheels":

Homesteaders were shown maps with lakes, woods, market roads. Locators for a considerable fee (from $500–$1000, or whatever the newcomers could afford) offered their services to "locate" the ideal homestead. Young and inexperienced, the veterans put up one-room shacks, or hauled in a frame cabin on a truck or wagon: a single layer of one-inch boards covered with tarpaper—one room, no wood, no water, no electricity, no roads. Some of them came to our ranch to fill their quart jars with drinking water. A few had their wives. John warned one who brought his wife and child on a motor bicycle of the difficulties he would meet. "Mr. *Love*," he told his wife, "Mr. *Gloom* is what he should be. These stockmen want to keep the land for themselves. He did not try to farm, the locators say." The man roamed the range trying to shoot coyotes, leaving his wife and little girl alone in a tarpaper shack. The child was badly burned. His wife left. Toys and aprons remained at the house. Then he abandoned his homestead.

David added in "Peace on Earth, Good Will to All":

Despite his own troubles, my father would clap the discouraged visitors on the back, smile, and say heartily: "Buck up, lads. While there's life, there's hope." He had taken this motto from the British humor magazine, *Life*, much-read copies of which occasionally came from friends in the East.[2] On the masthead a gallant knight in armor battled a terrible dragon. The inscription read: "While there's life, there's hope," which became an oft-repeated saying in our family.

With horse-drawn plows, the homesteaders gouged furrows in soil matted with thousand-year-old tangles of sagebrush and bunch grass, then planted grain on the dry land, unaware that there was no water anywhere for irrigation. To enclose their homesteads, they bought expensive, untreated, pine fence posts which began to rot immediately; there were no rot-resistant juniper or fir trees on the range to use as alternatives. They dug wells by hand, unaware that in most of this region the water table was 100–200 feet below the surface, and that most of the water was too alkaline to be of much use. They hoped for a bountiful harvest in August and September.

Ethel noted in an uncompleted draft of "Wagon Wheels":

One fearful woman met Harold, a respectable sheep owner from the JJ ranch, with a gun in her hands. He had stopped to get acquainted in friendly fashion and for a drink of water. "Now don't start any conversation. My husband is not at home," she said. There were children in that family, some buried near the house. The absent husband was a dry farmer from Nebraska—a hard worker. His fences were straight and strong. He even plowed land and tried to grow crops. He had mules to drive to keep his few furrows straight. To feed his few livestock, he fastened his tethered cow, a sheep, and a horse together along a pole and turned them out to graze. They became tangled in the brush, and he came as far as our house to hunt them. When taken away to school, his children had never learned about Christmas, or a rose, never seen an orange or perhaps a book, or even sung a song—and their speech was uncouth.

David added in "Peace on Earth, Good Will to All":

As could have been predicted, the hot, dry summer killed the grain seed-lings, the wind blew the topsoil away, and by fall most of the homesteaders had discovered how badly they had been duped. Then came winter, the wind howling around and through the uninsulated shacks, 40° below zero weather, no roads open to town for food, no shelter for livestock, no place for women and babies. Many families huddled in cellars they had dug in the frozen ground, barely heated by sagebrush fires. Some suffocated through their ignorance of ventilation and carbon monoxide.

One of the better-educated families was the Oneys. Tall and handsome, the gentle minister from Kentucky was also frail, a victim of the war. He was trying with all his strength, wisdom, and philosophy to keep his faith in God, government, and humanity. His wife, a tall, handsome, gentle woman, had been a schoolteacher.

In a few months, his savings were gone, and he began to realize that his labors had been in vain. Yet he and his wife remained on their homestead for nearly two more years.

Somehow nearly all of the veterans proved up, then went away and leased their land for grazing to sheep and cattlemen to pay the taxes.

Their abandoned shacks and fences crumbled and disappeared, grass invaded the plowed fields, erasing their desperate efforts to carve out a new life. I saw penciled on the wall of one shack: "I'm 90 miles from water and 100 miles from wood, so I'm leavin' this country, and I'm leavin' it fer good."

I don't remember that we had school that summer, but Mother's notes say that Mrs. Bailey, a grandmotherly lady, came to teach for the 3-month term. Diversions from our lessons were always welcome.

Ethel wrote of one such diversion in "Our George":

It was a memorable day for Allan when George and another hand drove the buggy the thirty-five miles to Shoshoni to have the tires set. He was eight years old and finally allowed to go. He rode a saddle horse which was to be shod. Another was tied behind the buggy. They stopped overnight at a deserted cabin. While the men were hobbling the horses, Allan explored. He heard a rattlesnake. There was a rake leaning against the house. He picked it up and beat the snake to death. Proudly he told George that he had killed a snake. George turned white. He seized Allan and stripped him naked as an ear of corn, Allan said later, to see whether he had been bitten. Then, satisfied, wiping his sweaty face with his bandana, he went to look for the snake. "You sure to God killed him, but don't do it no more. Call George or your Daddy."

George usually skinned the snakes they killed, and brought the skins home, the rattles still attached, wrapped in his red bandana. "The Missus likes them," he excused himself to any questioners, while he tacked the skin on the storehouse door.

David wrote of the following winter in "We'll Rebuild Again":

Winter came, with so much less insulating snow that Mother's flowers froze on the kitchen window sills.

To take advantage of the unusually large coyote population, Dad began to set out poisoned bait. Strychnine, and later cyanide, were carefully rolled in balls of tallow and distributed around cow carcasses well away from the ranch buildings. Once ingested, the tallow would melt in about five minutes, and death followed, usually before the hapless victims could go more than a few feet. Dad maintained that this was faster and more merciful than trapping, but later changed his mind. We were forbidden to approach the outbuilding where the baits were prepared, or to distribute them. A pea-sized bit of cyanide, Dad told us, would kill an elephant. There is no record of how many coyotes Dad killed that winter. He carried their frozen carcasses back to the ranch on horseback, making his rounds every other day, in all weather; coyotes buried beneath fresh snow were impossible to find.

Often, two or three frozen coyotes were stacked behind the kitchen stove to thaw just enough to be skinned. To Mother's distress, their fleas, which had been immobilized by the cold, revived and transferred allegiance to warmer bodies. We boys, however, got used to them because we were often involved in the skinning and stretching of the skins.

There could be no holes accidentally cut in the hide. The tail was never split; its bone core was clamped between two narrow laths and pulled out from within the tail hide, leaving it intact. A damaged tail reduced the value of the pelt. The body of the hide was pulled off the carcass almost as a sweater is pulled over the head. Hide on the legs was split minimally.

We made the stretchers of 1×4 inch boards about five feet long—two feet longer than the average hide—tapered with leather hinges at one end to approximate the shape of a coyote's head. The hide was slipped over the frame like a sleeve; the ends of the boards opposite the hinges were spread to stretch it tight, leaving an air space between the back and the belly. After carefully positioning the tail, legs, eyelids, ears, and lips, we dried the hides in the storehouse for several weeks, away from gnawing varmints.

Pelts as fine as silk were designated "silver," worth a few dollars more than those classified as "regular." Each properly prepared pelt brought about $10.00, at the time one of our two sources of income. Sold to the hide man,

Allan Love skinning his first coyote in front of the long building at Love ranch, 1921.
Love Family Archives

or sent east to Silverman's & Son, the coyote pelts were dyed and made into imitation silver fox furs.

I have no idea how my parents were able to pay any of their debts in 1920–21. A surviving ledger page shows that in January Mother received $4.18 for eggs sold, and $12.20 for live chickens. Six we ate, helped by the ever-increasing number of guests. This was the winter when the meat from one of George Rushton's horses was served at our table, and may have been the time Mother meant when she told my sister Phoebe years later, that she did not have the money to buy a paper of pins.

David's account of Christmas that year was his gift to his own family in 1967: "A Christmas at the Ranch."

Christmas Eve 1920 promised to be a dismal occasion for Allan, age eight, and me, age seven, because no one had been the 15 miles to town for mail during the last month, and therefore no Christmas packages had come. Visitors always brought our mail from the post office in Moneta, but this winter the snow was so deep that there were no visitors. We were old enough to understand the practical reasons preventing the journey to town: the round trip took two long, cold days with team and wagon, and Slopey, still healing from his injuries from the trace chain, was too weak to go that far in wintertime.

Our first five Christmases had been joyous occasions, or so I remembered, with trees we had cut in the hills east of the ranch, ornaments we had helped design and make, good food, store-bought presents, songs, laughter, affection, visitors, and excitement.

Then came the Hard Winter, preceded by a summer of no rain, little hay for the cattle and horses, no help because the cowboys had not yet returned from the war, and our struggle to recover from the Spanish Influenza sweeping the world. There was no Christmas that year, but during the long winter months we tried to keep our spirits up by promising each other that next year we would have a real Christmas again, one that we would remember for the rest of our lives.

Now the next Christmas was almost here. From snatches of conversations overheard, we boys knew that there was no money to buy presents. There were feed bills to pay, taxes, and leases for water and land. Mother and Dad put up a cheerful front and, although Allan and I pretended it didn't matter, deep down we were distressed, partly for our own selfish reasons and partly because we felt sorry for our parents who were feeling sorry for us.

We tried to make little surprise presents: pin trays cut from old tin cans, pot holders from worn-out socks, and whittled wooden objects of uncertain identity. Having had only six months of formal school instruction in our lives, and having known few other children, we were neither very imaginative nor skilled.

During the week before Christmas, Mother made pans of brightly colored gelatin candy (requiring a minimum of sugar, which was expensive), cookies, great puffy loaves of raisin bread, and many other things that we loved. We also knew that she was making scarves, mittens, caps, and coats from worn-out adult clothing. Nothing, however, could take the place, in our young minds, of something new, something store-bought, something completely outside our practical sphere of existence. The afternoon before Christmas Eve came, and dragged interminably. There was no tree to trim this year, again because the horses were not strong enough to make the trip to Castle Gardens where the trees grew.

To keep busy, Allan and I went out with Dad to feed the livestock while it was still daylight, rather than at twilight as we usually did. We finished our work, the wind died down, and as the sun sank lower, the rolling snow-covered hills grew pink from the lengthening rays of light. This was the "witching hour" that we loved. The three of us stood for a while on the sunny side of a haystack and looked out across the lovely ever-changing landscape.

Dad was short and broad. His powerful shoulders had nearly regained their strength after his long months of illness. He looked even bigger in his black buffalo hide coat, which fastened with wooden pegs fitted through loops of rope. His ruddy broad face with dark bushy moustache, topped by a straight broad nose and keen twinkling blue eyes, was framed in his brown bearskin cap. Putting his arms around our shoulders, he began to recite gently and softly at first, with a measured musical cadence, then with fire and eloquence, some of the wondrous and seemingly endless Scottish ballads he had learned as a boy that he knew we loved to hear: of crags and moors and lakes, fair maidens and heroes, great deeds and blood and battle in a shining world of constant adventure. On the now-red, glowing landscape in front of us, we could almost see the stories come to life. For a time we forgot the dismal prospects of Christmas Eve. This was his own special gift to us, and it made us feel very close to him.

Nevertheless, after the sun went down and the cold began to bite, and we had chopped and brought in wood, filled the coal scuttles and stoked the heater in the dining room, our spirits began to droop and conversation became forced. If only we would hear the jingle of sleigh bells and the tramping and snorting of steaming, frost-rimed horses signaling the arrival of company from town! There would be mail and possibly packages and news of the Outside World. Mother was bustling in the kitchen, concocting the spicy aromas of a Christmas Eve dinner so special that she hoped it would take our minds off the other inadequacies of the season.

By now the wind was howling again. With ever-changing tones, it whistled around the corners of the house. Each blast would suck a gust of air through the stove and set up a lively, poignantly haunting tinkling of the nickel disks which dangled loose when the dampers at the bottom of the stove were open—but they did not sound like sleigh bells.

Dinner included, among other things, roast chicken, special because there weren't many edible chickens left and each one eaten was gone for good. Other delicacies were hot rolls and homemade butter with lumps of sugared honey, chipped with hammer and chisel out of a 5-gallon can, canned asparagus—special because it was so expensive, and dried apple pie. In our restricted world, appreciation of anything was closely related to the amount of work and thought required to produce it, and we appreciated this meal very much. The occasion should have been festive, but there was nothing new to talk about. It did not occur to us that after the Hard Winter we should have been thankful to be alive and well, all together and very fond of each other. If it hadn't been considered unmanly for boys of our age and responsibility, we would have cried.

As we opened our pathetic little packages after supper, we tried to put on a show of surprise and enthusiasm, but all the presents had such a familiar, made-over look. Then, as Mother and Dad sat side by side beneath the yellow light of the kerosene lamp on the wall, we settled on their laps and listened while they read Christmas stories of the Outside World. The cold of the night seemed to seep through the walls. When the stories were finished, with wishes for a Merry Christmas, we were tucked in our beds and kissed goodnight. Then Dad and Mother shut the door behind them and went to the kitchen, on the opposite side of the dining room, to do the dishes.

Allan and I whispered for a while. How much better the Christmases of bygone years had been, and how disappointing this one had turned out to be. We were too old and too practical to believe in Santa Claus any more, and we knew that we had had all the Christmas there was going to be. Feeling very sorry for ourselves, we wished each other a Merry Christmas and dozed off.

Suddenly we awoke. Something out of the ordinary was happening. Dad and Mother did not usually stay up much later than we, and if they did, they read quietly to themselves. Tonight, however, a lively hum of conversation emanated from the kitchen, tantalizingly unintelligible through two closed doors. We were also puzzled by the sounds of bustling around, opening and shutting of doors, and the occasional giggle or smothered guffaw. This was quite out of keeping with the mournful mood earlier in the evening. It was too cold for us to get up and investigate, and we were not permitted to wander around once we had gone to bed, so we lay in the dark, speculating with curiosity as our excitement grew.

The commotion went on and on, until finally, after an especially loud burst of laughter and more opening and closing of doors, all was suddenly quiet again. Then came the rhythmic high-pitched jingle of bells, too high for those on the harnesses of any horses we knew, and the squeaking crunch of running overshoes in the below-zero snow outside. Someone banged loudly at the back door, and was greeted equally loudly by our parents.

"A-lain!" and "Dah-veed!" Our names were shouted, not as we usually heard them, but with an unfamiliar accent. Bounding out of bed, wild with excitement, we ran to the warm kitchen. There, dressed in a red coat with tiny bells around the bottom, shapeless red pants, long, white whiskers, and a red cap was the first real live Santa Claus we had ever seen! Wide-eyed, we stared at him, knowing that this couldn't be, yet was.

There were no other people in this part of the country; no sleighs and horses had come to the ranch or we would have heard them, for sound carries many miles in the still, cold air. Both our parents were clearly visible and obviously enjoying the situation. Who, then, was this person? Laughing at the expressions on our faces, he began to speak, shyly, hesitantly, in a curiously vibrant voice. His choice of words was unusual and we had the feeling that he was not only shy, but even perhaps not accustomed to speaking. Because we were shy as well, we felt an immediate bond with this stranger. He had tried to fly in with his airplane, he explained, because the snow was too deep for his reindeer and sleigh, but had had motor trouble, abandoned the plane on the Moneta Divide, six miles to the north, and walked to the ranch. He couldn't bring his pack of presents because it weighed too much, and he needed all his strength to struggle through the snow. Just the same, he couldn't bear the thought of our having no presents at all from him, so he had brought just one gift for each of us.

This story took quite a while to tell; he told it well, and the suspense became almost unbearable. Finally, reaching into his pocket, he drew out with a flourish two small identical packages. As he handed one to each of us, I noticed that his hands were brown and hard and the fingers and palms so callused that they shone in the lamplight. Eagerly we unwrapped the packages and saw with dazzled eyes two much-used, but clean webbed army belts with shiny brass buckles bearing the official raised insignia of the United States. These had been store-bought and they came from the Outside World, and they had been brought by an unknown man of mystery!

Our belief that there was no Santa Claus was severely shaken. As skepticism dwindled, I studied his face with care. At least the white moustache was genuine, for it was stained, perhaps with coffee, tobacco, or a pipe stem. The chin whiskers might or might not be his, but his story and his workman's hands and, above all, his actual presence in our kitchen seemed proof of the existence of the legendary figure. No ordinary man in his right mind would venture out on foot at night in the cold and snow of this rugged, uninhabited country just to bring two belts to two small boys, yet here he was and here were the belts, clutched tightly in our hands. By now, these belts had assumed not only extraordinary value, but also magical significance because of the mystery connected with them. We measured value and significance in our own terms.

Our shyness forgotten, we thanked him with profound sincerity and were startled to see his eyes grow misty as he smiled and shook our hands with a steely hard clasp. He still had a long way to go before him, he said, so bade us Merry Christmas and Good Night. With the belts, even the cold sharp buckles, held next to our skins, we danced off to bed. What a Christmas, beyond our wildest dreams! For a long time we chattered excitedly in whispers. In the kitchen we could hear more conversation while our parents fed the stranger Christmas Eve dinner and hot coffee to warm him before he started the long, cold trip back to the plane.

Next morning, Christmas morning, the event of the night before seemed like a dream, but in bed with us were the belts, warm now and symbolic of Christmas magic and the Outside World. In broad daylight, once again a bit skeptical, we would see for ourselves whether our nocturnal visitor was still here or whether he had actually gone as he said he would. Even Santa Claus would leave tracks, and there they were, coming in from the north in the direction of the Moneta Divide and going back the same way. The tracks were large and the stride long, and we followed them for a mile or more. Finally we stopped on a hill where we could look far to the north. The tracks continued on and on until they disappeared in the distance. Only then did we turn back.

For days we hounded our parents with questions, but the only answers were smiles and the comment that our visitor had come to give us the Christmas presents and then had gone. Our question as to whether there really was a Santa Claus was answered with the simple statement that we saw him and he gave us presents, didn't he? If we wanted to call him Santa Claus, it was up to us. When asked independently if they had ever seen this person before, both parents answered truthfully that they had not, nor had they known in advance that he was coming.

As we grew older and saw the Outside World and learned to ask more meaningful questions and to reason, we were able to fit bits of the story into place. Unbeknownst to any of us, a sheepherder known only as Frenchie had brought a band of sheep to the Moneta Divide a few weeks before Christmas. From his camp he could look down into our valley on clear nights and see the lights from the ranch house twinkling faintly. He had heard that two little boys lived there and, being observant, as people who live in the wilds must be to survive, he knew that no one had gone to or from the ranch for a long time. He reasoned that we weren't going to have much of a Christmas. Neither was he, far from his native France, with no family or friends nearby. From his meager possessions he had selected the two newest items, his finest gifts, the belts, and planned his Christmas trip.

He could not leave the sheep until they were bedded down at night, and he had to be back when they left the bedground at sunrise. It would take three hours to reach the ranch, nearly all downhill, and at best he had to allow four hours to get back. Further, if the wind came up and blowing snow obscured the stars and landmarks and he missed his camp in the dark, he would almost certainly be lost and die of cold and exposure. What were his thoughts as he weighed the risks? Would he, an unknown sheepherder and his little gifts be welcomed by a strange family on a cattle ranch on Christmas Eve? In some places where he had worked, herders were harassed or shot by cowboys. But he came, and was welcomed by our parents, who greeted him cordially as they did everyone.

They were immediately struck by his resemblance to Santa Claus, with his red, frost-blasted face, his white moustache bent with icicles, his warm smile and twinkling eyes. Furthermore, he had brought gifts. Our parents and Frenchie discussed how dismal Christmas Eve had been and how, with his help, this could be changed. On the spur of the moment, together they improvised the show and story I have just described. The costume was some worn-out long red underwear combined with one of Mother's old red college-day dresses. Chin whiskers were unceremoniously chopped from a pair of Angora goat hide chaps out in the barn. The bells on Frenchie's coat came from an old sled dog harness. For their success the conspirators relied on a naïve, completely surprised and uncritical audience, succeeding so completely that, forever after, this was in my mind our most wonderful Christmas at the ranch. We will never know what thoughts Frenchie took with him as he made his way through the dark and snow back to camp, but he entered so completely into the spirit of the occasion that I am sure it was a memorable Christmas for him, too.

Many years later the following brief obituary appeared in the *Wind River Mountaineer*, Lander's weekly newspaper: "An old sheepherder known only as 'Frenchie' died of natural causes last week in the county poor house at Lander. He had spent most of his life on the range in central Wyoming, left no estate, and had no relatives in this country."

Reading this disinterested note that summed up a lifetime of honest and hard work by a warm-hearted human being, I felt that he deserved better. Back came vivid childhood memories. They are probably inaccurate in some details because of the passage of time and the age of the youngest participant. Nevertheless, I have set them down, partly as a tribute to an almost-forgotten man, and partly as an example of the selfless nature, inventiveness, and wisdom of our parents and a stranger, all of whom made the effort to bring the spirit of Christmas to two little boys on a lonely ranch more than half a century ago.

Notes

1. "Muley" refers to the genetic strain of hornless cattle, not popular in the West then because they were defenseless against horned cattle. John probably got this one for next to nothing.

2. Later the title was bought by the American Time-Life Corporation.

CHAPTER TEN

~

1921

"Never a Light But One's Own"

A chinook blew in with the new year. The roads cleared, and the mail came, bringing the news of the death of Mrs. Mills. Having chosen to forego the comforts of the Outside World, she and Ethel may have shared the consoling thought that they could return to the cities for medical help if ever it were needed. Discovering that even a trip to Dr. Mayo's clinic could not save Mrs. Mills must have been devastating for Ethel.

The mail also brought a subscription to the Ladies' Home Journal, *a gift from Marion Hill. David never knew how his mother came to correspond with Miss Hill, perhaps through a mutual friend, or why Ethel saved copies, all typed, of her own letters to that kind lady from Brookline, Mass., or whether indeed they ever met. But once a year the magazine subscription was renewed, and Ethel wrote her acknowledgment, letters which gradually became résumés of the family's preceding year. No letters from Miss Hill have been found, but their correspondence lasted thirty years.*

January, 1921

My dear Miss Hill,

A card from you at Christmas time, and later the first *Ladies' Home Journal* of the year have come to me. I can hardly thank you enough, not only for the magazines alone, but for the sweet friendliness that prompted you to send them to a stranger. It was perhaps because of my last letter to Miss Jackson, which she wrote me was printed in part, or because you know her. So you must know a little about range life. The sheer aloneness of it is unique—never a light but one's own, at night. Days, weeks without seeing a

135

soul. No smoke from another's fire in sight. Miles and miles, twenty, thirty, forty without a house. I've often not seen a woman for months at a time. But this is slowly changing now.

I have two boys, seven and nine years old, and find my days full, with household duties and teaching them. I'm not very strong, about one cat power, so you can't think of me as the typical strong "ranch woman"—in fact I never saw but one of them, and she is from Indiana.

I will pass the magazines on to her or to someone else. May I hear from you? Sincerely,

Ethel P. Love

No publication in which part of Ethel's letter to Miss Jackson was printed has been found. In family conversations, David described his own perspective on ranch life and some of the tasks he had as a boy:

Although Dad had nearly regained his full strength, I remained underweight and not very energetic. One of the small jobs I could do was to keep the silver and crystal condiment jar on our dining table filled with mustard, which I prepared from mustard powder, salt, and vinegar. Mother kept me company mixing baking powder, from one part cream of tartar and ½ parts each of soda and cornstarch.

Mother also taught me to oil and repair our clocks. The alarm clocks, her Delft clock in its blue and white porcelain casing, the 8-day Regulator kitchen clock, and the Seth Thomas mantle clock, were placed on the dining table, along with saucers, feathers, screw drivers, kerosene and oil. I marveled at the cause and effect of the delicate gears.

I was not, however, permitted to touch Mother's tiny Elgin, or Dad's silver dollar-sized pocket watch, which was wound with a minuscule key. Its inscription read: "John Love, Dallas, Wyoming." We never learned the story behind it; the town of Dallas had ceased to exist long before we were born.

People who did not homestead, herd cattle or sheep, or prospect for oil began to drift into the area. Ethel wrote about some of them for a collection of short sketches she planned to call "Flotsam":

One of our most unprepossessing overnight visitors held a great fascination for our little boys. He had a crude wooden leg. They had heard of, but never seen such a thing. They hung about him and sat close, listening, enraptured, to his stories of rough violence. To John and me he was a most unsavory character, but finally his fascination for Allan and David outlasted his visit. At last they mustered courage to ask breathlessly the long suppressed question: "How did you get your leg cut off?" He leaned forward impressively. After a tense wait he said, "I didn't mind my mother!"

"Old Mica" drove to the ranch and camped there for a few days nearly every summer. His face, lacking an underlip, was hardly visible for the stiff, nearly white whiskers that grew from it in every direction. His shapeless hat fell around his ears. Two nondescript horses pulled his half-sized wagon. It had a high, rounded tin top made of flattened cans, some of them large five-gallon oil cans. What it would be like to sit inside during a rain or hail storm was a distressing thought. He had reinforced all four wagon wheels with various sized planks. Two were fastened close to the hub, parallel, one on each side of the hub. Two more were at right angles to these on the other side of the wheel, nailed or wired, or both, to felloes[1] and spokes. From every wheel, harsh groanings and squeaks announced his coming.

Old Mica was very proud of one of his horses, a poor old stallion he called "Bluebird," for its supposed color. He rode Bluebird, leaving his wagon in our field, on his yearly search over the country for a lost ledge of mica. This he remembered seeing thirty years before, near a German settlement. The mineral was scarce, valuable, much needed; bankers, he said, were ready to back him, if he could only find the place again.

Around us, German settlements were as scarce as any others. We suspected, without suggesting it, that gypsum crystals sparkling in the sun on a hillside, might have looked to him like mica. At any rate, he continued his hunt, year after year.

Occasionally we invited him to eat in the house. He was ravenous for green food, fresh eggs, and milk. He made an unforgotten impression on the children by noisily "saucering" his coffee.

In the winter he lived on the Riverton dump—and he looked it. He discussed this loquaciously: "Queer, what folks throw away; look at this coat and hat and these here shoes. I never have to buy no clothes. I git cans of stuff, squashed mebbe, but good, kittles and joolery. Do you like joolery? I kin git you some." And he did. A tangle of corroded and tarnished metal beads.

The last time we saw Old Mica, he was mourning Bluebird, who had died. The wheels of the tin-topped wagon were wobbling more than ever, clattering and squeaking more loudly. Occasionally after that we heard of him indirectly.

Six years later news reached me that southeast of Lander mica had been found. Strange to say, it was not far from the ranch which a German family had homesteaded, several generations earlier. A company had been formed for development, but the property was involved in litigation. Old Mica came again to my mind. Had he or his search anything to do with locating the mining claim? Could the company be trying to secure his share? Was he living or dead? Was there any basis for hope that Old Mica had at last made his discovery? We never heard the end of the story, and we never learned his real name.

Another driver of horses and wheels, a freighter, who stopped often at the ranch, was Bert Austin. He left us a photograph, later retrieved by himself, of his prized 24-horse string team. He enjoyed relating how, at his call, the horses would step into their places by the harness left on the ground; he'd crow about the few minutes it took him to hook them up; how he could turn his teams and four wagons around on the wide main street in Lander; how the horses worked together to drag the wagons out of the mud, first to one side, then to the other to loosen the wheels; how they could outpull any other teams; how if necessary, he would steal to feed them. One horse alone, he boasted, could start a freight car on a track. Bets were made. He hitched his best horse to the front of the car. After testing the load once or twice, the horse dug down, body close to the ground and strained forward. The car trembled, moved, then rolled along the track.

Bert claimed to be the first man to drive a freight outfit over the new [in 1889] Platte River bridge in Casper. Bridge, teams, wagons or load were insured. The bridge held up under the weight, and he drove over it safely.

Progress caught up with Bert. He turned to oil prospecting, and he was driving a car the last time we saw him at the ranch.

Ten or fifteen years later, David recognized the framed picture of Bert's string team on a wall of a remote highway store.

"Did you know Bert Austin?" he asked the woman at the counter.

"Sure. Obliging, friendly man. We got him to look after the store and filling station while we took a month's winter vacation in Arizona. When we got back he'd just filled up the back of a truck. He and the driver had been having a regular talk of it. 'How much?' the man finally asked. Bert just waved his hand, free and easy.

"'Nothing,' he said. 'Be seeing you.'

"'Who was that?' she asked him.

"'I can't say,' answered Bert. 'Friend of a Casper fellow I know.'

"We got back just in time," she added. "We looked over the stock and receipts. Bert's old time range hospitality set us back between four and five hundred dollars that month.

As David recovered his health in 1921, he and Allan helped with the livestock and also continued exploring their environment:

The spring of my 8th birthday, nearly all our surviving cows produced calves, Nature's perpetuation of the animals strong enough to have survived the previous winter. Allan and I were to watch for cows who appeared about to deliver, which gave us one more excuse to explore.

We carried picnic lunches in cloth bags: great slabs of homemade bread, with homemade butter, over which sugar and citric acid, usually in solution, had been dribbled. Not just tasty, the citric acid combined with our saliva was an ideal thirst slaker, especially when drinking water was limited. We also carried cookies or cake whenever there was any to spare.

Intrigued by the polished buffalo horns on our living room wall, although we had never seen the magnificent creatures which had produced them, we searched the range for vestiges of the great herds of another time.

In "Panorama," Ethel included her own observation of the bones they found:

Time and exposure were reducing the buffalo horns to mere shells. Allan and David hunted for them, and accumulated about fifty horns. Some they pried loose from the large skulls. They noticed the foot-long spines on the buffalo vertebrae. Rarely they found shreds of dried black hide clinging to the bones.

David remembered one particular discovery:

We found one buffalo skull whose horn spread measured between 30 and 36 inches tip to tip. The Shoshones and Arapahoes occasionally borrowed this prize to use in special ceremonies. They always returned it, and it remained for many years a conversation piece on our porch.

Ethel continued in "Panorama" to record her children's activities as they speculated about the pre-historic and historical contexts in their environment:

The boys chose the best of the horns to polish, and carried them to the top of the windmill. Sitting there on the platform, their feet hanging over the edge, they scraped the horns with horse rasps for the rough outer shell, and broken glass for the final polish. From that vantage point, they reviewed the landscape and speculated, undisturbed, on what they saw; their eyes could follow long unused trails made by buffalo coming down the long hill to drink at the Rat. The old trails were more washed and deeper than those of our cattle. In the meadow tall reeds marked the buffalo wallows from whose muddy edges they had pulled skulls of gray-blue, that bleached white in the sun.

In the short brush bordering the meadow they picked up broken parts of tiny agate bird points, shot from Indian bows. Wild ducks and sage chickens still nested where buffalo and Indians had gone.

"Under that cut bank by the bend in the creek they could have had a winter camp," said David. "We like to stop there ourselves to get out of the wind. That's where we found the tepee ring, and dug out the black stones where they had a fire. We find more chippings there, too."

Allan and cat, Ethel, and David Love under the windmill at Love ranch, 1921.
Love Family Archives

"Maybe there were muskrats in the creek, too," Allan reasoned. "Must have been once, to give it the name. I never saw but two. And the creek reached those banks. It was much bigger than now. Trappers were here."

"Do you think one of them had that flintlock Dad found in the field?"

"It says W. Chance & Son, England. Has a crest, too. Dad says they made guns like that in England around 1805. Dad and I gave it a good oiling. When we put a flint in the cover, it worked—you could pull the trigger. If we had some tinder now . . ."

"The sight is gold. It must have cost a lot. But somebody took the barrel for a picket pin. It wasn't round either—octagonal."

"What happened to the wood?"

"It was rotted away from the screws, just dust."

"He must have been killed. Nobody would leave a gun like that."

Could the owner of this gun, they wondered, have been that person whose skull was turned up by the plow, cutting across the bank of a small gulch below the Big Dam? John and his men searched in vain for a trace of clothing, or a weapon; but they found, and reburied, more parts of the skeleton. The upper arm bone was light-weight and short, just the length of my own. I had been having a toothache when it was found, so I noticed particularly that the teeth in the skull were perfect.

Indian or white, the boys cogitated; man or woman, young or old; seeking shelter in the gulch from a storm or hiding from an enemy; lost, how long ago; sick, starved, wounded; a trapper, a scout, a lone buffalo hunter; a gold seeker strayed from the Oregon Trail, not far away. The range had kept its secret well.

Prompted by the illustrations in my *Elements of Geology* book, the boys talked of the animals that lived then, and those far back in time. They could see the head of Muskrat Creek, 50 miles away. Fossil bones of a *titanothere*, 50 million years old, had been discovered there. David brought back a bluish tooth the size of my fist. They could see the nearer Chalk Hills, where, washed to the surface of a white draw, David found the bones and teeth of a prehistoric horse, no larger than a dog, that had once scampered over the very land across which the boys rode.

They visualized the forests that grew in a distant past in the prairie surrounding them, and thought of the ages passing before one of the trees turned to the petrified log on our porch or, in Castle Gardens, to the coal they dug, which showed an impression of leaves.

Long before then the sea had covered the land. When it receded, it left the shells they scraped from a sand bank not far up the creek, oysters, clams. Bill Grace brought us a fossil ammonite. It would have fitted neatly into a bushel basket. The iridescent pink and sheen of the shell, like mother of pearl, were perfectly preserved, a joy to see and feel.

Their imaginations took them no farther into the past, but they looked around for the milk cow, and locating her, came down from the windmill, with a long view of the passage of time over their world.

That summer David read *Elements of Geology* from cover to cover.

Relieved as they were to see David studying of his own volition, John and Ethel were growing more and more concerned about their boys' lack of formal instruction. In the 1950s Ethel wrote of their efforts to procure teachers in "The 3 R's":

Allan and David could read and write when Miss Evans, our first schoolmarm, came to teach. Allan had made and stained, with assistance in planning, a small sturdy desk for David to use, with a hinged top and a shelf below. It was pleasant to have a teacher, a companion about the house; to have meals on time, and to watch the cowboys' interest in her. Miss Evans took some of Allan's and David's work to a county exhibit, and brought back prize ribbons, before she went on to a town school in the fall.

"Ma Bailey," as our next teacher asked us to call her, taught 13 months in a year. This she managed by holding school on holidays, weekends and vacations, which suited everyone perfectly. She had grandchildren as old as

"Ma" Bailey, Ethel, Allan, David, and Dumpling. Love ranch, 1920s.
Love Family Archives

my boys. Results, to her, were more important than methods. She had gradu-ated from the Teachers' College at Greeley, Colorado with her daughter and, having a background of culture, business methods, and penmanship besides teaching, was in much demand for the small home schools she preferred. She came to us for three summers.

She had an unhappy condition of the stomach that demanded especial consideration. Her coffee had to be ⅘ hot water, but she had so many cups for breakfast that a cowboy was led to remark, "Why don't you take your coffee all in *one* cup, Mrs. Bailey?" Then her egg had to be boiled exactly 2 minutes. Homemade bread made some complications. She showed me once how it should be done, with a most dismal result. At butchering time we be-gan eating the more perishable parts of the steers—the brains, liver, tongue, kidneys, and heart. Ma Bailey was eagerly wanting steaks and roasts. "Do you always eat the offal?" she questioned. She enjoyed cucumbers, but could not digest the skin of baked custard or a raisin.

By the time the school term ended, each person at the table was imbued with preferences, wanting his eggs cooked differently from any one else. It was a relief when one stranger, asked whether he wanted tea or coffee, an-swered, "It don't matter. I'm not one of these here choicey guys."

I resolved that we were not to cultivate choicey guys. I installed a small white fine box on the table. David took it upon himself to compose and type out a sheet of rules. Infraction meant a one cent fine. The sheet read:

RULES FOR TABLE CONDUCT

1. Sit erect, keep elbows off the table, and the left hand in the lap, when it is not in use, or ask for food not served.
2. Do not find fault with the food.
3. If you want anything not on the table, go and get it.
4. Do not talk with mouth full. See that others are served before beginning to eat.
5. Eat quietly, with the mouth closed.
6. If you cannot reach it with one foot on the floor, ask for it.
7. Do not spear bread with your fork.
8. Use the side of the spoon for soup.
9. Do not play with the silver. Do not wave your fork in the air, or lift more than one bite on the fork at a time.
10. Do not smell of or blow on your food.
11. Do not read at the table.
12. Do not kick, bite, hit or otherwise abuse your neighbor.

These were the fundamentals. Rules were read aloud to guests and strangers. One good friend, back from sitting on the ground at roundup camp, found rule 4 impossible to remember. Her husband deposited a quarter in the box to free her from embarrassment. Proceeds from fines went for occasional oranges, which everyone could enjoy.

At the end of the summer, "Ma" Bailey departed to teach in a larger school. In nine months my boys could forget what they had learned in three. I kept on with their informal lessons, although every day there were at least two adequate reasons for not doing so, one indoors and one outside.

The house might be full of men, waiting out a storm, or riding on a roundup. I was baking, canning, washing clothes, making soap. Allan and David stood by the gasoline washing machine reading history or geography while I put sheets through the wringer. I ironed. They did spelling beside the ironing board, or while I kneaded bread; they gave the multiplication tables up to 15 times 15 to the treadle of the sewing machine. Mental problems, printed in figures on large cards, they solved while they raced across the long dining room to write the answers at the table—and learned to think on their feet. Nine written problems done correctly, without help, meant no tenth problem. There was no sitting or clock watching. Hearing a story fitted neatly into a cold day. Stitching shirts on the machine while dinner cooked and hearing a spelling match did well for the morning. Their stamp collections involved letters to foreign countries, geography, languages, and history.

In "Mirage," Ethel included more details about family time:

It was surprising in how little time they finished their school work, to ride horseback, trap, go to town or for coal, to watch the butchering, to help drive the bawling calves into the weaning pen, or to get to the corral, when they heard the hoof beats of running horses and the cries of cowboys crossing the creek.

We played games and sang songs on long buggy drives. They helped with the evening dishes, or irrigated the garden. By lamplight it might be chess, cards, cribbage, or Mah Jong. Through the years I read them the gamut of stories, from "Ab the Cave Man" to "The Three Musketeers" at bedtime.

David added his own memory of the boys' increasing awareness of how their experiences fit into a larger context in "Peace on Earth, Good Will to All":

Because of our stamp collections and the stories and letters read to us, we thought we knew something about the Outside World, although we'd seen almost none of it. In our geography book, I discovered a photograph of Lankin Dome, a bald, granite monolith, rising 1000 feet from the prairie below, a landmark, not far from where we'd picked chokecherries. That anything in our own narrow world might be worthy of being in a book had never occurred to me.

But our view of the Outside World and what could happen to people there was to receive a shattering blow. At some point during the summer, we learned that Willie, the trick roper we had loved, was coming through our country on the train. Badly injured in the war, he had spent a long time in the hospital, and had only recently been released. Finally the day arrived, and we all went to the railroad station at Moneta to greet him. We were totally unprepared for what we saw. Willie was helped down the train steps, on crutches, one leg gone, the other twisted grotesquely, livid scars streaming down one side of his face, one of his brilliant gray eyes gone. And his hands which had wrought such magic with a lariat could hardly be called hands any more. I ran to put my arms around him, crutches and all, too old to cry, too young to find words to express my shock. As we stared up at him, he looked down with a twisted grin, his gray eye expressionless, his deep voice slurred: "Son, it's been a long trail, and there ain't no glory at the end of it. Remember that." I do. Was this what war and peace were all about? "Peace on earth, good will to all"? Never again to see him twirling his rope, to hear his booming laugh, to see the joy of living on his face? The impact of seeing our friend, a real victim of a real war, was terrible. His broken body could not endure the jolting wagon trip back to the ranch. With sorrow too great to express, we helped him re-board the train and watched him disappear from our lives.

As winter loomed, George Rushton returned, just when he was needed. Ethel wrote in "Our George":

When Allan, at age nine, was considered old enough to be of help to George, he took John's place on the envied jaunts after firewood. George drove a four-horse team hitched to the heavy freight wagon, a wide rack upon it. No one lived along the little used twenty-mile road, which rose slowly, then abruptly, up the Deer Creek Divide.[2] George and Allan took hobbles and oats for the horses, a bedroll and a camp outfit for cooking. They wore warm clothing and overshoes, a precaution against November weather. On the Divide they collected fallen logs and stumps of pine. These they sawed into lengths that could be loaded on the wagon and chained into place. One tall stump too full of pitch to saw or handle, they left year after year. It may have been struck by lightning long before, for they called it "the black tree." Bits of it they chipped off for quick starting of their camp fire. They fried bacon, potatoes, and eggs for dinner. Home-made bread, milk, and sometimes cake completed the meal. They slept on the ground under a sky full of stars.

After loading the next day, the drive back to the ranch often lasted into the night. One evening when the horses were toiling along the road, George met a man from the oil camp in the area, an advanced advocate of the eight-hour day.

"What you doin', workin' this time o'night? Don't you know when to stop? The moon's shinin'."

"So what?" George responded easily. "Let 'er shine. You want me to stop here, when dinner's waiting at the ranch?"

As the boys grew, they became increasingly involved in the operations of the ranch. David remembered in "The Action Corral" how they learned about the process of butchering and its effect on him:

"Come, lads," said Dad one crisp sunny morning. "We'll be butchering today, and you are now old enough to see how it's done." It had to be done correctly; each animal killed was one part less of our dollar income. Dad no longer had the strength to fill the ice house, so our butchering was usually done after the cold weather set in and the flies were gone.

The designated animal (usually a 3-year-old steer, occasionally a sheep) spent its last night in the round corral without food or water to minimize fluid and digestive material. In the morning, cowboys maneuvered the luckless animal under the cross-bar above the heavy gate, and fired a single .22-calibre bullet behind its ear, carefully, so as not to tear the brains. A quick thrust of a sharp knife to the throat brought the end of life to the sheep. It was terrible to watch: the blood, the desperate gasps for breath, the struggle for, and rapid ebbing of life, the dimming and glazing of terrified eyes. As the animal fell, the rope and pulley hanging from the cross-bar elevated its hindquarters.

Toby Leitch often came to help, partly because he was a skilled butcher, and partly because he received part of the meat. With a stroke of his knife, Toby cut the steer's throat to drain the arteries into a bucket—the blood to be mixed with chicken feed. Then the hindquarters were lowered and the head raised. In one large piece the hide was stripped from the carcass and stretched over the top rail of the corral to dry.

With a single, precise knife stroke, the body cavity was opened from the rib cage down. "Forty years a butcher," Toby chanted, "and never cut a gut!" To cut a gut and soil the body cavity with dirt or manure would waste a lot of meat. In horrified fascination, Allan and I gazed at the innards. How efficiently they were compacted into the body cavity! Carefully the entrails were removed and carted away to be a feast for the chickens. The heart, liver, kidneys, tongue, and brains, special delicacies, were put in separate pans so that each unique flavor would not mix with any other. The empty carcass was thoroughly washed, cut into quarters and hung to age in the granary. The skull, too, was cleaned, and taken to the kitchen to be cooked into "potted heed," one of the most flavorsome rewards of the butchering process.

The amount of dressed meat varied with the size of the animal, but a steer would usually be from 500 pounds upward.

As I watched the butchering for the first time, I was both curious and horrified as the light in the animal's eyes gradually faded to dull gray. "Daddy, where did the life go? Did it just disappear, or did it go somewhere else that we can't see? Is it gone forever? If we die, will the light go out of our eyes, like the steer's? I don't want to make the light go out on any animal or person. Is death always like this, or are there exceptions? Why do chickens not die when their heads are chopped off, but keep running around for a while? Why do rattlesnakes keep coiling and striking and crawling after they are killed? Daddy, I'm afraid. Please tell me some answers."

Suddenly killing was a very real part of my world. My parents, who also hated the killing, were disturbed by my anguish. Dad, Mother, Allan, and I then discussed life and death, deliberate killing, the hereafter, and whether the life force in animals and humans disappeared forever. What is "forever"? We discussed passages from the Bible and philosophers whose work Mother knew well, and what our parents really believed. As we grew older and became more knowledgeable, they suggested, we might learn to be more at peace with the real but imperfect world. Yet, like it or not, butchering was

part of our life on the range, and we had to accept that other lives be sacri-
ficed to feed us. Throat-cutting became a symbol of immediate death in our
minds, so dreadful that we tried not to use the word "throat." When we read
of such incidents in stories, the sense of dread and finality persisted.

*In early December, Gardiner Mills wrote, rekindling the mirage of finding
wealth in the oil industry:*

I heard the other day that oil had been struck near Moneta but could not
learn just where. I hope it is true [. . .]. They say now that Sheep Mountain
is a dome in itself—they have always before referred to it as an "igneous
intrusion" or other derogatory term and said that if there had been no such
intrusion there would have been a great deal of oil here, and because of it
there was none. Anyway, a man who goes all over the world on such errands
was sent over from London to look at the place. He was out here twice &
then went immediately back to England to report—what, no one knows, but
by underground railway I understand favorably. Spring will tell. The Lander
representative of the "Royal Dutch Shell" has been out here twice. Isn't that
a fine name—do you know what it means?[. . .]

You knew that they had found oil at Carmody's on Twin Creek—where
the stone barn is. [. . .] They have a number of wells and are erecting tanks
to hold the oil. My horse knows there is something in the air down there for
it is hard to get him by the place.

This will reach you just before Christmas, so I do wish you all the very
best wishes of the season—if it could only be something more than just *wishes*
. . . G.S.M.

*Against this backdrop of anticipated change, Ethel put some of her thoughts
about the timelessness of the coming winter into verse:*

"Earth Changeling"

In the white twilight of the falling snow
    Like a new look upon a well-loved face
A mystery has come on all we know.
    Old certainties of distance and of space,
Familiar lines of mountain, bluff and hill,
    Color and form, are spirited away
In shadow-whiteness. Earth and air are still
    As if in breathless sleep an angel lay.
Oh brown earth of our common days!
    The soil of our age-long defeat, success, and toil,
This garment of the sorrow of the years
    Slips from thy shining shoulders, and appears
This exquisite, white wonder of a thing
    Shown to earth children for their worshipping.

Notes

1. The part of the rim of a wheel into which the outer ends of the spokes are inserted.

2. Later renamed "Cyclone Rim" by uranium prospectors.

CHAPTER ELEVEN

~

1922

"Earned, Not Given"

With no oil mirage in sight, the family finances were minimal. While Ethel's writing rarely mentions their financial issues, the boys, 11 and 9 at the beginning of the year, were learning the importance of their own contributions to the ranch operations. Ethel focused on the simple pleasures of family life in her annual letter to Miss Hill.

Moneta, Wyo., 7 Jan., 1922

My dear Miss Hill,

Your thoughtful kindness put one of the letters in the spelling of our Merrie Christmas this year. It was a simpler time than we expected, thanks to snow and wind and cold, that make keeping warm and fed so engrossingly difficult. Our little family spent Christmas alone. It was a shame, for a friend sent us a twenty-pound turkey. Usually several unattached men-folk drop in from the highways or byways and share our Christmas, but this year they must have stayed in their holes like the rabbits, for we had one of the worst days for years. We had a tree and much candy; a few books and games for the boys. They used the water flowers[1] you sent at once, which froze by the window at night. One of your cards is to be a bookmark in a Christmas book, and the little diary is just what I wanted for my own use. I am glad to have the Magazine again. I pass the magazines on, ten or fifteen miles when I finish them. The beautiful pictures will surely begin their use day after to-morrow when the boys begin their lessons again. Stamps I find a fine way to teach geography. Both boys have albums and collections. The younger boy is especially enthusiastic over any addition to his collection. Several friends sent him some for Christmas, and he now has over nine hundred varieties.[2]

I must tell you of what happened at the Christmas school program in the Moneta school of seven children. Little William, aged nine, was reciting his pledge to his country.

"I pledge my heart, my hand, my . . . " William was stuck, but hopefully supplied, "liver." His six-year-old sister waved her hand and cried, "Teacher, Teacher, I know what William should have said, 'guts'."

"Oh, no," said the teacher. "People don't have such things."

But little sister was not to be suppressed. "Yes, Teacher. You have guts, I have guts, and chickens have guts."

Curtain.

My boys have been coasting, falling off their sleds into the snow, "heels over head," as one of them said. Since December first we have had zero weather and much snow and wind. My husband has not been to town for nearly a month, and no team or car has been over our road for ten days. Still, people go around the drifts by another road, for five men were here today from sheep camps. One bunch has had over a hundred sheep die already, in spite of feeding corn.

I wish that you would write me again, Miss Hill. I have some lovely memories of Brookline;[3] and didn't I have some jolly times in the swimming school! Friends are few and far between now, and I should like to have a new one.

With many thanks, and best wishes for your new year.

Sincerely yours,

Ethel P. Love (Mrs. John G. Love)

John Love still occasionally hired out to help sheep outfits, where, in addition to wages, he was given mutton to supplement the family's meat supply—a godsend, not only for the family, but also for the increasing number of visitors. Ethel kept a record of their visitors:

Eight men might stop in a day, then no one for a week. In October 1922, I initialed on a calendar the names of those who came to the house, nearly all for a meal or overnight. There were sixty-six. Unrestricted hospitality did not extend to the towns, and was a vanishing "custom of the range." Word was passed along, "go to Johnny Love's. He'll put you up." Only one man was ever turned away hungry, and that was because I was asleep in the afternoon.

David added in "We'll Rebuild Again":

After the bunkhouse burned, the only place for guests to stay in winter was the house, as the long building had no source of heat. Our family crowded into one bedroom; the guests, depending on their number, occupied the other bedroom, and overflowed onto the couches in the dining and living rooms.

Ethel's January diary read:

  1   Chinook −2° to 32°
  2   S. McK. [McKenzie] brought mail. J. back with lambs. Thaw?
  3   Snow. G.[George Rushton] & R. here. 630 lambs . . .
  5   J. brought mail from fence corner. R. left.
  9   John & George got coal. Mr. Peterson here. A. [Allan] hurt coasting.
 10   J. & Allan to town. T. [Toby] came for bucks. George here overnight.

Years later David elaborated about "A. hurt coasting" January 9th in "The Scar":
The winter that I was nine and Allan going from ten to eleven was the last one when we had no formal schooling at the ranch. Mother taught us for part of each day, but we had plenty of time between our lessons and the chores for skating and sledding on sunny days.

When the wind swept the snow off the ice on Muskrat Creek, we could skate for half a mile, a mile, and once two miles. We also used the frozen creek to reach the sledding hills half a mile west of the house, jabbing pointed steel coyote trap anchor pins into the ice to propel our sleds along.

One sunny afternoon, Allan and I sledded to these hills. The wind had combed the snow into deep drifts over the east-facing terrace edge, 60 feet above the flood plain. Although only half an inch wide, our steel sled runners did not break through the crusted snow enough to stop the sleds, and we had never had better coasting. Ever searching for steeper sides of the terrace to make faster descents, I found one so steep that my sled might fly. We were wary of that particular slope, however, because a barbed wire pasture fence extended diagonally along the base of the hill. I sailed off the jump first, was airborne, then landed with a crash as the sled runners broke through the snow crust, stopping so abruptly that I was catapulted forward into soft, un-crusted snow. I was well short of the half-buried fence. Yelling with delight, I urged Allan to try it. After considering the fence, the momentum and the snow conditions, he started down just as I reached the top again.

Lying prone on the sled, he soared off the terrace with an exultant whoop, was airborne, and hit the soft snow below—but his sled did not stop. It ca-reened toward the fence. Allan's face hit the barbed wire, his head snapping back sharply. The wire tore through the staples on the posts with a metallic scream as the sled went through the fence and stopped a few feet beyond. For a few terrible seconds, Allan lay writhing on the sled, his hands over his face. Staggering to his feet, he half turned, and in a strangled voice croaked: "I think my throat's been cut. I'll try to get to the house. Bring the sled."

Blood poured through the fingers he pressed tightly against his face, damming up against them and filling one eye socket. Another pool covered the front of the sled. Stumbling, falling, then struggling to his feet, he started for the house, one hand holding his face, his head tilted to one side.

My brother, my idol, my antagonist, one third of my world! Would he die like a butchered steer? If I could get him to lie on the sled, maybe he would last until we got to the house. Half blinded by tears, and gasping great sobs, I dragged my sled through the fence, grabbed his sled rope, and ran as hard as I could to catch up with him. My stubby legs were too low in the snow. Each place he fell was marked by a fresh patch of blood. The sleds kept catching on the greasewood, so I abandoned my smaller one. Dear God, help him to last until I can catch up. A hundred yards from the house I caught up with him, now staggering and weaving, one hand still holding his face together. I put his other arm over my shoulders, trying to shift his weight onto me as his knees buckled. Blood dripped from his open mouth and when he inhaled, he wheezed and coughed. Was this the death rattle I had heard the steers make?

Mother rushed to the door as I screamed for help. Her mouth tightened as she saw Allan, her eyes grew wide and tragic. Carefully we laid Allan on the sofa. I ran to get old clean sheets, stoke up the fire, and bring a basin of hot water. His eyes closed, Allan was in deep shock, his skin sickly white, in stark contrast to the patches of bright red blood beginning to darken and clot around the edges. His breathing bubbled. One eye socket filled slowly with blood which spilled along his nose, one cheek a puff of raw open flesh. Not a whimper, not a tear. Was his windpipe cut? No! He had yelled at me just after he went through the fence.

Gently Mother began to clean his face and neck to determine the extent of his injuries and whether emergency measures had to be taken. A gash rimmed the lower eye socket, but the barb had not punctured his eye. The main wound was a Y-shaped tear which crossed his entire cheek, so deep that he was bleeding through his mouth. Another gash had grazed the jugular vein throbbing blue beneath his skin.

Carefully, Mother put her arms around him and said: "Allan, you're going to be all right." He opened his eyes and tried to smile, but that started the bleeding again.

Dad and George Rushton, digging coal at Castle Gardens, would not be back until dark, so I was Mother's only help. From her surgical kit, she took a curved needle and a string of catgut and sterilized them in a pan of boiling water. Carefully she arranged the central flaps of the Y so that they were even, saying, "Allan, this will hurt. I'll be as careful as I can. Please help me by not moving, if you can stand it." We had no anesthetic in those days, no aspirin, and our whiskey bottle, for adult emergencies only, was in the root cellar. I held Allan's head on one side and Mother began to sew. Putting the curved needle through the flaps of flesh, she carefully positioned them, drew them tight and tied the stitches, those deep inside first, and finally the skin itself. Occasionally Allan twitched or gasped, but made no sound, no other movement. Finally it was finished and covered with a clean, neat bandage.

Liquid through a glass straw was essential because Allan had lost so much fluid. Solid food might infect the wound, and chewing it would start the bleeding again.

In early evening, Dad came home. Immediately he went to Allan, eased himself down on the sofa, and put a hand on the small shoulder. "Laddie, you're a real man." Then he embraced Mother, and whispered: "Lassie, I'm proud of you, and your father would have been, too."

The next day, Dad took Allan by buggy to Moneta and from there by train to Riverton, where Dr. Tonkin examined Allan's face. There was nothing more he could do, he said; he couldn't have done a better job himself.

Allan's scar was a terrible reminder for me because it was my fault. He was perhaps a little more shy and reserved because of it, but his friends and family merely took it for granted. Many people, including my father, had facial scars just as bad, most resulting from lack of prompt medical attention. The emotional toll on my mother cannot be measured. Her journal merely said:

11   G. left. Very little thaw.
12   J. & Allan back. Dry farmer here for bull.

Ethel's calendar recorded a month of snow, wind and below-zero temperatures. Dumpling disappeared. People came and went. The egg tally was 235. Chickens and eggs were taken to town. Her entry for February 25 stated:
J. & T. back from town with freight—phonograph.
In 1999, David wrote of the importance of that day for him in "Childhood Without Music":
As children, Allan and I had lived in a world of adults, with little contact with children our age. Something else was totally lacking as well, and we weren't even aware of it: We had never heard any real music. There were no radios or musical instruments in our house; we could not afford any. The cowboys we knew never sang around campfires; they were too tired at the end of days which began before dawn and ended at dark. Dad chanted Scottish battle ballads on a few cherished occasions, and more often Bobby

Burns' poems; and although they had rhythm and cadence, they were not real music. Mother had once been an accomplished pianist and had sung at performances during her college days. When I was ill, she would hold me and sing lullabies, but to us, "music" was just a word without meaning.

The summer I was eight, we were invited to dinner by the Clark family in Moneta. I don't remember ever having been invited to dinner away from the ranch before. Allan and I were coached in all aspects of behavior as prospective guests, but nothing could have prepared me for the experience ahead.

Mr. Clark, the station master for the Chicago & Northwestern Railroad, was a large, dynamic, personable man with the baldest head I had ever seen. His wife, a small, gentle, kind woman, was completely dominated by her husband. They had three children, Ralph Jr., Harriet, and Ruth, all slightly older than I.

On the appointed day, Dad, Mother, Allan, and I drove our buggy to Moneta where we were to stay at Kanson's Hotel. (The Clarks lived in part of the railroad station, but had no guestrooms.) In their living room stood a piano. I didn't know what it was. They fed us a wonderful dinner with fresh vegetables and lettuce brought in on the train, luxuries we seldom had at our ranch.

Seated between the two girls, I was petrified. Only once before had I even been close to a girl nearly my age. The Clark girls were so clean and so beautiful in their pink and green flouncy dresses, the like of which I had only seen in the catalogs in our outhouse. Fortunately, I didn't have to say anything. The younger girl, Ruth, a skinny extrovert, was interested only in horses. All evening she pestered me about how soon she could come to our ranch and ride horses, any horses, wild or tame. Allan and Ralph Jr. immediately became kindred spirits and ignored the rest of us.

After dinner, we all gathered around the piano and the Clarks began to sing. They had fine voices and clearly enjoyed singing together, drawing wondrous music from the instrument. Overwhelmed by the new and beautiful sounds I had never heard before, I dissolved into tears. When Harriet sang an especially moving song in her glorious, clear voice, I broke out in goose pimples, wishing with all my heart that the song would never end. Surprised, and somewhat embarrassed, the Clarks and my parents made light of my emotional reaction by singing even livelier and louder songs. My mother even contributed rollicking songs from her college days. I had never seen her so delightfully animated before—she was like a young girl. Dad stood quietly by but did not sing. Allan and young Ralph paid no attention.

That night at the hotel, I could not sleep, but savored again the wonderful evening in my mind, melody by melody, especially the voice and image of the older girl. Our Bible at home had paintings of singing angels. Harriet must have stepped out of one of the paintings and into real life.

On the buggy ride back to the ranch the next morning, Dad and Mother were unusually quiet. From time to time, during the rest of the summer and fall, Mother reminisced about the Clark's party, hinting that we needed to add music to our own home, perhaps as a Christmas surprise. When I hounded her to tell what the surprise was, she only smiled and said that the word for it began and ended with the same two letters. I could find no word that matched.

Somehow, perhaps with help from the Bear family (we never knew), money was found to buy the musical surprise. On a snowy day, Dad and Toby returned from Moneta with our bobsled[4] loaded with a ton or more of cotton-seed cake. The four-horse team, encrusted with ice, was blowing steam from ice-rimmed nostrils. Dad, in his buffalo hide coat and bearskin cap, eyebrows frosted, icicles dripping from his moustache, wore a broad, triumphant grin. On top of the load lay a rectangular plank box about five feet high and three feet on the sides, labeled in block letters: "Fragile—Phonograph, Handle With Care." I stared at the label. The same two letters began and ended the word for an object I had never seen before.

Very carefully, we carried the box into the house. Dancing with excitement, Allan and I begged to open it immediately, but Dad reminded us of a bitter experience the year before: A wind-up toy engine had just arrived on the sled from town, and in my haste to see it whiz around the track, I wound it up before it had thawed. The frozen mainspring snapped, and the motor was permanently ruined. So, we waited on tenterhooks until the next day.

What a magnificent sight the phonograph was. Nearly as tall as I, it was of golden, polished hardwood, with an arched, hinged top to cover the felt-covered turntable which held the record. A chrome arm with a complex knob to hold the steel needle swiveled out over the turntable. Ever so carefully, the needle would be placed by hand in the outermost groove of the record and the turntable manually started with a lever. A crank on the outside of the case wound the motor to run the turntable. Swinging doors in the base of the case hid vertical slots to store the records. Half a dozen records came with the purchase, large black, Bakelite discs, nearly ½ inch thick and 12 inches across. A label in the center, with ornate gold lettering stated the name of the piece, the composer, and the musical artist.

We boys had to read and re-read the instructions and repeat them back to our parents before we were allowed to play any of the records. Even then, we could play them only with permission, when the time was suitable. We wound the crank, placed the record on the turntable, positioned the needle carefully on the record, released the lever. Suddenly the pinched, quavering sound of "Thaïs" played by the New York Philharmonic Orchestra filled our ears—the first music ever to come to our house. It wasn't like the Clarks' music at all, but it was wonderful! Enchanted, I played it many times the first few days.

Our new world of music appreciation expanded quickly. Friends shared their records and before long, we had quite a variety. "La Paloma," "The Land O' the Leal," "Eileen Alanna," and "When Irish Eyes Are Smiling" sung by the great Irish tenor, John McCormack, were among the first records we heard. We thrilled to Sir Harry Lauder's "Bonnie Mary of Argyle," Robert Burns' "Scots wa hae wi Wallace Bled," "The Battle of Kille Krankie," and other of his poems set to music, often accompanied by bagpipes. At the sound, Dad would suddenly appear, silently, an expression of sad remembrance on his face. "Sahara, I'll Soon Be Dry Like You" commemorating the Volstead Act, was added to our collection. Mother felt it inappropriate for her young boys, so we played it only when she was out of earshot.

Later, when I was in college and had access to a radio, I delighted in the Sunday night concerts by the New York Philharmonic Orchestra. The vibrant, baritone voice of host DeWolf Hopper invariably concluded the broadcasts with: "The song is ended, and the words? Well, choose them for yourself—for the words that music brings are those closest to your heart."

The egg tally for February was 500; visitors, 22.

Ethel's March diary, similar to that of February, recorded cold, snow, chores, and visitors. The boys ice-skated on Muskrat Creek on sunny days, and roller-skated in the hay house on snowy ones. Spring song birds began to appear. Ethel noted there was a sick cow. David later explained that the cow had been mired in the wallow where her skin was pierced by a bone fragment in the mud. Infection would contaminate her milk, and she had to be destroyed—a major loss for the family. Snow complicated the annual Easter egg hunt.

The egg tally for March was 1,174, visitors: 9.

In April several of Ethel's journal entries stated: "J. & boys after wool." In 1975 David wrote what lay behind his mother's notes in "Earned, Not Given":

April, 1922. Allan was eleven years old and I was nearly ten. The winter just ending had been severe, and the animals on the range had suffered acutely.

Then spring came with a rush, the melting snow exposing the carcasses of hundreds of frozen sheep—not ours—scattered across the sage-covered hills north of the ranch. They had belonged to many outfits, but no one wanted them now. Within a few days the bodies began to thaw and then to rot. At a certain stage in decomposition, the wool could easily be pulled out in great handfuls. This "pulled wool" brought a lower price than sheared wool because it was dirtier, though the fibers were longer. It could be sold for cash to the Jewish hide, wool, and junk man who came to the region every spring to buy whatever was for sale. His price was always minimal: "Take it or leave it." It was always taken. Anyone who pulled wool probably desperately needed the cash it brought.

We had always looked with contempt at "wool pullers." This spring, however, with no warning or explanation, Dad announced: "We're going to pull wool. You boys will help." Mother's lips tightened, but she said nothing. Our bodies, clothes, and the house would reek of decayed flesh for days, and, more seriously, the risk of infection was high. Before the advent of antibiotic drugs, blood poisoning was a dreaded scourge of the range.

Each morning we hitched Slopey and Darky to the now dilapidated and topless buggy and drove with no enthusiasm across the roadless hills to look for carcasses. At just the right stage, their toothpick legs sticking out straight from their bloated bodies, we could strip a carcass in five minutes, stuffing the reeking wool and accompanying maggots into gunny sacks. Our stomachs heaved when we turned these sheep over to get the wool from the slimy undersides. Carcasses on sunny slopes were harder to pick and dirtier, because chunks of skin came off with the wool. The price would be reduced accordingly.

Carcasses in gulches and on shady hillsides were frequently half-thawed and half-frozen. We flagged those that were not yet ripe with a piece of cloth to "pick" a few days later. Coyotes were everywhere, yapping, overstuffed with carrion, arrogant, unafraid. They seemed to know that we would not shoot them because, at this time of year, they were shedding and their fur was worthless. We resolved that next winter, we would set out a trap line and even the score.

From dawn until twilight we worked, filthy, reeking, hating ourselves and our parents—but we salvaged hundreds of pounds of wool. Every six pounds meant a dollar, but it was poor compensation for the humiliation, stench, flies, maggots, and visual impact of so much decaying meat. We could not eat lunch the first day, and after that did not bother to bring food.

At night, we stripped in the outer entry of the ranch house, checked our bodies for ticks, bathed in the laundry tub, leaving our clothes outside to be worn again the next day. Only after this purification, hurried, because after sundown the temperature dropped rapidly in the unheated entry, were we allowed, naked and shivering, inside to dress in clean clothes before supper.

Two weeks passed, each day worse than the one before. There was little conversation as we worked; talking meant drawing air through the mouth, which heightened the sense of smell. Also, the big, buzzing blowflies, with their gunmetal blue abdomens, were so thick around the carcasses that they were all too often inhaled. The only words uttered in an entire day might be, "There's one," "Not ripe yet," and "Too far gone," generally followed by Dad's, "Get all you can from it anyway."

The breaking point came suddenly one day. In an outburst which erupted from the depths of our souls, Allan and I demanded that Dad tell us if this misery were really worth the money. Then we stopped, appalled, at our breach of custom. We never, ever questioned orders or talked back to our parents. There was a long silence. Dad looked at us steadily with his keen blue eyes. Then in his soft Scottish burr, he said: "Laddies, I don't like this work any more than you do, but someday you will learn as I have that the things of real value in this life are earned, not given. None of us can afford to be too proud or too squeamish to work for these goals. Twelve years ago I owned our ranch and nearly a million dollars' worth of livestock, all earned by my own labors. I was proud to tell people that nothing was given to me. Twice since then, Nature has wiped me out. Pride has gone; determination hasn't. I'm 53 years old and have your loving mother and you bairns to take care of. Nearly all our cattle died two years ago, and before they died they ate three thousand dollars' worth of feed. The bank is threatening to take the ranch to pay for the debt. They almost got the ranch once before."

This was one of the longest speeches Dad ever made to us. His currents of thought ran deeply, and I suspect that he had planned precisely what he would say if it were necessary. The financial problem was now clear, and the revelation about the ranch was a shock. There was a strained pause. Horned larks twittered faintly in the distance. Not a breath of air stirred and the brilliant sunlight bathed us, but we felt cold and uncomfortable.

With a sigh, Dad resumed: "Right now our family goals are to keep the ranch and to get out of debt. With luck and hard work we may make several hundred dollars from this wool. Some of it will go for food and taxes. Maybe a hundred dollars will go to the bank for part of the debt. It's not much, but it shows the bank people that we are trying to do the right thing. This is very important, laddies. Your mother and I need your help. Someday you will have your own goals and you will try to earn them as men should, but you may require a little help, even as I do now."

In a few minutes on that sunny hillside, we grew up.

Shutting our minds to the messes before our eyes, the smells seemed a little less nauseous. Challenges flew: who could find the most carcasses, who could pick the fastest and cleanest? We were no longer quite as cross at night because now we understood the family goals, and were helping to achieve them. Long after the wool-picking was replaced by other onerous chores, the memory of this conversation remained, but we never discussed it again.

Ethel's egg tally for April was 1,170; visitors, 10.

Her journal for May lists rain, snow, heavy snow, calves born, calves dead, washing, visitors, her garden, and the school board meeting in Moneta. For the first time, the Loves were allotted a teacher for four months instead of three, and arrangements were made to have "Ma" Bailey return.

Her entry on May 17th says: "Man stopped."

Remembering the day, sixty years later, David wrote "From Father, Christmas, 1901—The Gold Watch":

Shortly before dawn one May morning, Allan and I were awakened by a sharp knock at the front door of the ranch house. Peeking through the curtains of the bedroom window, we saw a saddled horse, head down, legs braced apart, sides heaving, foam-flecked, tethered to the fence.

The low rumble of male voices came from the living room. We knew not to interrupt or to interfere with man-talk, so we returned to bed, to wait impatiently until our usual rising time. By then, the visitor had departed, not waiting for breakfast. We thought that strange, but were relieved to learn that Mother had provided him with food to eat while he rode. The code of the range demanded that all visitors be fed.

Who was this stranger whom we had not seen and never would see? Any visitor was of interest, but this one was especially intriguing because of the condition of his horse, his time of arrival—he must have ridden all night—and his hasty departure. Dad merely smiled and said that the matter did not concern us. We knew there was more to this story, and remained on the alert.

Sure enough, about mid-morning, five riders raced over the hill from the south. Galloping through the south pasture, they splashed across Muskrat Creek and thundered up to the front gate. Like that of the mysterious visitor, their horses were lathered and gray with dust, as were the grim-faced riders. Each saddle scabbard carried a rifle, and the men wore six-shooters and full ammunition belts. Dismounting, they warily spread out around the ranch house, guns drawn.

Ignoring their suspicious behavior, Dad greeted them pleasantly by name. They responded in kind, but with no cordiality. They were the sheriff of Fremont County and his posse of deputies.

"Johnny, we're after P.H.S. He killed J.F. on the Sweetwater yesterday and we're going to bring him to Lander and hang him. He can't be far ahead of us. You must have seen him. Which way did he go?"

"Yes, he was here," Dad replied mildly, "but he didn't say which way he was going and I didn't watch him leave. Why do you want to hang him anyway? You know he's a fine man. You also know that J.F. has needed killing for years. It was just a question of who would do it and when. P.H.S. should be rewarded, not hanged." The truth, apparently, but not what the sheriff wanted to hear, especially in front of his posse. The capture of a killer could further his career.

"None of your lip, now, Johnny," he growled. "He's guilty of murder and he's gonna pay for it. We rode 60 long, hot miles yesterday from Lander to the scene of the murder, 40 miles this morning, and we're in no mood to argue. We've no time to waste."

They spurned the offer of breakfast, but pumped and drank a lot of water, knowing that ours was the only potable water in 65 trail miles. While they watered their horses, Mother, deliberately slowly, fixed sandwiches for them to take along. Dad seemed to be prolonging their questioning, delaying their departure for an hour or more.

Finally, the posse departed, galloping north toward Moneta, too fast to see any tracks that the fugitive might have left, unless he had made them in the dust of the two-track road. Later we learned that he had not gone to Moneta at all; he disappeared and was never heard of again.

Gradually we learned more about the pre-dawn visitor. Not telling Dad of the killing, P.H.S. had merely said that he needed $5.00 and would leave his watch for security. When Dad hesitated, the visitor turned steely. "Johnny, we've known each other a long time. I want to be honest, but, by God, if you won't trade, I'll have to rob you. I don't want to use my gun on a friend." Realizing that something serious must have happened and he'd better be serious, too, Dad agreed to the trade.

The watch was an Elgin, 15-jewels, in a 14-K gold hunting case, emblazoned with a stag and a shield bearing in script the letters "P.H.S." Inside the back was engraved: "From father, Christmas, 1901." The watch was, even then, worth many times the $5.00 that Dad gave the man, but he never returned to reclaim it. Dad never told us who P.H.S. was or how they knew each other. It was not wise to pry too closely into a man's background, or to talk to others about it. We did not know, then, that Dad, himself, had been involved in some way with Butch Cassidy and the Wild Bunch a little more than 20 years earlier. I have found no P.H.S. among the names of the Wild Bunch and their associates. Could the watch have been stolen from the real P.H.S. and the thief merely assumed those initials? Or was he the real P.H.S., whose father gave him this expensive Christmas present? We will probably never know.

Ethel's journal recorded that Mrs. Bailey arrived May 20, to teach her third and final term with the family.

The Love family and a friend picnicking at Castle Gardens near the Love ranch, 1922. A saying on the range was: "If summer comes on a Saturday, we'll have a picnic."
Love Family Archives

Despite the spring snows, garlic, squash, beans, beets, and sunflowers sprouted. Kittens, calves, and colts were born. A new gate was put in the garden fence. The egg tally for May was 1,186, visitors, 10.

David's notes included the following memories:

Despite Mrs. Bailey's best efforts to teach us, our lessons were often interrupted. The spring roundup came, and range tramps, including a man named Liechman, whose body bore putrid sores he called "irresipilis." Mother refused to let him in the house. He kept a human skull in his wagon. Neighbors named Sharp and Oney proved up on their homesteads. We had picnics at Castle Gardens.

Desperately wanting a tree, I dug up a small cottonwood, which had washed down from the Little Dam several years before and taken root. Hauling it in a wheelbarrow, I planted it in the front yard. Several years later I transplanted more little cottonwoods and some Russian olives from a river bank near Shoshoni. As the water table dropped during the next 20 years, they gradually died, but my first tree, hoary and free-form, was still alive more than 80 years later.

Ethel's notes recorded the summer's events. A driller named Gilbourne and his wife arrived, and some surveyors, reviving the family's dreams of riches from oil. Mrs. Gilbourne had beautiful white hair. She told Ethel that she massaged drilling oil into her hair before rinsing it.

A roundup crew branding a range cow at Love ranch, 1917.
Love Family Archives

The egg tally for June was 762; visitors, 24.

In July a group of cowboys, George Rushton, Brocky Jones, A. Jammerman from the JJ ranch among them, came to help with another cattle roundup. The Loves branded 30 of their own calves.

Ethel's sister Faith and her friend Mrs. Tovani arrived from Denver July 7th to take Ethel to Yellowstone Park—the trip she and John had attempted on their honeymoon twelve years earlier. In Faith's Ford they crossed the Continental Divide on a dirt track at more than 9,000 feet, over what is now Togwotee Pass. A few photographs of geysers, bears, Tower Falls, and Ethel wearing her first slacks are the only record of their trip.

During the ladies' ten-day absence, John and Toby Leitch took Allan and David by buggy to Long Creek on their first real fishing expedition. No one recorded what occupied Mrs. Bailey during their absence. They returned 24 hours later with 24 succulent trout. The egg tally for the month was 801; visitors, 15.

The egg tally for August was 733; the visitors, at least 30. On the 22nd John went to Moneta to oversee an election, and returned with a load of precious fresh vegetables.

Ethel Love in her first slacks at Yellowstone Park, 1922.
Love Family Archives

David and Allan were now old enough to participate in the process of haying,
which David described in "Haying at Mud Spring":

Dad announced one morning at the end of August that the hay at Mud
Spring was ready to harvest. Despite being mostly coarse swamp grass and
sedges, and less nutritious than the finer grass harvested in the meadow, it
was half the lifeline which fed our gradually expanding herd of cattle. In
previous years Allan and I had only been allowed to open and close gates
as our two heavily laden hay wagons toiled slowly down the long slope
near the sledding hills toward the hay pen. This year we were old enough
to really help.

We were taught how to sharpen the sickle blades for the mower on our
grindstone, and check the rest of the equipment for cracks or breaks. We
examined the wheels on each wagon to be sure that the wood had not dried
out or the spokes shrunk enough in our dry climate to loosen the iron rims.
(If any were loose, the wheels were removed and soaked in the creek, or as a
last resort, taken to Shoshoni to be "reset" by the Scottish blacksmith, who
heated then shrank the wooden felleys or felloes and refitted them with new
iron rims and rivets.) We daubed thick, black axle grease on the wheel hubs,
and helped wrestle hay rakes and racks, mower, food, drinking water, grain
for the horses, and bedrolls onto an extended supply wagon.

At Mud Spring, the hay was mowed, raked into shocks and spread to dry
for two or three days before it was pitched onto the wagons to be brought
back to the ranch.

After tethering the lead horses, either Allan or I drove the wheelers,[5] from
shock to shock, while the other helped the men pitch hay onto the rack. The
boy on the hay rack distributed the hay evenly across it, making sure that
the corners were filled. The boy on the ground, usually Allan because he was
stronger, had to pitch heavy forkfuls of hay five to ten feet above his head.
I have no idea of the tonnage of a load, but the hay, even cured, was very
heavy, and it took about two hours to load each wagon.

The trip back was the best part: the serenity of the landscape, the jingling
of the links on the harness tugs, the creak and smell of sweaty leather, the
fragrance of the fresh hay, the cadence of the horses' hooves, and the knowledge that we had done men's work.

The two-track road to Mud Spring crossed about 100 yards of sand in a
nearly dry channel of Muskrat Creek. (There was no bridge; the creek was
usually only 8–10 inches deep.) Digging in their pie-pan-sized hooves, the
horses struggled to gain footing in the sand. Mid-way across, they rested
on a grassy island, their muscles quivering, lungs heaving, and their bodies
dark with sweat. On the other side, they rested again, while Allan and I

Allan Love pitching hay at Mud Spring at Love ranch, 1922.
Love Family Archives

searched for Indian artifacts: bird points[6], thumb scrapers[7], *manos*,[8] or other arrowheads. But when the wagons started again, we were expected to be on board. Once, as Allan ran to climb aboard, he slipped and the rear wheel passed over the instep of his foot. He screamed. Miraculously, his foot had sunk into the sand, and no bones were broken. Dad just looked at him and said nothing.

Back at the haystack yard, the horses were unharnessed, fed grain, and turned out to pasture, where they shook their great bodies, then rolled, only to stand and shake again. We men did the chores, splashed water on our faces and hands, and went to the house for dinner.

The next day in the hay pen, Dad and George outlined the stacks, about 10 feet wide and 50 feet long. Then Allan and I spread the hay within the outline, building the stack, layer by layer. The sides had to be vertical, even, and interlocked with the hay in the center or the stack would topple or fall apart. At the height of 10-12 feet, the stack was peaked with a crown of hay, and packed tightly to shed snow and rain.

Both men and horses rested for several days. Then haying at the buffalo wallows meadow could begin.

During the mid-1920s, a cloudburst upstream from Mud Spring raised Muskrat Creek to flood-stage. The water cut through the "gooseneck" of the stream meander, destroying the spring and spreading a solid sheet of sand across the hay field, ruining it for all time.

Ethel's August journal noted that Brocky Jones, T. Graham, O'Conner, and Albert Jammerman had spent the night at the ranch. In 1981 David wrote of one of their visits in "More Speed, To Hell With Direction":

Autumn was the time of the annual fall cattle roundup when a dozen or more large outfits along the Sweetwater River trailed their herds northward, past our ranch to Moneta. From there the cattle were shipped to Omaha or Chicago, depending on the market price of beef. The Chicago & Northwestern Railroad provided feed and water for the livestock in transit and free passage in the caboose to ranchers shipping with them. The Union Pacific and Chicago, Burlington & Quincy rail companies shipped from equally near sites, but were reputed to not look after the cattle in transit, so the cowboys chose not to use them.

That fall about 1,000 head of beef were trailed past our ranch, at 10–15 miles per day, so that they would lose as little weight as possible. About 20 cowboys, plus a cook and horse wrangler, accompanied the herds. Young, lively, and single, the men anticipated a roistering good time after the cattle had been shipped and they had been paid.

Mother noted that the swaggering 16-year-old son of a successful neighboring rancher came with his mother for the occasion:

"Billy D., wearing new boots, was blustering about the corral. Omar admired them. 'You don't want to lose them boots. Better put your brand on 'em.' Billy hunted the 'J' iron, first letter of his father's brand, heated it red hot in the fire, then pressed it firmly on the instep of his right foot. For a few seconds the leather heated unnoticeably. Then Billy threw the iron from him, leaped into the air and grasped his foot. Hopping, cussing, jumping, he ran for the creek only to stop and grab at his foot, to the delight of the seasoned hands in the corral.

"On another occasion, Billy had so annoyed the cowboys that while he was sleeping in his henskin, they lassoed his bedroll and dragged him into the creek. Enraged, the boy threatened to kill them all, but foreseeing trouble, the men had removed the bullets from his gun."

That autumn we had about 20 two-year-old steers ready to ship with the Sweetwater herd. The boss of the group was Brocky Jones, a tough, bowlegged bantam who claimed he could whip his weight in wildcats, ride anything with hair, and drink any man under the table. About five feet, five inches tall, and very erect, he wore boots with high, tapered heels to keep his small feet from slipping through the stirrups, and thus prevent him being dragged by his horse if he ever lost his seat. Flat-heeled shoes to wear when he was not riding were tied on his saddle. Nobody ever poked fun at him for that foible more than once. His cauliflower ears and a stubby broken nose were trophies of bare-knuckle fights. His eyes were blazing blue, keen, honest, his voice deep and distinctive. His real name was Jean Jones, but to everyone he was "Brocky" because his face wore a mass of freckles.

He was a hero to Allan and me, for he often took the time to tease and encourage us, and to show us riding and roping tricks. That autumn he agreed to let us ride with the other cowboys as equals in the drive to Moneta. Dad would come by road in the buggy to be on hand when the brand inspector checked his brands before the shipping, and to bring us home when the hubbub was over.

The 25 citizens of Moneta braced themselves for the annual onslaught of the Sweetwater bunch. These drovers would bring in hundreds of sorely needed dollars, but Adolph Kanson, and his sons Omar and Ivan, whose hotel-bar bore the brunt of the invasion, always wondered afterward if the breakage and fighting were worth the money. Ivan, a giant of a man and the bar's bouncer, had frequently whipped as many as six men at a time. Even Brocky was careful to avoid those ham-like hands and enormous arms.

The cattle cars were waiting at Moneta's stockyards when the herd arrived. The animals were watered and put to graze overnight on the range outside of town before the journey to Omaha.

Brocky set up his camp a mile from town, and would allow no one to go in, knowing what could happen if his cowboys scattered. The next day came the jockeying of the stock cars with the little steam engine, the dust, heat, flies, and the prodding of reluctant cattle up the chutes into the cars. Finally, the last car was loaded, the train assembled, and, with a wave and a blast from his whistle, the engineer started east. Dad, Allan, and I departed in our buggy for the ranch.

Brocky paid each man in cash; then, himself in the lead, they all headed for town.

By early morning nearly all the whiskey had been drunk, the fights fought, and most of the cowboys had staggered, or were dragged back to camp. Most, but not all. Brocky, flush with new money, bought Adolph Kanson's topless Model T Ford, and with a few roistering cronies decided to drive back to the Sweetwater in style, leaving the other men to bring the cavvy and chuck wagon when they were able.

So, they started out. Brocky was driving, but wouldn't admit that he scarcely knew how. It hadn't been long since his first automobile ride, when he panicked as the driver sped down a steep hill so wildly that Brocky jumped out and broke his arm. This day, he missed the turnoff along the old freight road to the Sweetwater and found himself on the dead-end dirt road to our ranch. About dawn we heard them coming, eight men draped in and on the tiny car, whooping and hollering, sustained by the bottles of whiskey which Brocky had thoughtfully cached there.

Roaring southward off the steep terrace above the ranch, the Ford whizzed across the flat past the ranch buildings, shot into the air off a 10-foot cut-bank, and landed with a splash in the shallow water of Muskrat Creek.

Not pausing to see if any of the tangled bodies of his friends had fallen out, Brocky pushed the low gear pedal, revved the motor to a whine, turned the car around, and roared up out of the creek bottom. As they reoriented on the flat by the buildings and raced back up onto the terrace they had just left, we heard Brocky's gravelly voice yelling at the top of his lungs: "More speed! To hell with direction!"

This immediately joined the list of stock phrases in our family. Brocky would have appreciated the colorful legacy of inverse advice that he left us!

Ethel's egg tally for August was 733; visitors, excluding the roundup crew, 31.

David remembered one youthful prank on a trip to Moneta:

For the steers shipped to market, we received a small amount of hard cash, some of which went toward paying the debts of the Hard Winter. Our heifers, now Herefords, were kept to augment our breeding stock.

On our trips to town for winter provisions, we often visited the Clarks. One day Ralph Jr. persuaded me to put my only 50¢ piece on the railroad track to see what happened when a train ran over it. Gleefully, we waited beside the tracks as an engine chuffed slowly into sight. Suddenly my delight turned to horror. The engineer stopped the steaming locomotive a few feet from us, climbed down from the cab, tucked my hard-earned coin into his pocket, and, with a grin at us boys, climbed back into his seat.

We got even, though. While the engineer was having lunch at the hotel, Ralph and I applied a little axle grease to the tracks beneath the locomotive. As we giggled from behind the station house, the wheels spun, the steam hissed, the locomotive stood still, and the engineer, knowing who had done it and why, swore as he shoveled cinders and sand onto the tracks to regain traction for the gigantic wheels.

Mrs. Bailey's last 3-month term at the ranch ended when her winter term in town began. Ethel wrote of what happened next in "Too Much Wild Duck":

Mr. and Mrs. Oney moved into our guest room for a month in the fall. He had been gassed during the first World War while serving as an Army chaplain. Hoping that the dry Wyoming air would help his lungs, he took up a homestead and brought out his timid southern bride. Her light brown hair fell like a heavy shawl nearly to her knees. She wore it piled simply about her head. The reason for their coming was that she might teach the last four weeks of our unfinished term of summer school. The school board had made an exception by allowing a married woman to teach, perhaps because Mr. Oney was a veteran.

David remembered other details about the couple as well:

We watched in awe when he coughed blood into his handkerchief, and tried to be kind to him. With no income but her husband's disability payments, his wife, a tall lady with a charming southern accent, was grateful to have even a temporary job.

Ethel's account continued:

Both were congenial members of our household. Our boys enjoyed listening to Mr. Oney's recollections of war and of travel about Japan distributing Bibles, even of eating fried grasshoppers in a Japanese country home.

Despite his ill health, Mr. Oney joined in the affairs of the ranch, riding horseback, riding with the men on a wagon to dig coal, or going to Riverton thirty-five miles across country for a load of vegetables and a ham. He especially enjoyed hunting. But on Saturdays, Mr. and Mrs. Oney returned in their little car to their homestead cabin for a quiet Sunday by themselves.

He was sitting in the ranch living room one afternoon during lessons, when I came to the door from feeding the little chickens. I whispered to Allan, "Where are the shells for your .410?"

"What do you want to shoot?" he exploded, jumping from his chair. David and Mr. Oney had an immediate reaction. Forgetting school and teacher, they plied me with questions. "A badger? Killed all the little chickens! It turned and hissed at you? On the path by the kitchen door? Still there?" They ran for other guns and shells. By that time I needed none. Man and boys hurried from the house and killed the badger.

At that time there was no closed season for shooting game birds or limit on numbers. Mr. Oney particularly enjoyed shooting—and eating—wild duck. Since he did not have a gun of his own, he borrowed one of John's, a single-barreled, eight-gauge shotgun, now outlawed. This when fully loaded had a tremendous recoil, but the advantage of a wide shot pattern which could bring down at one shot a large number of birds. There were many varieties on the pools up the creek: teal, blue-winged and green, golden-eyed duck, spoonbills, redheads, pintails, and mallards.

Sixteen ducks were killed by the men one Friday; early the next morning Mr. Oney shot twenty-eight more. The rule that a hunter must dress his own game was not practical with forty-four ducks. Moreover, the next day was Sunday, when it was against Mr. Oney's principles to work. He would not pick or clean ducks, although he would shoot them, on Sunday. We did not want to do anything to offend him, so we set to work that Saturday on the ducks.

Mr. and Mrs. Oney sat in the kitchen picking ducks. Allan and David worked at their hinged table. I picked beside them. John drew and cleaned the birds and took them to the cellar. Dry picking was slow.[9]

We separated, for pillows, the down and small feathers from the larger and stiffer ones. The bloody feathers John put into the fire in the range, where they burned with a long stench. A light snow fell all day. We worked while morning dragged into afternoon and afternoon approached evening. Some man came before dinner and was put to work. I am sure he never forgot his share in the tedious picking, as we struggled to finish before the Lord's day. Feathers piled up in dishpans. Cloth sacks were filled. Feathers strewed the kitchen floor. When the outside door was opened, they blew through every room in the house. They caught in our clothes and hair. At last, by lamplight, the forty-fourth duck was stripped and ready for cooking.

The Oneys went peacefully to their cabin for Sunday. I tried to sweep and capture the still flying feathers and clean the house. I really worked on Sunday. For dinner the large oven of the range was filled with wild ducks roasting, one to a person with some extras. After a few days, I needed to cook only half as many. Mr. Oney asked a blessing at every meal and gave hearty thanks for the ducks.

By the end of the week, still exhilarated by his success, on the eve of his departure from Wyoming, Mr. Oney wanted to hunt for the last time. John sent the boys to the long building to find some new shells for the eight-gauge gun. There were no more.

"We'll have to load some," said Allan, reaching slowly for the equipment. "Get some used shells. I don't really care for any more ducks. My fingers are still sore from picking feathers—all day, too."

"I don't feel like eating any more duck," chimed in David. "Every day we bow our heads and thank the Lord for ducks. I'm not thankful any more; and there are still lots of ducks in the root cellar." He put a four-inch brass shell into the loading stand to pry off the cap. "Shall we give him what Dad calls a squib load?"

Allan was thinking deeply. "We'll fix just three shells. This first one . . ."

David watched him press in the new cap, pour bird shot through the funnel, and add wads, tamping them down. "No powder?" asked David.

"No powder," answered Allan, grinning. "Now the second." After capping another shell, he filled it with wads.

"No shot?" asked David.

"No shot and no powder," said Allan.

"Let me do the last one." David carefully dipped black powder from the can until the shell was nearly full, then topped it with wads. They arranged the shells in a small square box for Mr. Oney.

Flocks of ducks were swimming on the water up the creek. The two conspirators lagged behind Mr. Oney to let him get near enough for a good shot. They held their breath while he aimed and pulled the trigger. There was a small pop and the shot dribbled slowly out of the gun barrel. Nothing else happened. The ducks were not even disturbed.

"Must have been a dud," said Allan.

Mr. Oney removed the used shell from the gun and reloaded. Again he took a careful aim to get as many ducks as possible with one shot. Again he fired. There was a louder pop, and strings of brown felt wads sprayed out a few feet. The ducks were alarmed, rose, circled, but returned to the water. Not one fell.

"You've still got another shell."

Mr. Oney looked puzzled as he put the last shell into the gun.

"Do you think he will swear?" asked David in a whisper.

There was a terrific explosion as the heavy gun kicked. Mr. Oney reeled and staggered down into the brush. Smothering their delighted sniggering as the ducks took safely to rapid and distant flight, the two boys quietly disappeared.

Back at the house, Mrs. Oney was preparing to leave the next day for Kentucky. She and I tied up the four-foot, seamless sack of feathers and down for her to take with her. John was in complete ignorance of the boys' part in the shooting that day. It was some years before David confessed what they had done.

When the hunter came in empty-handed, "What luck?" John asked.

"None," was Mr. Oney's brief reply.

Notes

1. Tiny paper flowers which emerge on threads from small clamshells when the shells are placed in water.

2. In one of Ethel's fictional stories written in the 1950s, "Clash in the Old Stamp Album," she imagines conversations among stamps from various nations as they discuss their places in the United Nations.

3. Massachusetts.

4. A sled with two sets of runners and a freight-size wagon box.

5. Stronger horses.

6. Small arrowheads one inch or less long.

7. Sharp chipped stones used to scrape hides.

8. Hand-held stones for grinding grains.

9. Wet plucking is easier: the bird is dunked in boiling water to loosen the feathers so that they may be stripped off easily (J.D. Love, personal communication).

CHAPTER TWELVE

1923

Daily Life on Muskrat Creek

Not every year had catastrophic weather or medical events; some years were only marked by the ebb and flow of family life and growing children, punctuated with visitors and infrequent contact with the Outside World. As Ethel reported to Miss Hill:

7 Jan., 1923

Dear Miss Hill,

It is very sweet and friendly of you to send the *Ladies' Home Journal* to me for another year, and I certainly appreciate it. After I have finished reading it, I will pass it on to someone else.

This year we had almost no Christmas celebration—a tiny artificial tree on the table after dinner, and packages under it. This we repeated on New Year's day. In between, my two boys and I spent a week with friends in Lander, about a hundred miles away. The boys had a splendid time, hunting, skating, going to the movies (which they don't often do, for the nearest ones are forty miles away, and I am often thankful for that fact), sitting up late, playing caroms, checkers, or rummy with our friends, and eating popcorn. I celebrated with a small operation, necessary and inconvenient, but not enough to incapacitate me much. Since coming home after even a week's absence, I found my hands more than full, mending, washing, cleaning, the usual ritual of a country housekeeper especially exacting after a holiday.

Why is it that things disintegrate just at Christmas time? I've noticed it before, and this year tried to forestall the disaster, with some degree of success too, except as regards stockings.

It's been a beautiful holiday season, sunny and not too cold. I've some narcissus in bud and blossom that are a joy.

My two boys have been trapping, and caught four coyotes, two badgers, and an enormous bobcat (our local species of wild cat). The plan is to sell the coyotes, which are in demand this season, and get a correspondence course in taxidermy and a rifle. They can get a very good course second-hand. Then they will make the bobcat skin into a rug for their new room and make me a muff from the badger skin—q.e.d.[1]

With very best wishes for your New Year,

Sincerely yours,

Ethel P. Love

David described the importance and process of trapping in "We'll Rebuild Again":

Finally, Allan and I were old enough to run our own trap lines. Pelts were a needed cash crop, and we were eager to begin.

A government trapper named Frank Ramsey became an occasional guest at the ranch. Short, with the battered face of a fighter and years of riotous living, he had spent 30 years in U.S. Army campaigns all over the world. "No woman was ever sorry she knew me!" he boasted. Now retired from the

David and Allan Love with a bobcat they have trapped at Love ranch. (It is dead.) Dumpling is in the foreground, 1922.
Love Family Archives

David Love with badger pelt at Love ranch, 1923.
Love Family Archives

Army, he had become a professional trapper and traveled around the region in a small, battered car. Paid by the government for quotas met, he eradicated coyotes and other "nuisance" animals, and depended upon the ranchers in his assigned area for food and lodging.

Patiently he showed us the tricks we needed to be good trappers. First, we would have to think like a coyote. After determining places that coyotes would like, in a small sagebrush fire we lightly smoked our old gloves and two traps for each site. Trapped coyotes may chew off a trapped foot to free themselves, so, cruel as it sounds, we set one trap to capture the front feet and the second for the hind feet. Then, after positioning and staking the traps, we sprinkled the area around them with Ramsey's secret, evil-smelling scent, reputed to drive coyotes to be reckless. We covered the traps with a weathered page of newspaper and a layer of fine dirt, careful not to spring the traps and catch a finger. With a carved wooden replica of a coyote's foot, affixed with leather pads dipped in scent, we imprinted fake tracks around the traps. No trace of human scent could remain.

My coyote trap line was a 4-mile square with the ranch house in the center. I also set badger and bobcat traps at Castle Gardens. We used horsemeat, or any other carcass found, as bait.

Dad expected us to make the rounds of our trapline at least every three days; it was inhumane to let trapped animals suffer. Hating it, I killed the animals I caught quickly, with a single shot from my .22 rifle or pistol, being careful to not damage the pelt. Dad paid us 50¢ apiece for skinning and stretching his own coyote hides and $2–3 for badgers and bobcats, which he shipped to furriers in the east. For the first time in our lives we felt the thrill of anticipated wealth.

With some of my earnings I bought the Northwestern School of Taxidermy correspondence course books. The rest was deposited in the Shoshoni Bank as a lesson in the merits of saving money. I began by tanning a badger and a bobcat, although similar pelts tanned by our Native American neighbors were much more beautiful. Coyote pelts were too valuable a cash crop for me to learn on.

Someone had given our parents a magnificent horned owl, stuffed and mounted, clinging to a branch. I hoped to learn to mount a bird just as spectacular of my own.

Apparently responding to news of Ethel's and the boys' Christmastime stay in Lander, Gardiner Mills wrote March 17th:

Truly a fine day—easily the worst storm of the winter! How the snow must be blowing across the Muskrat flats today when we get it as hard here in the hills. We shall see in the paper of someone caught out in it and frozen—it is only ten above zero here. I hope you are warm & comfortable[. . .]

How much we miss by living in the wilderness & how thankful that the "movie" was not invented in my time I am. I saw Ed Farlow in Lander [. . .] who told me of [. . .] helping to make a moving picture of Emerson Hough's "The Covered Wagon" [. . .] 60 miles out in the [Utah] desert. He had charge of the Indians [. . .] from here as well as of some Utes & Bannocks from Idaho. It was made under the Lasky Player Management[. . .] They had over a thousand people to transport, lodge & feed, to say nothing of the Indians [. . .] Farlow suggested that the latter would feed themselves if given the chance[. . .] They were to have all the beef they could eat [. . .] and firewood was hauled in front of their tents for them. Farlow told me it was heaven to them—& they all got fat—he was sure Yellow Calf gained 25 lbs [. . .] The Indians from here had been to Cheyenne and Lander so many times on the 4th of July that they took their parts in all seriousness, but some of the Bannocks would stop and laugh and so spoil the film. There were two hundred four-horse wagons of regiments, men, women & children[. . .] They had to build a road & bridges and hire all the motor trucks to haul supplies, had a herd of cattle for fresh beef and hay to be provided for them[. . .] Think of the expenses, and for only part of the picture. The rest would be made in California. The book of "The Covered Wagon" was published in the *Saturday Evening Post* [. . .]

Ethel recorded another example that the Old West was changing in an undated note left with a gift from one of their visitors:

Mrs. White Antelope, wife of an Arapahoe sub-chief, stayed at the ranch for a few weeks. She spoke almost no English, but she and her son visited almost every day. When Mrs. White Antelope left, she gave me a belt I had admired made of reddish, black, tan, and olive green wooden tubular beads joined by ivory-like[2] tiles. I asked if she had made it. Mrs. White Antelope smiled, shook her head, and said "Me buy in London." Apparently she and her husband had been part of an Indian troop that Ed Farlow had taken to London in the 1910–1920s. The belt may have come from India.

David described how the boys themselves learned about the wider world even without leaving the ranch:

With the Oneys' departure, our formal schooling stopped until the following spring when the school board hired a new teacher, but Mother continued her lessons as before. Whenever a letter from a faraway place arrived, we learned more about geography and contemporary history. We placed the globe, atlas, and massive dictionary on the dining table, and brought out our stamp collections. Letters from friends in Belgium, New Zealand, and China were read aloud and discussed, their words transforming the dots on the world map into living places.

Spring brought David's 10th birthday and another horse roundup. Ethel noted the attending excitement, and wrote a sketch for the collection of characters she planned to call "Murderers I Have Known:" The completed collection has not been found.

The P Lazy 3 was Jack Peterson's brand. He always came on horseback, being the horse foreman for the Delfelder outfit. I used to climb to the roof of the granary and watch the range horses being driven into the round corral to be snubbed and branded. Twenty, thirty, or forty at a time would be collected in the outer corral, whinnying and crowding away from the cow-boys, scattering, pushing, darting—"the canny ways," John quoted his grand-father, while the riders tried to quiet the frantic animals. In exchange for the use of our corrals, the round-up crew helped brand our horses and cattle.

While running a bunch of range horses, Peterson, small, wiry, with straight white hair and sharp features, a moustache above a close thick mouth, had been kicked by a stallion, his leg broken. He had been cooking for the horse roundup. Jack was hard, lean, with a pistol and a bottle close at hand, and a joke on his lips. "You aren't much of a cook," he told me once. "I can cook more in a morning than the camp can eat in a week—but you cook and there's nothing left."

Buck Camp used to be a hang-out for those who were riding the bread line. A trapper, staying there in winter, was sitting by the window reading a paper he'd found. Jack rode by and thinking, he said, to scare him, shot the man through the window and killed him. Jack was taken to the jail in Lander, where he was kept for some time. It took Delfelder's influence to free him and bring him back to the ranch. He told me of it afterwards. "I did it for a joke, but for a while it looked as if it might be serious."

The cowboys on this roundup roguishly locked him in a sheep wagon and went riding. He began cursing, shooting from inside at the lock. The bom-bardment brought my curious boys to the scene.

It was not just the ignominy of being locked in. He was so angry that he was nearly speechless. Jack finally called to my boys to come let him out. But since he was shooting wildly at the door lock of his wagon, they took refuge in the blacksmith shop where they could still get glimpses of his white hair blowing about his face, his stiff short moustache going up and down with the fury of his cursing, while half of the cartridges of his heavy old .45 revolver failed to fire. Finally in a lull they approached timidly. "Want to get out, Jack?" they asked unnecessarily; one climbed the tongue of the wagon and turned the key still in the lock of the door.

The following year Ethel began a poem to commemorate Jack's passing:

> Is Peterson back with the round-up this spring
>> Back to the range's open sky
> Back, on the way from the billiards in Lander,
>> Laid in the potter's field, last fourth of July . . .

Ethel wrote of another event of that summer in "Porch Chair":

Reading was and is a family vice. Piles of newspapers, magazines and catalogues, coming in full mail sacks, accumulated on tables and bookcases. The household magazines I read all too seriously—for building family unity, one said, all members should join in home improvement projects. We did—and not only our family, but nearly every man who came along had had a share in putting up a shelf, nailing a quarter-round at the ceiling, or doing other odd jobs. To be ready for a volunteer, I continued to keep a list on my kitchen reminder.

There had come a lull in the home improvement activities. In a catalogue the picture of a handsome porch chair, generously sized, from wide arms to high, fan shaped back, "so easy to assemble, a child can do it, shipped complete in a flat box," showed just what we needed to supplement our porch swing, and the two onion crates that made comfortable low stools.

John was considered the best of story tellers, but he had been accused of not being able to drive a nail straight or saw a board. Uneasily I faced the prospect of his undertaking, practically alone, the construction of a new chair.

The chair arrived. Included in a mail sack which had been retrieved from the corner of the fence, the kit contained a large box of boards, which I put aside to await a propitious day. After a hailstorm, at last there was a weekend of the usual summer drizzles. We were alone on the ranch.

"Are you doing anything today?" I asked my husband cautiously, and somewhat guiltily, early in the morning. "No," he boomed, loudly, suspiciously, warily.

"Let's open the box and look at the pieces for a porch chair." This committed him to nothing. Allan and David tore open the box and packings.

"The pieces aren't all here," John objected. We spread them out over the kitchen floor. "Besides that, this one's broken—there aren't any directions." But found in the bottom of the box was the paper with a diagram and instructions.

"No nails or screws with it." A large manila envelope of these discovered, he grumbled, "Not enough anyway."

"Let's see where this goes," said David, experimenting eagerly.

"It won't work," John objected.

"Is this right, Daddy?"

"No, it goes that way. O yes, I see it, and there's another one like it."

John ceased to struggle and gave orders. The boys scattered to bring hammers, screw drivers, more nails, glue and a furniture clamp with, "Where's that piece?" and "Hold this tight." The long project started.

While I prepared dinner, skirting about the work and the three workers on the littered kitchen floor, I produced bits of gossip and news saved to lighten the unhappy situation I anticipated. "It was Charlie Cunningham who hi-jacked the truckload of whiskey while the driver was having coffee in the store at Moneta. He drove it up the Lysite road several miles and into a gulch, where it couldn't be seen."

"Idiot! He might have known it could be tracked."

"They say he drank some, took more bottles and left the truck."

"Worse yet. Of course the sheriff got him."

"Yes. Do you think he'll be sent to Rawlins?"

"That's where he belongs. There'll be few regrets. Where did you hear all this?"

"Ramsey came by yesterday while you were gone. He was camped by the Big Draw when the news came. He told Mack to put the wagon on a hill, but the campmover set it in a low spot. He was out with the sheep when the hail came. He said he tore up a big sagebrush and held it over his head, the stones were so big. When he got back to camp there was water all around the wagon. Mad! Mad! He said they should give him a boat next time. Did him good to let off steam."

"Hand me another nail. This strip cracked." The boys were in their element. John was holding up well, but I was feeling the strain. Dinner was ready, and I produced the dried cherry pie, baked the day before, for the emergency.

The chair was taking shape, but was far from finished. The slow rain had stopped.

"Bud Daly was with Ramsey. He wanted to know when we're getting another teacher. Do you know his real name? He doesn't usually tell. It's Rosebud—and he looks like a piece of old saddle leather. No, it was not that reason—He was born on the Rosebud Indian Reservation. In South Dakota. Who was Old Gilbert?"

"Oh, he herded for me years ago. Good herder, but a spiteful man. He hated coyotes. Whenever he shot or poisoned one, he kept it by the wagon and cussed it every day. Bye and bye he had quite a bunch of coyotes—hauled them around in the supply wagon, dumped them out when he camped, and every morning he gave 'em a cussing: 'Here's a fine day ye won't be getting none of my sheep. How do you like it to be dead, ye devils? That's what ye are to my sheep, they're as dead as ye are.' When he moved camp he hauled the dead coyotes with him till they thawed out in spring. By March he had seven he was hauling.

"Bye and bye it became impractical to haul around all the coyote carcasses, desiccated by Wyoming's dry air, so near Coyote Springs, he left a cord of his carcasses—5 feet high, 3 feet wide and 10 feet long."

John began one of his favorite chants as sign of satisfaction:

> They made her a grave too cold and damp
> Her heart so warm,
> So all night long by the porch lamp she came . . .[4]

Late in the afternoon the chair stood complete and surprisingly sturdy, ready for red paint and its long life on our porch. A loud knocking came at the kitchen door. Jim and Bill Gray, who had been hunting sage chickens, entered, and looked around.

"What have you been doing?" Jim asked of John. He straightened and answered, importantly.

"I've been making a porch chair."

They admired it properly, while John proudly stood by between Allan and David.

I was limp and ashamed. Never again did I try to coerce him for the sake of family unity.

David recounted another visit that summer in "Bill Grace and the Rattlesnake Dinner":

The summer of 1923, Allan at eleven and I at ten were already full-fledged cowboys, riding the range, bringing in cows and calves for branding, earmarking, castrating, and shuffling bulls and cows to ensure the following summer's calf crop.

One hot day in July, we were riding near the Sulfur Spring (a prime bit of meadowland which Allan homesteaded many years later, but lost while he was in the service during WWII), along some brown sandstone ledges marking the southwestern margin of Castle Gardens. A gigantic rattlesnake crawled out from under a ledge, coiled, rattled furiously, and struck at Allan's horse.

In those days, we killed every rattler we found. Our dog Dumpling had nearly died while protecting us when we were smaller, and while riding the range, we occasionally saw a cow staggering around with a grotesquely swollen head after having been bitten on the nose. This particular snake was so big that, after killing it with rocks and cutting off its head, we coiled the body in our lunch sack to show at the ranch. From previous experience, we knew that the word of small boys could be questioned.

At the ranch we hung the rattler up by the neck and stripped the skin down like the casing on a sausage, careful not to tear the skin on the belly. Mother admired the cream-colored, chevron-striped muscles—more than two pounds of clean, unblemished flesh.

The deer, antelope, and elk populations in our area had been nearly eliminated by severe winters and sport hunters from town. Domestic sheep had been trailed to the mountains for the summer to escape the heat of the plains. There were no fish in Muskrat Creek, and fresh trout were a day's ride from the ranch. Young sage chickens were too small to shoot, and egg-laying chickens too valuable to eat during the summer. So, the only meat we had during the warm months was beef butchered the previous winter, and "bottled" in quart Mason jars. This fresh, tender rattlesnake meat would be a treat.

Busying ourselves with the preservation of the snake skin, we carefully spread and tacked it to a plank so that it would dry properly and not be flyblown. The largest rattler we had ever seen, it measured five feet nine inches without the head. (Later that summer, David Andrews, nephew of naturalist/explorer and author Roy Chapman Andrews, a graduate student at the University of Missouri, who was collecting fossils in the region, offered us a dollar for the snakeskin. We accepted.)

Late that afternoon, Bill Grace arrived on horseback. He had homesteaded about six miles south of our ranch and was currently trying to promote an oil well on his property. Like most of the cowboys we knew, he was a tall, lean, taciturn bachelor. Dark-complected, with thick black hair tinged with gray, he was handsome in a rugged way, but had deep, grim lines around his mouth, and a brooding, violent glint in his eyes, especially when he was complaining about people or things not to his liking. Rarely did he show compassion or humor.

Ethel had written about two of Bill's previous visits to include in her sketches of "Murderers I Have Known":

A group of convicts came late one afternoon to the kitchen. They were trustees who had been sent under guard from the state penitentiary in Rawlins, about 100 miles away, to repair roads. But they had stopped work to hunt sage chickens. Several were serving life sentences for murder, including Bill Grace. No one was at the ranch except myself and my two small children. The trustees had guns. Our saddle horses were in the corral. It would have been simple to try to escape, but all they wanted was water. While they pumped and filled their water bags we exchanged the usual small talk of the range.

Later Bill Grace was pardoned. At the dragging close of our hardest winter, known as "the Equalizer," he came to the ranch again. John and David were both sick. To make soup for them, I asked Bill to kill a rooster. "Me, kill a *chicken*!" he objected, this man convicted of murder, "I couldn't kill a *chicken*!"

David resumed:

Despite Dad's assurances that his victim had needed killing, Allan and I were wary of Bill, although he did not seem to be as inherently vicious as some of the other known killers who had been at the ranch. He was courteous and respectful to Mother (as the cowboys invariably were), but ignored Allan and me, which was all right with us.

Mother invited Bill to supper and, while he was washing up, both she and Dad cautioned us not to refer to the meat dish as rattlesnake. If identification were necessary, we should call it "chicken." Possibly Bill, like many other cowboys, had phobias about rattlesnakes in any form.

Supper was the more-or-less formal meal of each day. Mother always spread a clean tablecloth over the battered oak dining table. Places were set with sterling silver—a wedding gift of long ago—unless the roundup crew or strangers riding the grub line were joining us. (These men cut their meat with such vigor that they bent the shafts of the soft metal forks to right angles, or broke the fork tines.) We all had cloth napkins in silver napkin rings (changed once a week, more often if necessary). The kerosene lamp on the wall cast a mellow glow in the dimly lit dining room. In the center of the table stood a heavy, shiny black French .75mm artillery shell, whose explosives chamber now held kerosene. The lampshade depicted villages in France ruined by the war. A copper band above the base bore the inscription: "They shall beat their swords into plowshares, and never wage war any more." (Dad grumbled that it had to be filled more often than the other lamps.)

When there was company for supper, Allan and I sat on the same side of the dining table, watching each other, ever mindful of the behavioral rules that Mother had had us make for ourselves. We were advised, however, that it would be discourteous to impose these rules on our guests who might have different standards of etiquette.

Mother had filled a large baking dish with the rattlesnake meat, minced in small flaky pieces, added fresh cream mixed with spices and a little flour, and dusted the top with paprika. It did indeed resemble the white meat of chicken. Served on thick slices of homemade toast, this steaming dish was a joy to behold. There may have been other dishes, too, but I don't remember them. As Allan and I concentrated on the one we had helped provide, we found it more and more difficult not to boast. In fact, gradually we forgot our parents' injunctions and began skirting around the subject of rattlesnakes.

We asked Bill if he had ever seen a den of them on his homestead. How big was the largest one he had ever seen? We told him about the large one we had killed in Castle Gardens, but didn't say when. Our parents shot warning glances at us. We told how once we had come upon a rattler in the process of hypnotizing a gopher. Careful not to get too close, we watched through field glasses as, almost imperceptibly, the snake's head had moved from side to side, back and forth, until the gopher, transfixed, was unable to move. Suddenly the snake struck. Fanged jaws clamped around the little animal, and gradually the gopher disappeared, whole, down the rattler's throat. Immediately we killed the snake and released the gopher, stunned, but still alive. On another occasion we killed a rattler with a swollen belly and cut it open to see what it had swallowed. The bulge turned out to be four tissue sacks, each containing two baby rattlers about eight inches long, just ready to be born. Wondering if the babies were already poisonous before they were born, and if they were immune to their siblings' poison, Allan cut open one sack, noting that the babies could already coil and strike. He positioned one so that it would strike its twin, and the twin died almost immediately.

Warming to our subject, our parents' caution forgotten, we commented that we had heard fresh rattlesnake meat, if cooked and seasoned well, was considered by some people to be very good eating.

Our words died in our throats. Mother and Dad were looking sternly at us. Too late! His dark eyes ablaze, Bill Grace slammed his fist down on the table so hard the dinner plates bounced and the French .75mm lamp wobbled. His steely voice rose almost to a shout: "By God! If anybody ever gave me rattlesnake meat, I'd kill 'em!"

The silence which followed probably lasted only a few seconds, but was, to me, an eternity. We two boys sat, catatonic. With her quick and lovely smile, Mother passed the serving dish to our guest. "More chicken, Bill?"

"Don't mind if I do," he replied, matching her smile with a rare one of his own, as he refilled his plate.

David later wrote of his continuing efforts in taxidermy:

One day in August, my father shot some sage chickens. As he approached one of them, a Swainson's hawk swooped down, alighting on the sage chicken to claim it. When Dad challenged the hawk, it attacked him with beak and claws. Dad kicked it in the head and killed it, then brought it home for me to mount. It was a beautiful specimen, feathers, skin and bones intact. In the hot weather, I had to work rapidly to mount this bird, or it would have decayed and the feathers would have fallen out. I mounted it in a pouncing position with wings outstretched, beak open, and talons extended. Despite my best efforts, the results were a mockery of this beautiful bird, but I knew that with practice I could do better.

I now wanted to work on an eagle or a blue heron. Although they were plentiful and it was not illegal to kill them then, Dad would not let me shoot either one. Later that summer, a driller from a nearby oil rig brought me a magnificent golden eagle. He had shot it when it flew over him, the bullet going upward through the bird's head. Either he was a terrific marksman or he had made a very lucky shot. I mounted this nearly perfect specimen in a soaring position with wings outstretched, tail feathers fanned, legs tucked in, and its talons in a striking position. Steel cable held the wings, which extended more than six feet from tip to tip. But with the eagle my taxidermy career came to an end.

Ethel added:

David hung it with the wings extended over the head of his bed, their tips reaching almost from wall to wall. There it hung for years, until one night the cord gave way. The eagle fell upon a cowboy sleeping in the bed. It attacked him, he thought, in his dream. After the fight, little was left but the wings and the tail of the eagle.

In 1987, David wrote of the end of that summer in "The Runaways":

There had been occasions in previous years when, individually or together, Allan and I had been sufficiently angry at our parents to think about running away. At least once, I had hidden out alone for most of a day, feeling sorry for myself until hunger, cold, and other practical considerations reshaped my philosophy. We had never been abused. Ours was a loving home, but one where parental rules had to be obeyed and without question.

I don't remember the fancied insult which prompted our decision to leave, but it had something to do with the drudgery of everyday chores. In the thousand uninhabited square miles surrounding our ranch, there were no other children with whom we could share our grievances, and our nearest neighbors, adults and childless, 15 miles away, would not be sympathetic to our complaints. Worse, with no more attractive places to run away to, we might be trading one set of troubles for another.

Nevertheless, on this particular day, our accumulated resentment had reached such a point that we felt our only option was to run away—not far at first until we saw how well we could survive. We planned our caper with what we considered to be care and foresight. Only in hindsight did we realize how naïve and inexperienced we really were.

Two sougans[3] and a thin, partially waterproof henskin, a small frying pan, a small aluminum kettle, two canteens of fresh water, a hunting knife, two spoons, wooden matches, and several pages from the Montgomery Ward catalog for toilet paper and fire starters, comprised our equipment. For food, we took a three-inch slab of bacon, salt, potatoes, and dried apples. Allan brought a single shot .22 calibre rifle and 50 shells. We would live off the land and hide out at least until the cold weather of late fall set in.

Backpacks and pack boards were unknown, but we had seen Indian pack frames on the Wind River Reservation, so we rigged copies for ourselves. If our parents were watching our clandestine preparations with secret amusement, we never knew.

It took us a day, between chores, to assemble our gear, which we cached in the greasewood behind the barn. Dumpling devoured the bacon almost immediately, and was sick all over the yard. So we had to steal another piece. Expensive, bacon was monitored carefully, and this shortage might be discovered. Our tension the night before our departure made sleep difficult.

By morning neither of us was angry any more, but pride kept us from admitting that we wanted to change our minds. After a hearty breakfast, we shut Dumpling in the hay house to be sure he stayed behind, slipped away past the barn, put on our packs, and began our adventure.

We planned to go east about two miles to "the pinnacles" in Castle Gardens, a maze of white sandstone spires and turrets capped by a layer of orange-brown sandstone. Among the pinnacles was a labyrinth of passages, some of which ended in vertical unscalable walls, others in cliffs. Here we could hide indefinitely from searchers (if there were any) just as the Indians had. Their workshops, in sunny places sheltered from the wind, were littered with red-stained campfire rocks and stone flakes of artifacts. Barricades of rocks and rotted logs lay across a few passages as barriers of defense.

We began our journey on a bright sunny day, with many qualms, often looking back toward home. Silently we wound through greasewood higher than our heads, emerging into the wild hay meadow east of the house. In the center were the buffalo wallows, 100 yards or more in diameter, a constant source of discovery. In summer they teemed with red-winged and yellow-headed blackbirds, snails, and frogs. In the dry season we could excavate old buffalo skulls mired in the accumulated vegetal debris. The wallows were also treacherous. A calf or even a small boy could sink quickly out of sight in the ponded bogs, whose watery approach path to the point of disappearance would return in minutes to a tranquil puddle, showing no trace of a tragedy. We had once watched in horror as a high-spirited calf galloped into one of these pools, thrashed wildly for a moment, and disappeared beneath the froth of bubbles expelled from his drowning lungs. Dark green swamp rushes called Phragmites rimmed the margins of the bogs, along with a dense growth of light green jointed reeds, which we cut for pipe stems, straws, blowpipes, and whistles.

Hungry by the time we reached the largest wallow, we ate the pancakes we had squirreled away at breakfast. We tried to pad the sores that the pack frame ropes were wearing into our shoulders, and explored the bird rookeries to relieve our mental distress. Always we kept a watchful eye out for wild range cattle, especially cows with calves. (These animals were fast, thin, and aggressive, not like the heavy, docile breeds we see today, and would lower their horns and charge any threat, two-legged or four, to their calves.) Allan and I knew that, encumbered by our packs, we could neither run nor dodge very well, and there were no nearby trees, rocks, or cutbanks to afford protection.

Sure enough, some cows spotted us and came galloping and snorting after us. Against our better judgement, we plunged into the thickest of the reeds in the bog, hoping that the footing was strong enough to support us. Our enthusiasm for continuing our adventure was rapidly diminishing. When the cows finally wandered away to graze with their calves, we crept quietly around them, trudging another mile out of the meadow through stabilized sand dunes, to enter the pinnacles. The sun was now low in the west, a chilly wind had begun to blow, and dark clouds were scudding across the sky.

In a sheltered spot, we made camp. Allan shot a rabbit. We skinned and gutted it, built a fire of sagebrush, cooked some bacon, and fried the rabbit in the grease. Pouring some of our precious water into a pocket of clay, we made enough mud to encase two potatoes, which we baked in the coals from the campfire. Castle Gardens had no water at all to replenish it.

The world now looked brighter and our thoughts turned to our parents. They would worry. There were other dangers besides bogs and range cattle, rattlesnakes being among the most obvious. A large one had recently been killed on the porch of our house. Jimmy Fraser had been sitting on a creek bank not long before when a rattlesnake bit him on the wrist. He galloped to our ranch, where Dad gave him his fastest horse and some hobbles. Dad told him to use the hobbles, heavy and clattering, as a whip, and the horse would know where to go—to the livery stable in Shoshoni. The man at the livery stable would know what to do, and so would Dr. Jewell. Knowing that Jimmy would lose consciousness before he reached help, Dad tied his feet under the horse's belly to keep him from falling. As predicted, Dad's lathered horse reached Shoshoni, Jimmy Fraser slumped unconscious on his back, where Dr. Jewell saved his life.

Besides snakes, we had trapped several enormous bobcats among the pinnacles, and cougars were known to be present.

Mother, in particular, would worry. Dad would counter that he had taught us to be careful. If we got into trouble, it would be our own fault. We hoped that they would be sorry they had been so mean to us, and that if we ever returned home, they would treat us with more respect.

It was a long night. With only one sougan over us and another beneath, the sandy ground was hard, lumpy and cold. We had not yet learned Dad's trick of heating the spot for our bedroll first with a campfire. The wind howled around the pinnacles, carrying a blizzard of sand which filled our eyes, ears, and mouths. We began to understand how the pinnacles had been sculpted. Sand swirled into our food and stuck on our unwashed dishes. Toward morning a cold rain began. Our efforts to start a cookfire were in vain; the wet sagebrush would not burn. We ate some dried apples, sand crunching between our teeth, and drank the last of our water for breakfast.

The rain continued, the wind blasting it in gusts against the sides of the pinnacles. What if the rain lasted several days, as it sometimes did? Our dried apples would be gone, and raw rabbit meat and cold, raw potatoes had no appeal. Our sodden jackets and henskin afforded little protection. Our teeth chattering, we thought of our warm beds at home, and our parents. They tried to be fair and were obviously fond of us. Perhaps Dad shouldn't have to do the chores alone when he had two able-bodied boys who could help. He always said that a horse who wouldn't pull its share of a load should be shot. Were we pulling our fair share? The rain continued. Perhaps our parents deserved one more chance to be appreciative.

We packed our gear and started home. The sodden blankets and henskin were much heavier than the day before, and we felt weak from the unaccustomed lack of food and sleep. Facing into the blasting wind and rain, we returned to the ranch, slipping and wallowing in the mud for the last mile, ever alert for wild cattle. Caching our packs behind the barn, we sneaked down the hill to the ranch house. By then it was late afternoon. Hearing voices in the kitchen, we crept quietly in the front door and tiptoed into the dining room.

Before we could decide what to do next, the door between the kitchen and dining room slowly opened. We just had time to dash into the front bedroom and dart under the bed. Dad and Mother entered the dining room, clearly discussing us. Mother was nearly in tears with worry; we might have sunk into the bog and never been found. As she imagined other disasters, more horrible than those we had considered, Dad, the realist, said: "They will come scuttling home like drowned rats before dark."

How could we reappear and still save even a little face? We decided to wait until Dad had gone to start the evening chores. Alone, Mother would be so glad to see us that Dad wouldn't dare make caustic comments or punish us. He had never laid a hand on us before, but we had not previously run away.

As soon as Dad had departed for the barn, we crawled out from under the bed, tiptoed out the front door, around the house, and walked into the kitchen, trying to look as nonchalant as our bedraggled appearances would permit. Mother put her arms around us and wept. We had never seen her cry before and the knowledge that our thoughtless behavior had hurt her so deeply made us cry, too. It was the last time I saw Allan cry. He was always so manly and composed that crying seemed out of character and that made me cry even harder.

At this moment Dad came in. He looked at us a long moment, then said quietly: "Laddies, let's finish the rest of the chores before it gets too dark." We went out silently, meekly, each to his usual tasks. Not a word was spoken then or later of the entire affair.

That fall, the school board awarded us our first and only 9-month teacher: Miss Robinson, a tall, thin, homely woman from Arkansas, with minimal education and no experience. Her outspoken disdain for the backward people in Wyoming did not endear her to the natives. She and my father frequently argued, occasionally vehemently, mostly about grammar and methods of teaching. On one occasion, she shouted: "Mr. Love, I am NEVER mistaken!" After that, he gave her the silent treatment; the rest of us delightedly added this to the list of Family Sayings.

Ethel wrote her own view of Miss Robinson in "The 3 Rs":

Aside from the best recommendations yet sent to the board for her first school, a neat appearance and lovely red hair were the assets of the girl from the Ozarks, who was our next teacher. Her custom was to sit and read from a book by the fire in the living room, then ask the boys questions on what she'd read. Her grammar appalled us. Doubtful, I asked Allan about how much he was learning. He responded with characteristic candor, "No more than I can help." A friendly trapper stopping by regularly was also from the south. They greeted each other formally, with a "Good eve'nin'!"

On Hallowe'en we were to have a party among ourselves with special games for the occasion. It was very cold, with some snow. Two men drove in and asked to spend the night. Toby's sheep wagon and our remaining one were on the hill by the woodpile.

They were offered our wagon, where they would be warmer than in the unheated long building, and invited in to dinner. Dinner progressed merrily with the five men, two boys, Miss Robinson and myself. When we had nearly finished I went to the pantry to bring the pie. Through the window overlooking the hill I saw and heard flames.

"The wagon's on fire," I called, forgetting the pie.

"Which wagon?" shouted Toby, leaping toward the kitchen door. We all hurried outside in the snow.

Already it was too late to save anything. Flames were over the top of our wagon. Boxes of cartridges in the drawers were exploding, like a bombardment. Fortunately there was no wind. We gloomily watched, until the quick flames died down.

The men had piled wood too close to the stove, perhaps, after making a hot fire to warm themselves.

We came back to the house, without appetite for the pie. David asked, "Are we going to have the party?"

"Of course," I told him, and we did, with apples.

When the men left the next day, I found an old coat of John's for the one to wear whose coat had been burned in the wagon.

"Better luck next time," was his farewell.

In later years, David reflected on the challenges his parents faced and the deci-sions they had to make:

From the unending hard work, financial loss, and whims of the weather, Dad was learning that ranching on his small scale held no future for our fam-ily. Yet he had no choice but to continue. Allan and I, however, gradually realized that although we were growing up on a ranch, we were not being raised to be ranchers. Our parents had other plans for us. Letters from family and friends reflected the queries Mother had been making about schools and the cost of living in town.

Ethel's Wellesley friend Win Hawkridge wrote of a Christmas surprise:

I have been meaning to ask you how Allan's school is progressing. You know, as his godmother, I am responsible for his college career, so when you are ready to think about that date, let me know[. . .]

I have hit on something that you would all like—a new kind of radio set[. . .] I remembered that both Allan and Mr. Love had a mechanical turn. It has given me so much fun already to think of Allan and Davy listening to San Francisco and Denver. With your high clear atmosphere you ought to have good luck[. . .] It will be sent to you by express, and may with luck, come by Christmas, and surely by New Year's[. . .] A Happy Christmas to you Loves, big and little, especially Little Bear. Win

The radio set arrived. Powered by a single-cell battery, it was housed in a hand-some wooden case, and had an ear phone to allow one person at a time to listen. Ethel's notes recorded:

For the first time we had the company of voices—cultured voices, chil-dren's, eastern, somber, affected, safe voices, hard, soft, any number of voices.

David later told his children about the transformation this small radio brought to ranch life:

It brought into our narrow world the notion of time, and the sounds of what we learned later were the Roaring Twenties. I remember the voice of Mme Schumann-Heinck, reputed to be the greatest singer of her day, singing in German. She sang even into the 1930s, when she labored through then traditional carols—vestiges of glory in her aging voice.

Notes

1. From the Latin *quod erat demonstrandum*, meaning "which has yet to be proven."
2. Bakelite, an early plastic.
3. Heavy wool blankets.
4. John's version of Thomas Moore's Ballad: "The Lake of the Dismal Swamp." In Thomas Moore's *Complete Poetical Works*, Boston: Thomas Y. Crowell & Co., 1895, p. 129.

CHAPTER THIRTEEN

~

1924

"Problems of Education"

*As the children grew, the Loves became increasingly concerned about the boys'
education. The school board intermittantly sent teachers to the ranch, but the boys
continued to learn many of life's lessons from their environment. Ethel summarized
the previous year in her annual letter to Miss Hill:*

27 Dec., '23

Dear Miss Hill,

Many thanks for the dainty handkerchief in the exquisite Xmas folder and
also for the gift of the *Ladies' Home Journal*. The card of presentation came
direct, and such a beautiful thing it is: Fra Angelico's Virgin and child in the
center, and angels on the two half panels.

This year we have a schoolteacher with us for nine months. She also en-
joys the magazine, and when we have read it sends it to her sister. Last year
I sent it to different sheep camps.

The boys had a lovely Christmas this year, as David said happily, "everything useful." The boys had clothes as usual, but thanks to the state of their
wardrobe more than usual!

We had a tree cut four or five miles from here in a spot similar to the
Garden of the Gods in Colorado. Our beauty spot is called "Castle Gardens,"
although neither castle nor garden exists therein. Allan spent one morning
fastening the tree into its box. David helped trim it. We had home-made
wreaths of cedar for the windows, and opened our presents Xmas eve before
the fire grate.

Many old friends and some new ones remembered us. That is the joy of Xmas largely, isn't it? The boys were sent a set of Mah Jong which has so fascinated us that we have played every evening since. No bedtime has been prescribed this week, for they go to bed at eight and eight-thirty all year. One night we all played until eleven, the next night until ten, then nine-thirty, so habit is gradually settling the matter. I remember at their age how I longed to stay up late once, as if the later hours of the night would somehow be more wonderful than pre-bedtime hours.

All best wishes to you at this time, and may 1924 be very good to you. Sincerely yours,

Ethel P. Love

Faith wrote Jan. 8, 1924, expressing her concern not only for the boys' education but also for Ethel's welfare on the ranch. Although Ethel's family and friends may have envisioned a different life for her, Ethel was committed to her choice, and never wrote about wanting to leave the ranch or her marriage.

1560 Downing, Denver, Colo., 2 A.M.

Dear Ethel,

I came home & found your and the dear boys' letters awaiting me & you cannot know how glad I was, for I haven't had a letter for over a month from you[. . .]

You ask my advice about school. I could not see you leave the ranch soon enough! [. . .] only if I loved a man with my whole soul & I wonder if even that could hold me on a place such as you are[. . .] What would you think of a man who would take me off to a desert where I saw few people, who promised I should never work & who made me his slave body & soul. Ethel [. . .] can't you see how I feel because I love you so, can't you see how it cuts to the very quick? [. . .] I have wondered how you ever stood it[. . .] You have never complained. It has changed you more than you know.

But it is John's duty to realize his responsibility, and so long as you choose to stay with him, he should be made to feel that responsibility. If he were sick or unable to work, it would be different[. . .] I appreciate John's good points & he has many[. . .] But it seems to me a true love would be an unselfish love & that he would want you to have some of the life, the pleasures and comforts other women enjoy[. . .]

Will you not come right out & tell me? What does John do? How does he earn a livelihood for his family? I can only judge from what I have seen when I have [visited you] & I would not like to misjudge him [. . .]

It's the middle of the night & my soul waxes bitter with indignation as it does at times. So if I have said what I shouldn't, forgive me & set me right.

Living is terrifically high in Denver[. . .] A year ago I heard it was on the same par with New York, Washington, etc.

Heaps of love dear. It is 4 A.M. and I must try again to get to sleep. Faith

David remembered that a handsome leather suitcase arrived in the mail from one of his mother's former suitors, a token invitation to leave the hardships of her life on the ranch. His father was not happy. The suitcase was never used.

The isolation of the ranch sometimes led to mysterious visitors. Ethel described one such visit in her notes:

The dishes were done and put away, the kitchen floor mopped, that cold and snowy night, and an undisturbed night's rest followed. In the morning when John built the kitchen fire, he saw large overshoe tracks on the floor. The coffee pot was on the stove, there were crumbs beside the breadbox. This would not have been surprising, but there was no man staying on the ranch. We discussed the situation in the light of a report that an insane man had escaped from the state asylum at Evanston, and ranchers were asked to watch for him. The boys found the man's tracks and followed them for a mile to the main road where they disappeared. For a long while this was one of the mysteries of Muskrat, but eventually we heard what had happened. The night before the tracks were found, an Irishman with a 4-horse team had spent the night with us. He was lost in the storm and wanted to know the way to the Fish cabin—this was his story. He started out in the morning, drove all day, perhaps in a circle, and by night recognized the fence corner again. Ashamed to admit that he had been lost a second time, he tied his horses and walked to the house. How long he stayed in the kitchen we did not know—probably until daylight. Our dogs had recognized him and did not bark.

David's untitled notes recorded a family outing that spring:

Robins, meadowlarks and redwing blackbirds had begun to appear. One morning before dawn, bundled in our warmest clothes, we crept silently out to the meadow, where we sank without a sound to the ground. As we waited, hardly daring to draw breath, in the pre-dawn light, sage chickens appeared from the underbrush, like dancers on a stage. A rhythmical drumming began, as the gray speckled birds, tails in spiked fans, began their courtship dance. The males wore chest ruffs of white feathers, as fine as ermine, through which their egg-shaped air sacs inflated and disappeared in time to the drum of their feet. The females feigned disinterest, but remained. As the rising sun cast long blue shadows across the new day, suddenly the birds were gone, vanished into the greasewood and sage. We returned to the warmth of the house and breakfast.

In "The 3 Rs," Ethel described Miss Robinson's departure:

The boys' school year dragged to its close. A roundup was at the house, and somehow a car was there. Miss Robinson was to be taken away in style, although mud was deep on the road.

When she and her bags were loaded and the driver ready, the car could not make the hill between the buildings. Cowboys rushed to the rescue. It wasn't until John accused them of pulling the car back, instead of pushing it up the hill, that teacher and admirer got away.

Ethel wrote of a more serious event that spring in "Marlinspike":

The Basques are splendid shepherds and sailors, a proud people. Every man is a nobleman. Juanech Echevarrias, straight and tall, had too long been called "lord of the house." An only child and no stranger to trouble, he was a newcomer from the Pyrenees to the lambing camp at Box Springs on Muskrat Creek.[1] He had not yet become adapted to the ways in Wyoming which differed from those of his country.

In the sheep wagon, Bader, the 3Bar foreman, was trying to explain to Juanech the method of persuading a ewe whose lamb was born dead to accept, instead, a stunted twin, by jacketing it with the pelt taken from the dead lamb. Both men knew that the mother recognized her lamb by its smell.

Through the open door, the sound of voices and the fragrance of mutton stew and biscuits baking reached a third shepherd, Pedro, as he swung easily from his horse, dropping the reins to the ground. Seven hours after his sunrise breakfast, he was content with the world and the weather, pleasantly tired and hungry, anticipating dinner. He broke happily into a snatch of "La Cucaracha." He had been handling newborn lambs to make certain of their taking that first life-saving taste of milk which assured the bond between mother and offspring.

Juan looked at him. "Dirty," he said. "*I* eat first."

Pedro's song stilled. He turned to the tin wash bowl on the keg by the wagon.

"You will eat with all the men," Bader told Juan abruptly. "Do what the others do, or leave this job, pronto."

The Basque jumped upon him without warning. He threw Bader down in the narrow space by the stove. He seized a chunk of firewood, and began beating him over the head. Bader reached for the kerosene bottle on the floor, and over his shoulder hit the Basque a blow on the head that knocked him senseless. Then Bader lifted the man and dumped him out of the wagon. Pedro slid inside and sat down to eat without a word, then hurriedly caught his horse, and rode back to "mother up" more lambs.

Bill and Slim took their places then at the small sheep wagon table. When the Basque regained consciousness, he stood, swaying and holding one hand to his head. "OK," he said, "You the boss. I stay. We friends?" They shook hands. Juan ate and went to work along with Bill and Slim. Bader thought the matter settled.

Except for this troublesome Basque, he had a fair crew. Winter hadn't been too bad; he had kept his count of black sheep.[2] Weather was fine, so far, grass greening fast, lambs coming along well, ewes had plenty of milk. Already he could reckon his percentage of lambs, roughly; more twins than usual made it run high. He would have a good report for the boss next week.

Juan, moving the drop herd[3] slowly, saw a recently deserted oil rig about a mile and a half from the spring. There he found a sailor's marlinspike, a pointed, T-shaped, steel implement used at a drilling rig to splice the thick rope which wound around the bull wheel. Concealing the marlinspike under his blue denim jumper, he waited his chance.

A few days later, after the men had eaten their noon dinner and returned to the herd, Juan lingered around camp until he saw Bader, alone, head down, cleaning out the barrel in the spring. As Bader lifted his head, the Basque gave him a terrific blow behind the ear with the marlinspike, beat him about the body and legs, tied his hands and feet, and carried him to the creek, where he threw blankets upon him, expecting Bader, if not already dead, to drown.

The Basque then went to the sheep wagon about a hundred yards from the spring. He ate again, heartily, put meat and flapjacks into a flour sack, and rummaged in the drawers, filling his pockets with gun shells. Taking Bader's rifle and all the cartridges he could find, he caught the bay horse, which, always kept saddled and bridled, was grazing near the camp. He roped a second horse, tied his bedroll upon its back, and started away, riding one horse and leading the other.

He was topping a long hill, when my husband and twelve-year old Allan approached Box Springs. They had driven in the buggy ten miles up the creek from our ranch, looking for flatiron cattle.

The clamor of the sheep and lambs put an end to their desultory talk about Box Springs. It once had been a stopping place for the stage between Casper and Lander, the next station east of Old Muskrat. All traces of buildings and corrals were gone; only the name remained. The water in the Box was clear and cold but scanty. In summer, riders sometimes left a few cans of tomatoes in it to retrieve on a hot day. Enough water ran in the creek for spring lambing, although it was not good for drinking.

Before them, father and son saw the freshly broken brush, the clutter of the camp, scattered sheep and supply wagons, some holding bed rolls and saddles, nose bags and ropes, some piled with grain sacks, tightly covered by tarpaulins. On the ground strewn in disorder, were extra tepees, lanterns, and a great pile of empty tin cans.

The main bunch of sheep was unseen, but the incessant blatting of the ewes and the maa's of the lambs, the smell and the flies showed that they were near. Not a man was in sight, not even a dog or a horse. John drove directly to the nearest wagon. Standing by the wagon tongue was Bader, washing blood from his face, badly cut and puffy, in a washbowl of red water. His movements were like those of a very old man, slow and painful.

"What happened to you?" John asked. "Horse fall on you?"

"No . . . that damned Basco . . ." Even his voice faltered. "He sure worked me over . . . that there hammer . . . at the spring . . . when I come to . . . I was layin' in the water . . . . The crick was cold, it brung me about. I'd a drowned. . . . What he wanted, I guess. . . . He'd tied my hands and feet. . . . Good thing he tied my hands in front of me. . . . At that, had a hell of a time getting my knife out of my pants pocket. . . . Opened it up with my teeth and cut my legs loose. . . . I clumb over the crick bank to the wagon here . . . got the axe 'atween my knees and sawed the rope off'n my hands."

"Where's the Basque? Was that him on the hill?"

"The devil was riding off when I crawled out of the crick. I could a shot him, had him dead to rights, but he stole my gun—keep it by the wagon . . . for the coyotes."

"What started the whole thing?"

"Oh, we got into a argyment, three, four days ago, and a fight in the wagon. He give up. Didn't think no more about it till he jumped me today."

"You should get to a doctor, Bader. You look bad. Can you make it into the buggy?"

Bader could hardly lift his feet. He had stiffened too much to reach the buggy step. Allan found a box to help him. Then the boy picked up the marlinspike at the spring. He went to the creek to see the ropes that had tied Bader's feet, the soggy blankets, the blood in the sand where his head had lain. He noticed the tracks of the horses.

"Tell Bill what happened . . . the boy can find him yonder . . . tell him to take over . . . outfit short two men . . ."

"We'll drive you to town." At the road fork from Puddle Springs they met a truck returning from an oil camp there. The driver helped Bader into the truck, and drove him, not only the twenty-five miles into Moneta, but eighty-five miles farther to the hospital in Casper.

The alarm for the Basque spread so rapidly that the following morning a posse from Lander, composed of a number of broad shouldered, six-foot cowboys in chaps, Stetsons and boots, reached the ranch. They wore wide cartridge belts loosely on their hips, and more pistols per man than I ever saw. No doubt they had rifles, too, in the car.

The sheriff, in his sixties, was small and wiry, stooped and bow-legged. His steely blue eyes under bushy gray brows gave the impression that he would be the man to take any prisoner, although he wore no more formidable weapon in sight than a fountain pen in his pocket.

All stayed for noon dinner to question John and Allan and to examine the marlinspike. Who was working at the 3 Bar? What was the location of the camp at Box Springs? Which way was the Basque headed? Did he take food with him? What were the colors and the brands of the horses? Were they shod? What guns? Then the posse left to pick up the trail.

The man they were following showed even less intelligence in his attempt to escape than he had in his crime. He made his way toward the Sweetwater River, but at a crossroad he turned west, possibly thinking of the hundreds of his countrymen who lived, worked, and prospered in the sheep business about Boise, Idaho. Each year they held a colorful Basque "sheepherders' ball," a social event, invitations to which were highly valued. He should arrive in plenty of time for that, he may have mused, as he jogged along. However, the road he chose led to Lander, to the very door of the jail, town authorities before him, and the posse hot on his tracks. He was promptly arrested, tried and sentenced to serve several years in the penitentiary.

Bader was a long time in the hospital. In fact he never entirely recovered from the beating his legs had received, although he was eventually able to return to his work in sheep camps. A great lump remained behind his ear, the stitches showing clearly around it. "Just give me one shot at that man. His life isn't worth a plugged nickel. Or a knife would make him remember me. When he's out of the pen, I'll be ready," were the mildest of his threats. Word must have reached Juan, who never returned to our part of the state. At the ranch, a reminder of violence on the Rat, the marlinspike remained.

The challenge of providing schooling for the boys was on-going. David wrote about the last school board meeting the Loves attended in "Our Last School Meeting, June, 1924":

School District Number 20 encompassed roughly 1,000 sparsely populated square miles in central Wyoming, extending 45 miles north from the Beaver Divide to the Bighorn and Owl Creek Mountains, and west 20 miles from the east boundary of Fremont County nearly to the Wind River Reservation. In the southern half of this area were only three ranches with school-age children: the Loves with two, "Mule Man" Orr with three, and a disabled World War I veteran with two. In addition to cattle and sheep ranches, the district contained segments of the Chicago & Northwestern, and the Chicago,

Burlington, & Quincy Railroads. Taxes on these and the three small towns with stores, bars, filling stations, and post offices were significant. Moneta had a population of about 25, Lysite about 50, and Lost Cabin about 50, each with a school, with one teacher for grades 1–8. No high school was available.

Between 1919 and 1923 Allan and I had had three teachers. The rest of the time Mother taught us, but despite her good education and previous teaching experience, as a married woman, she could not be certified to teach us—or anyone else—the 7th and 8th grades. Without this certification, even if we passed the obligatory state exam, we would not be permitted to enter high school anywhere in Wyoming. Therefore, our parents' attendance at the school meeting at Lysite, 26 miles north of our ranch, was of paramount importance. Allan and I did not know then that Mother, who was nearly 42 years old, was four months pregnant, nor were we aware of the risks she was taking to make such a trip.

At last the day arrived. The buggy was packed with baggage and grain for the horses. Allan and I rode facing backward, our legs dangling off the wooden packing boxes in the back. To shade herself and Dad, Mother carried a tattered, black umbrella whose ornate silver handle was engraved "EPW"— a relic of her more affluent past.

Dad kept Slopey and Darky at a walk, three miles per hour, and it took five interminable hours to reach Moneta.

Facing directly into the sun, Allan and I fidgeted, hot, sweaty, and bored. As we grew grayer and grayer from the dust churned up by the wheels, we began to giggle over who looked the ugliest.

In Moneta we collected the mail, then splashed the dust off our faces, necks and hands at the horse trough beneath the railroad water tank. The public privy was dirty, as it always was, with a box of corn cobs and a catalog for major events. The inside and outside were painted red-brown, and tex-tured with fine sand, an exigency of the railroad to discourage railroaders, hobos, and small boys from carving their initials or unacceptable messages on the walls.

Now presentable, we went to see Jacob Epstein and his wife Rebecca at the railroad depot. Jacob had replaced Ralph Clark as stationmaster, and as such had become an important man in the region. As we ate the lunches we had brought, we visited with them around their dining table. The only Jews in the area, they had come to Wyoming from Germany after World War I because Rebecca could not face crowds of people. A survivor of a terrible pogrom, she had been gang-raped, beaten many times, and finally left for dead. I can still see her scarred and broken face, her twisted lips, and, when she laughed, her shattered teeth held together by a filigree of gold. Her eyes, haunted at quiet times, generally glowed with a zest for living. Her voice was hearty and cordial, her English broken but enthusiastic. Unable to have children of her own, she lavished affection on Allan and me. Having worked so passionately for peace, Mother felt a special bond with Rebecca, but she never wrote about this kind woman, whose heroic spirit never accepted defeat. Perhaps Rebecca's story was too sad to tell.

Tall and thin, Jacob was darkly handsome, with sensuous lips beneath a hooked nose, and expressionless eyes. Well-educated and competent, he was so reticent that we knew only that he, too, had been terribly abused during the war. I liked him especially. Together we had put pennies on the railroad track to be flattened to the size of quarters by passing trains.

After lunch we drove the eleven miles to Lysite. Friends who could also accommodate our horses had invited us to spend two nights with them. They too had horses, beautiful matched bays, to pull an elegant white-topped, yellow-wheeled phaeton buggy. For the first time, I was ashamed of our mismatched team and tattered buggy, and became aware of the stigma of being poor.

The remainder of this story has two versions: one written by Ethel in a short vignette, and the other as recalled 70 years later by David eleven years old at the time. Ethel wrote in "The 3 R's":

"I'll never go again. I'll never go again. I'll never go again! I want a bath." The four of us were at home again after the dusty 50-mile round trip to the annual district school meeting to request a teacher.

The schoolhouse where the meeting was held stood on the top of a west-facing hill, the building painted white, as were the two outhouses in back. In front was a hitching rack, where the pupils from outlying ranches tied their horses while attending school, this day used by those of people attending the meeting. The small schoolhouse was crowded with parents and other voters, sitting one or two in a seat. Overalled dry farmers were in the ascendant at that time.

"Farmers!" sniffed one man, "They don't have enough water out of season for a radish. Homestead inside a man's fence, live on sage chickens and antelope, vote themselves school money, prove up, lease or sell the land, leave the state—or fence a rainwater hole, when they ain't got a head of stock of their own. Dry farmers! They're dry all right. Well, the Oneys were OK and the Sharps."

Those with children who stayed on the range were given teachers, or school allowances to take the children to town.

"School meeting!" I wrote in my diary. "Such a mess, five people talking out loud at one time. The chairman among them, hustling along the aisles, doing verbal battle, first with one side and then another. We voted teachers for families with one or two children in each. Everyone fighting for something."

A woman from Austria was accusing another from Czechoslovakia: "You're no citizen! You can't vote. You haven't been neutralized yet! You're a-lyin'." A hushed expectancy fell over everyone, but nothing happened. I realized later that "alien" was what she meant to say.

David's version of the meeting was less restrained and more descriptive:

Molly, the Czech woman, was young, pretty, and vivacious. By her own unabashed admission, she had been a prostitute in her country during the war. Charlie, a lean, bald, lantern-jawed career sergeant, was stationed in her home town so they saw a lot of each other. She married him and soon produced a thin, red-haired daughter. When the war ended, Charlie retired on a full disability pension and they came to Wyoming, where a grateful government allowed him to homestead 320 treeless, waterless acres of open range about half-way between our ranch and Moneta. Charlie's pension, plus an allowance for his wife and each child, made the difference between survival and the inevitable bankruptcy which beset the other veterans in the area before they abandoned their homesteads and moved away.

Charlie, Molly, and their daughter stayed on. Several more children were born to the couple. Wags commented that it was a good thing Charlie had waited until he was old and feeble to marry and have children, or he would have bankrupted the nation. At the time of this school meeting, however, only the oldest daughter and the oldest son were of school age.

Having quickly taken the measure of the all-male school board, Molly knew she would get what she wanted, which is why she ignored the spat with the woman from Austria.

The chairman of the school board, "Old" Doug Fuller (as distinguished from his son, "Young" Doug) with a full thatch of white hair and piercing blue eyes, resembled Uncle Sam, minus the beard, on the war posters of that era. He wore real cowboy boots, not the low-heeled boots which characterized dudes and flatlanders.

The secretary was Ed Knapp, a short, fine-looking man. Well-informed and efficient, he ran the meeting with an iron hand, yet was obviously softened by Molly's charmingly tearful plea for a school. The board voted to give Molly's family a live-in teacher for the nine-month school year at their dry farm.

In contrast, the "Mule Man" (as Mr. Orr was called because he was the only dry farmer in the region with mules) demanded a school for his family 20 miles down Muskrat Creek from our ranch. Big, powerful, and raw-boned,

Orr was blustery and accustomed to having his own way. His luxuriant brown handle-bar moustache hung beneath a large overhanging nose inset with wide nostrils. He was moderately handsome, but unkempt. When he became excited or angry—which was often—his long, pointed tongue would dart out of his mouth, lap up over the left lobe of his moustache, and disappear into his left nostril. Then it would rapidly retreat, shift to the right side, to disappear up his right nostril, not unlike a cow clearing her nostrils before beginning to chew her cud. It became almost a game to agitate the "Mule Man" so that he would repeat the procedure, oblivious to the giggles from the audience. Eventually, reluctantly, the school board voted him a teacher.

Two bachelors began to argue in the back of the room. Jim, a chunky dry farmer in overalls, was in favor of educating his children, if he ever had any. Joe, a lean, hard-bitten cowboy, countered that giving money to dry farmers was a waste. They would go broke and leave, and the community would be out that much money. Shouting, with descriptions of the illegitimate offspring of canines and references to the amount of horse effluvium in each man's stomach, soon turned to shoving. "Old" Doug marched down the aisle and commanded the adversaries to settle their differences outside. Ladies were present.

Growing bored, Allan and I slipped quietly outside to find Jim and Joe squaring off near the hitching rack. Joe, taller, with longer arms, was the more agile, but although Jim was short, he was solid and more powerful. In a flurry of wild and vicious blows, blood began to flow and Jim wrestled Joe to the ground, where they really began to brawl, first one on top, then the other. This violent, noisy activity nearly under their feet spooked the horses tied to the hitching bar. Pulling back almost in unison, they tore the log bar off its posts and galloped off down the street, ignored by the crowd of partisans who had gathered to watch the fight. As blood mixed with mud from the horse urine beneath the hitching rack, the bare-knuckled scrappers became less recognizable. Straddling Jim's chest, Joe began to knock his bloodied head from side to side. Then, inspired, he stuffed a handful of the manure beside the hitching rack into Jim's mouth, shouting: "By God! I'll show you who's full of horse shit!"

Gasping for breath and choking on the manure, Jim did the only thing left to do: his teeth clamped hard on Joe's thumb. With a howl, Joe tried to pry Jim's jaws apart, fearing the severing of his thumb, but to no avail. His eyes scanned the cheering crowd in a wordless plea for help. No help was offered.

Finally, with tears of frustration and pain in his eyes, he rolled off Jim and muttered: "Let's call it quits." Jim released Joe's thumb. Staggering to their feet, they shuffled to the horse trough to clean up, shook hands and melted quietly away into their respective partisan crowds.

Inside the schoolhouse, the board voted a second nine-month teacher for the two boys at the Love ranch.

One day not long after the school meeting, David told the story of his father's decision to take the boys on a short camping trip, a trip which later influenced David's interest in geology and vegetation patterns:

"Come, laddies," said Dad. "Let's give your mother some time to herself. David has always wanted to see the Lankin Dome whose photograph in your geography book so intrigued him. It's just beyond the agate beds near the Sweetwater. You'll also see the Split Rock—a landmark to travelers along the Oregon Trail. We'll only be gone three days." In the mid-July lull between calving, branding, and haying, we could spare the time. The buggy was loaded, farewells to Mother were made, and off we went. As the horses shuffled in front of us, Dad talked about his early days in the country. Always interested in rocks and associated vegetation patterns, he had observed that cedar trees didn't grow anywhere north of the Sweetwater, or in Castle Gardens, only pines. Even where there was sufficient water, very few cottonwoods, willows, and chokecherries grew between Lankin Dome and our ranch because the geology just wasn't right.

Water and pasture were always the prerequisites for a good campsite. Sage Hen Spring—a 40-mile ride from our ranch—had both. To reach it we crossed the agate beds—open patches in the sagebrush where ideal geological conditions beneath had formed these gently-edged smooth stones. Sweetwater agates are characterized by what resembles dark gray or brown moss in a nearly clear or white-gray silica background. The Shoshone Indians believed that a warrior who carried a Sweetwater agate in his medicine pouch into battle would not be killed, though he might be wounded. To see their beauty before the stones were polished, Dad told us, we should put them in water, or spit on them. Allan and I scrambled to fill our pockets and small sacks.

Southeast of the agate beds, Lankin Dome rose stark and bare 500 feet from the meadow at its base. The unbroken, gray-brown granite face extended nearly half a mile in length and was about one quarter of a mile wide. Why was it here? What had happened to form it? Were there any more?

Over our supper of fried eggs, bacon, flapjacks, fried potatoes and cake, Dad told us about Gus Lankin, who had homesteaded in the 1880s at the base of the dome now bearing his name.

A bachelor, Gus had gone to Rawlins one day, nearly 20 years before, for supplies and some female company. There, under the influence of the demon rum, he was jailed for misconduct. Humiliated, he hanged himself in his cell. The state took his homestead for taxes.

The next day as we explored the abandoned homestead, we found the point of a war arrow embedded in the center roof beam.

The terrain around the homestead was unique: good soil, good water, a meadow, trees, abundant wild gooseberry bushes, and the magnificent dome, constantly smoothed by the wind. It was here that I decided to be a geologist, the beginning of my chosen way of life.

We returned to Mother the third day, our pockets full of treasures, our minds full of the trip, and many unanswered questions.

In "We'll Rebuild Again," David described the beginning of a new chapter in the family's life:

"Come into the living room, boys," said Mother shortly after we returned. Quietly she closed the French doors. "I have something very important to tell you, and I want there to be no interruptions." Allan and I glanced at each other. Mother was rarely so secretive. Drawing us down on the horsehair davenport, she put an arm around each of us. "I want you boys to be the first to know. You are going to have a little brother or sister in November, if all goes well." There was dead silence. We had given up on being big brothers years ago. Then simultaneously, we cried, "It's going to be a girl! This is the best news you could have given us!"

"This is all I have to tell you at the present time. Go and think about it." She hugged each of us, and the talk was over.

Allan and I spent the afternoon talking on the sunny hillside where, not long before, I had buried some cats-eye marbles and a padlock, my special treasures. Of course the baby would be a girl. We had seen other families with girls. Having a little sister would be a little bit of heaven. Only four months left!

Ethel wrote of her own preparations for the addition of a new baby in "Our George":

George Rushton's last stay on our ranch was when we were making preparations for the birth of my third baby. John, Toby, and George began work on an outside entry of logs to make the kitchen warmer, and have a place for the many coats, slickers, chaps, sweaters, jackets, overshoes, boots, spurs, hats, caps, gloves, and mittens.

They added a laundry, which Allan immediately appropriated as his bedroom, and bedroom it remained ever afterwards. The room between it and the kitchen was for a bathroom, although years passed before it held a conventional tub. They built in a seat the length of the wall. Under it were drawers for towels, and bins, one for soiled clothes, one for clothes not yet ironed. The outhouse continued its function for the remainder of our time on the ranch.

David moved into the narrow bedroom built off the living room. His eagle swirled above his bed in the breezes from the window.

Following the decision of the school board in June, Ethel resumed her story of "The 3 R's":

That fall we were given nine months for school. John went to Riverton, and came back with a teacher—a man, named Harris. He was not young, rather large and soft-looking. Unpacking, he showed me his medicines. There were many bottles and powders, with hints as to their purposes. He also brought a seamless sack of soiled shirts, socks, and underwear for me to wash for him. While he had a wash bowl and pitcher in his room, he carried away the ones used in the kitchen when he wanted to shave. Already we had three men and two boys at home. He made six, and my baby was due in little more than a month. I cried that night for the first time in years, and the last time for years to come. I filled one ear with tears and then turned over and filled the other ear.

The boys accepted him. He took them for a good walk that October day. They came into the kitchen as I was emptying an ovenful of fragrant cinnamon rolls on the cabinet shelf. He picked up and ate several. "Hot bread," I warned him, for in spite of his infirm digestion, he had an enormous appetite.

Dinner followed. We were all at the table around the French .75mm shell lamp, and again he bolted the rolls and his platefuls of food.

Suddenly he struck out with one arm, then the other, barely missing the lamp. He flung himself about wildly for a moment, collapsed on George Rushton's shoulder, righted himself and dashed out of doors. Toby ran after him.

We were stunned. What had happened? Was he mad? Sick? What might he do? Fall against the stove, set the house on fire, lose his balance on a horse, a constant danger to himself and to us. "Epileptic," we decided rightly by morning. He had kept this a secret when he applied for the position. It was a hard but necessary thing to tell him that we could not keep him. But what a blessed relief to see him leave!

David added in "Problems of Education—and Our Last Country Schoolmarm":

Dad and one of the cowboys took Mr. Harris to town, where he departed on the train to parts unknown. We learned later that he had a long record of *grand mal* epilepsy, and in those days no drugs were known to help the poor man.

No more school, we thought! We could concentrate on our traplines and work with the men.

During the hiatus between teachers, Ethel wrote in "Our George":

David's long urging to go after wood with George was at last successful. All started happily enough, the drive in the country, the hunt for wood, work on the two-handled saw. They ate and went to sleep at dark in the canvas covered bed-roll.

During the night a cold snowfall blanketed the Divide. Thanks to the black tree, they had little trouble with their breakfast fire, but it was difficult to catch, harness and hitch up the four horses, skittish from the cold. George would have his hands full to control them and brake the top-heavy wagon down the steep, now slippery, hill. Fearing that they might run away or overturn the wagon, catching David underneath the jagged load, he made the boy follow on foot.

At Iron Springs, where the ground became nearly level, and the horses were more manageable, George climbed stiffly down from his seat, beating his arms against his chest.

"We both got to walk now to keep warm. Make the blood circleate." He encouraged David, "It ain't too far for us." David, so challenged, and George walking beside the horses while he drove them, covered together the sixteen more miles to the ranch.

Occasionally George spoke, a few words at a time, giving the only advice David remembers hearing from him.

"Don't be a quitter . . . your folks aren't quitters . . . that's why I like them . . . my own son was a quitter . . . don't you be one."

Hours later, at dark they saw the light of the house. They reached its warmth almost too tired for the food ready for them. After the day-long walk in the cold and snow, David was glad of the tub of hot water, and his own bed.

In November 1924, the Shoshoni State Bank failed. David remembered in "We'll Rebuild Again":

As Allan and I deposited the earnings from our traplines the previous year, we had believed the promise of "STRENGTH, SAFETY, SECURITY" carved in the stone lintel above the door. Now, suddenly our money was gone. Dad and Mother tried to explain, but their answers made little sense. It seemed like stealing to us, and that was wrong. Their meager savings as well were gone, and the additions to the house had yet to be paid. There would be no more cattle money for another year. Little more was said within our hearing, but their faces wore a tired, desperate look.

Dad immediately enlarged his already extensive area for coyote trapping, every day making his solitary rides to sites farther from the ranch, regardless of the weather. Seeing his exhaustion, Allan and I tried to shoulder more of the chores at home and doing what we could to spare Mother, who could risk no strain. One stormy day, Dad's horse slipped on ice and fell on his leg. Only with great difficulty did he succeed in remounting.

This penciled scrap of Mother's poetry reflected her personal anguish:

Outlasting (Dublin in Ireland)

I have known men bereft of all they had,
    I have seen women stript of trinkets rare,
A thousand towns may fall, their streets be sad
    Their fame to be echoless upon the air.
But I have never known a dream to die
    And I have dressed in dreams for many years
And I have seen around me careless lie
    Their trinketry as bright as tears—
For only the Impossible is true
    And only the Impossible can stand
At last the long uncertainty will do.
    For I have found it so in every land . . .
I live by the dream.

Knowing that John would pay them when he could, Toby and George continued the improvements on the house. Ethel wrote in "Our George":

The men were putting up doors and windows when John took me to Moneta to meet the once-a-day train to the doctor in Riverton. The boys were to continue their lessons without me, and send me daily reports. My baby, Phoebe Elizabeth, was born on the sixteenth of November.

David remembered that Ethel stayed with the Tonkins during her confinement and for several weeks afterward. She saved the boys' letters, which chronicled their activities during her absence, but the family archives do not include either the telegram announcing Phoebe's birth or Ethel's letters to the boys.

Although a few of the letters are typed, most are on tablet paper. Allan's are often in ink, and the writing is beautiful, thanks to "Ma" Bailey's instruction. David sometimes typed his and described the news of the day:

November 13, 1924

Dear Mother,

When did you get to Riverton?

After you left George and us chinked and daubed the cow stable [. . .] While we were doing that we saw a blue heron going south.

Daddy and Toby got in about 7 o'clock with two boxes of apples, George's freight and a lot of mail.

My shoes came and my watch. The shoes were not like my other ones. They have no straps on them and they have rubber heels and the toes are very soft and in two places. They sent a new watch and it works fine. Thursday George and us went riding after a cow to butcher but we did not get her. We brought in all the cattle in the meadow, and put cans on the noses of two yearlings that were suckling a roan cow. This morning we went down to Toby's place for some two-by-fours and Allan took the gun along, we saw 5 hawks owls and three hawks. Allan nearly got a hawk.

We got back at half past one and had dinner. Toby's bread was not a success because it did not rise.

Toby has cut a doorway into your bedroom and has cut down the closet. I put a new comfort on our bed so now I am nice and warm. Allan is sleeping with me now while Toby fixes the bedroom and makes improvements. Toby has the door on hinges and has the lock on and the fancy knob. He stirred up a ghost odor[4] in the closet and nearly fainted. Daddy had to get Toby's Arabian perfume[5] from his writing paper box to stop him. Toby's bread rose and after it was baked it was fine and we ate a whole loaf for supper.

Daddy got two chickens in the evening.

Saturday we went riding after the beef cow . . . We saw a very big eagle and a lot of rabbits. We got in at three o'clock and had dinner. Toby is finishing the closet now. . . .

Monday Fred Crowley and Charley Furgesson[6] came to help butcher the cow. One of them was a professional butcher so it was all done in 3 hours. Crowley wanted to lease some land from daddy. Daddy went off with Crowley this afternoon.

With much love, David

P.S. Daddy has taken spelling in hand and we are doing two pages a day. I have not missed any words and Allan has missed nine[. . .]

Allan wrote:

Moneta, Wyoming, November 14, 1924

Dear Mother,

Since you have been gone we have wanted you back very much. For instance, last night I lost my nighty and had [to] hunt all over the house for it. I finally found it in your bedroom.

The day you left I went out to the barn and fixed the top of the cow shed door. I had just finished nailing the last board on when I found that it was too long. George started to saw the board when I got my finger in the way. It got sawed and I put some salve on it. It is doing fine and I am wearing a bandage to keep it clean.

When Daddy got home George, David and I were playing Rummee and Flaggs. I won one game of Flaggs.[7]

This morning we got through with our lessons. Just about the time George was going down to Toby's for some planks Daddy asked me if I wanted to go too[. . .] I took the gun along and when we were just about there George said he would walk the rest of the way if I would drive the wagon. I told him to take the gun and some shells because he might see a rabbit[. . .] I was driving along when all of a sudden a coyote came out from behind a bush about 50 feet away and stood and looked at me while I passed[. . .] Daddy made some bread that he says is so good that all throats want it.

November 15, 1924

This morning we got up fairly early and hoped to get thru with our lessons early and go out on the ice for a while. We had just gotten up when we heard daddy say that all hands were to go up the creek after cattle. We hurried during breakfast and got a little of our school work done[. . .]

This morning daddy said we would ride for the beef cow again[. . .] We thought we saw some cattle over by a round hill with a monument on it[. . .]

This afternoon daddy and George started to fix the weaning pens so that he can wean the calves pretty soon. He said that in the sand where he has to set posts the sand is frozen for four solid inches. He said that he was none too soon starting to fix it or it would have frozen too deep.

I think we are going to have beef tomorrow[. . .]

P.S. I am enclosing a French lesson.

The letters continued in the same vein for the next four weeks. On December 7, Ethel and Phoebe took the train to Lander, where they rested for several days with the Clarks, who had been transferred by the railroad to manage the station there. John and the boys went to visit their two Phoebes at the Clarks' home. David remembered that Phoebe was a perfect little miniature, all pink and white like their mother's cameo pin. After the trip, John wrote to Ethel:

Dear Pettikins,

For a wonder we are all alone to-night & I have been doing a little writing & now at 12:25 A.M. I will write you a few lines to tell you like Faith "that I still love you." The boys keep you posted on the events of the day. I finally got some wheat but the vegetables were not worth sending, so I am ordering 120 lbs cabbage, 50 lbs white onions & 50 lbs of beets from Denver. I also sent to Lovell for more apples. Store bill at Moneta for Nov. $100.88—cow feed, chicken feed, & horse feed, 200 lbs flour etc., etc. Only about an inch of snow on the ground at present. Toby just got the bread out of the oven at midnight.

Toby made a cupboard to-day for Mrs. Graham & some other things for her & is going to take them to Moneta to-morrow. . . We are still waiting Thanksgiving dinner until you get home. David has not yet sampled or produced the ginger ale.

David was telling Toby about the baby & wound up by asking "do you think there will be any more?" If you can get a [news]paper with the court docket, please do so. Also George wants one of those razor sharpening outfits from Mr. Clark & says to send him the bill & he will send a check for same. Four eggs to-day. David made the butter all alone, therefore nothing would do but that a pound had to be sent up to you. Hoping that you are enjoying life I remain with love & kisses for the two Phoebes,

John

A few days later, Ethel and Phoebe took the train to Moneta. David remembered their arrival:

With our new little sister in her arms, Mother was helped down from the train. She was thin and pale, but her eyes glowed with a softness that made her even more beautiful than before.

Toby may have offered the use of his car, but Dad wanted only his family along for the homecoming. In the bitterly cold weather, Dad had equipped the buggy with a charcoal footwarmer, heated soapstones from the fireless cooker, and a metal hot water bottle, all buried under mountains of buggy robes to keep his family warm on the 30-mile round trip.

Ethel wrote of her and Phoebe's return to the ranch in "Our George":

When I reached home I found two large lard pails of yellow horse fat that the boys had rendered, and about as much grease on their new, sheepskin-lined coats. The beautiful, light brown horsehide, tanned so that it was soft and pliable, George used for the rest of his life to cover his bed.

Our friends the Frasers had sold their range sheep. After a long visit at home in Scotland, they had come back to Wyoming. They bought a small farm near Lander, but stayed to spend Christmas with us before moving, and to help with the new baby.

Allan constructed and painted white a small cupboard for baby clothes. David matched it with a low bath screen. John made a large diaper box with a hinged lid. Toby sent for an armless rocking chair for me. George bought a silver cup for the baby.

Discreet bets, I heard later, had been made around town as to whether the newcomer would be a boy or a girl, odds being on a boy.

November days had been as alike and shining as gold beads on a golden chain. A month later they were darkly cold and growing colder. It was close to Christmas when I reached the ranch, and unwrapped the pink blankets from around my baby girl. Her hair was the color of my wedding ring. On her cheek the fingers of one hand were outspread like a small, pink starfish. She was passed from the arms of one person to the arms of another, and found welcome everywhere. The next morning I gave Phoebe her bath in an oval, white enameled pan on the dining table near the heater.

Lizzie Fraser was enraptured. "Oh, the precious darling! See the little hands and feet of her! See the little nails! Jimmy, come see the baby in her bath! Dimples she has already, on her hands and knees. I'll help her splash. And she smiles! Not much more than a month old and she smiles!"

Toby took pictures of her holding the baby, whom he boldly called his little sweetheart. He took a picture of me holding the baby. The boys felt immensely proud and important to have a sister, and John showed a new glow of fatherhood.

George spoke seldom but wore a constant smile. He was the oldest among us, the only other one to have had a child. His son had been no joy to him.[8] Our children seemed a compensation.

We had no Christmas tree that year. Although the bank which had held our few savings failed in November, the rejoicing over the birth of our new baby made that our happiest Christmas.

I had written my sisters and friends not to send presents. We would share the baby with them on our part. But packages piled surprisingly high on the dining table. There were dainty garments, enough for triplets; blankets, pink, blue and white, handwork to bring tears to my eyes. So many gifts to open, so much to see and try, we forgot all about Christmas dinner, until Toby produced my huge preserving kettle full of beef soup, fragrant and thick with vegetables. In a box with other gifts I found a tiny plum pudding, sized for John and me, which we stretched with plentiful sauce for eight of us.

The next days were the coldest we ever had. In the morning I could estimate the cold by the frost on the nailheads of the inside kitchen door frame. At ten below zero, the nails for a foot above the floor were white with frost. At forty below zero the frost made white buttons of them as high as the doorknob. But even with the protection of the new entry, that January the frosted nails set a new height record. Our outdoor thermometer could register no colder than forty below, but we heard, and believed, that it was fifty-five below at Riverton.

I left Phoebe's basket at night close to the heater, where the fire was always burning. I put a hot water bottle among her blankets, but she woke at midnight, crying with the cold, until I took her into bed between John and me.

Phoebe's first winter was the last that we were all together at the ranch. How glad we were that George had Christmas with us! The Frasers moved to their new home near Lander. George drove one of the wagons for them, and stayed to help on the farm. He left his horses and saddle at our ranch.

Notes

1. The spring was dug out and its sides lined with a bottomless wooden box or barrel—hence the name. Water seeped in to fill the box and flowed out the top.

2. Herders generally put one black sheep in each group of 100 white sheep so they could easily approximate the size of a herd by counting the black sheep.

3. Ewes about to deliver.

4. Reminder of the unsanitary family which had occupied the ranch house 14 years before.

5. Probably smelling salts.

6. Sheepmen who leased land from the Loves.

7. The player who could match the most flags with the correct country in the shortest time won.

8. George's son had spent time in the penitentiary in Rawlins for robbery.

CHAPTER FOURTEEN

~

1925

Changing Horizons

1925 was a year of both looking forward as their children grew, and looking back at the changes in life on the Love ranch. The Wellesley Record *of 1925 reported:*

Ethel Phoebe Waxham, M.A. University of Colorado

(Mrs. John G. Love)

Moneta, Wyo.

Allan Galloway Love, December 30, 1911

John David Love, April 17, 1913

Phoebe Elizabeth Love, November 16, 1924

"Ethel says that her 'baby is so new and engrossing' that she neglects everything else and so she has written no life history. It seems to the committee that the list of accomplishments that follows Ethel's name speaks volumes."

January 4, 1925

Dear Miss Hill,

You have my delighted thanks for the lovely garden picture you sent me. It hangs over my desk, like a glimpse of paradise. The earth here, now so white, is almost always white or brown; such a riot of color is unknown. We do have it in the sky, however, at sunset. I thank you, too, for the subscription to the *Ladies' Home Journal.* I value it the more, for I have let my other magazines go for this year.

You must hear the reason: I've a new baby girl, two months old, and she absorbs a surprising amount of time, considering her size. The boys are delighted, and so are the rest of us. Little Phoebe is a darling, and smiles at us in a most engaging manner. She is a very satisfactory baby, growing as she should, and responding nicely to her training. But she has had colic since I came home to the ranch, and I don't wonder. It has been dreadful weather for new little babies, as well as for man, woman, and beast. We had for a time the coldest weather we ever had, fifty below zero. Since then the days have grown warmer, above zero most of the time for a week. There is not very much snow, and cars go back and forth to town occasionally.

We did not do anything for Xmas this year, but the boys hung up their stockings, and many friends and relatives sent presents. The baby was the best present we could have, and needed all the time and strength I had.

I hope that you had as much joy at Xmas time as she gives us and that your new year will bring you the bread I know you habitually cast upon the waters.

With very best wishes for your New Year,

Sincerely yours,

Ethel P. Love

Wyoming weather, which can change capriciously from one extreme to another, was and is a constant concern. David's Christmas chronicle for 1984 recounted his own experience during the frigid winter of 1924–25 in "Hypothermia":

The weeks before Christmas 1984 were times of record low temperatures across the nation. On our enclosed back porch in Laramie, Wyoming, the thermometer read –12°F, outside, –25°F; in Casper, –35°F; Butte, Montana –65°F. The bitter weather of 1984–5 reminded me of the winter I was eleven. The ranchers then fought the elements alone, dealing with whatever losses fate dealt them. It never occurred to them to ask for help from the government.

For several years I had been running a trap line to supplement the family income. One of my most successful sites was in Castle Gardens, where in addition to other traps, I had set a pair of large No. 4 Newhouse coyote traps among the sandstone pinnacles. Because I had to break trail through deep, crusted snow, it took most of a day to check them all. I killed the animals I caught, then cached them to retrieve on horseback the next day, and moved the traps to a new site.

January 1925 had been bitterly cold, with a wind chill which could kill a human in a matter of minutes. This particular morning, I had missed two days on the trap line, so, feeling guilty, I was anxious to get started again. The temperature was about 10°F below zero, and the wind was beginning to rise. Dad paused as he fed the livestock, to squint up at the pale fuzzy sun through the frost crystals swirling in the light breeze. "I'll come with you, laddie. Maybe we can shoot some rabbits for supper. Pack some sandwiches for us, put on your warmest clothes, and get the .22 rifle and some shells." Dad would make the long trek less dreary. He was wise in the ways of the range and always had a fund of new ideas and stories. Little did I realize that he had sensed something ominous in the weather.

The word "hypothermia" was unknown to us then, but people who spent winters on the range were all too familiar with its effects.

The ominous weather made Dad think of Thomas Mahoney, who had worked for him the winter of 1909–10. In a letter to Mother that January, Dad described him as a big, strong, good-natured Irishman with a wife and two daughters in Iowa. He had educated his daughters, and provided well for them.

Why such a gregarious, fun-loving man as Tom would choose the lonely life of a sheepherder on the desolate range of Wyoming was not known. Many men came west to start a new life and no questions were asked. Despite Tom's lack of experience with sheep, Dad entrusted him with a herd of 2,000 and two of his finest sheep dogs: tall, yellow and white part-collies, experienced, and indispensable to the herder.

The bond between Mahoney and his dogs became extraordinary, the dogs devotedly following his commands with a skill and enthusiasm they had not accorded previous herders. Despite the vicious weather in December 1909 and January 1910, Tom and the dogs managed to keep the sheep from scattering, being buried alive by snow in ravines, or stampeded by the ever-present coyotes.

Tom lived in a sheep wagon, with a canvas roof stretched over arched oak bows. Inside were a built-in bed, a table which pulled out from under the bed, a wood-burning stove, and wooden seats on the overhang above the iron-bound oak wheels. The canvas kept out the wind, but when the stove fire died down, the heat immediately disappeared.

At night Tom brought the dogs into the sheep wagon and, by the light of the kerosene lamp, gently broke off the balls of ice which clung to the hairs between their toes. Without these ministrations, they might have frozen their feet and gone lame. Then the dogs were fed and let out to burrow under a snowdrift, sleeping curled in a ball, ears ever cocked toward danger.

Every few days, Dad or his campmover came to bring mail and fresh provisions. Thus it was discovered that Tom had not returned to his sheep wagon the night of January 1, 1910.

On January 4, 1910, Dad wrote to Mother that fifty-one sheep had frozen to death in temperatures of more than 30°F below zero, and that there was no trace of the herder and his dogs.

A search party was sent to search for Tom, all within sight and sound of each other, yelling and whistling, hoping that Tom's dogs would bark in response if they were still alive. Finally, through the blasting wind, faint barks were heard, shrill, fast, desperate. The men raced toward the sound, their horses lunging and floundering through the snow. On the lee side of a low hill Tom Mahoney staggered slowly toward them, an ice-encrusted dog crowded against him on either side.

Tom had been dressed in the customary long wool underwear, two wool shirts, sheepskin coat, wind-proof wool cap, and heavy mittens when he'd left the sheep wagon three days before, his feet in wool socks and felt shoes, wrapped in bundles of gunny sacks. His face was nearly black, his eyebrows and moustache rimed with frost. His eyes were dull and bloodshot, his nose an ominous gray.

As the men hurried toward Tom, the dogs moved in front of him, snarling protectively, teeth bared. "Down, lads," Tom mumbled. They retreated, but remained on guard. Stiffly, he reached down to pet them, and whispered with a ghostly flicker of his affection: "Great doggies. They kept me walkin' and wudna let me die."

Tom was lifted onto a horse and taken the several miles to the nearest sheep wagon. One man started on the all-night ride to notify Dad and the other search parties, and return with a buggy and fast team of horses.

A roaring fire was built in the sheep wagon stove and hot soup and coffee were fed to Tom while the men rubbed his hands, feet, and face with snow in a desperate attempt to restore circulation. Frostbite was a dreaded condition on the range, because aside from rubbing with snow (we did not know then that it is the worst thing that could be done), the only solution was amputation of frozen limbs—or death. Left outside, the dogs refused to eat, keeping watch through the night and the next day.

Tom's hands were probably saved by the warmth of the dogs as he clung to them, but his nose, feet and body had been badly frozen. His delirious ramblings during the following days revealed what he had endured during the storm.

Taken to Moneta in a covered spring wagon, Tom wanted the dogs with him. When he was carried into the Moneta Hotel, the dogs came as well, the ice balls on their toes clattering on the linoleum floor. Beside his bed, they continued their vigil, refusing food and snarling at visitors. When spasms of pain racked him, the dogs licked his hands in wordless comfort.

A telegram requesting a doctor was sent to Casper by railroad telegraph. For six days of high fevers, Tom raved and screamed before the train returned from its circular run to Lander to take him to Casper. His kidneys and other internal organs had ceased to function; catheters were not available. He died on the train.

Other herders offered to buy the dogs, but Dad brought them back to his ranch where they spent the rest of their days doing what they liked best—herding sheep.

In March of that same year Dad found the body of Ed McClatchie, one of Delfelder's herders, on the range, another victim of the same storm. He never forgot either man.

On this day in January 1925, Dad wore his usual winter attire of long underwear, wool pants, two wool shirts, wool sweater, buffalo coat and bearskin cap, a heavy scarf and thick mittens. His feet, in wool socks, were wrapped in the *New York Times*, then stuffed into felt liners inside rubber overshoes. I was similarly attired, but on a smaller scale. Too many clothes immobilize a small boy. My mittens were lighter, too, so that I could fire the rifle quickly if a rabbit suddenly jumped up. It was a privilege to be entrusted with the rifle and the responsibility of shooting rabbits. We never did it for sport.

Like robots we shambled along the course of my trapline, gauging the easiest route across the crusted snow; in the cold we had little energy to spare.

The traps around the buffalo wallow were empty and undisturbed. We skirted them to avoid leaving our scent. Around noon we stopped for lunch in the shelter of the pinnacles. Our bottled meat sandwiches were half frozen and the water in our water bag was mushy with ice. (Vacuum bottles, with their thin glass liners were too fragile to use on these trips, but how welcome hot soup or cocoa would have been!)

The traps in the labyrinths were likewise empty. As we started back to the ranch, I shot three cottontail rabbits, proudly carrying them and the rifle. Dad carried the heavy wood and leather clamps used to set the trap jaws in the open position.

As the wind whipped up, swirling snow and frost crystals began to obscure our vision. Ice crystals blew under our scarves, melted, and refroze, covering our skin with ice. Icicles tangled in Dad's moustache. I wiped my nose and face on my mittens.

About a mile from the ranch house, I realized that the rabbits kept slipping from my grasp. Then I dropped the rifle, something absolutely forbidden. Why was I so clumsy? I did not feel cold, only slightly numb, dull-witted and very tired. From behind me Dad suddenly spoke up sharply: "Laddie, put down the gun and rabbits and run to the house. RUN! Don't stop for anything! Don't wait for me! Don't lose your bearings! I'll be right behind you." "Why?" I thought dimly, but when he used that tone, I did not question him. As I tried to run, I fell repeatedly; my stiff muscles would not obey my commands. Standing after each fall became more and more difficult. My whole being cried out to rest—just for a few minutes—but Dad's voice, behind me, would not let me stop.

Gradually, I began to hurt, first my feet, then my legs, then hands, then arms, then my entire body. I was not aware of screaming with pain, or the tears freezing on my cheeks. I became confused and lost my bearings, only to have Dad set me straight. As the sun disappeared behind the scudding snow clouds, the biting wind intensified. My numbing mind began to fix on goals: three quarters of a mile, half a mile, a quarter.

At last I could see the ranch buildings through the falling snow. Home! Staggering and sobbing, I skidded down the hill to the house. As I blundered through the door, Mother took a hard look at me, shivering, incoherent, dull-eyed, gasping. Quickly she stripped off my ice-caked clothes in front of the kitchen stove, and began to rub my feet, legs, arms, and hands with dry crystalline snow. It rasped like sandpaper, and I expected my skin to come off. One kind of pain was replaced by another as my circulation returned. Gradually, the spasms of shaking subsided. Hot cocoa thawed the inner boy. Dad arrived with the rabbits and rifle. Looking me over carefully, he nodded and said gently: "A close call, laddie. We won't let it happen again."

Perhaps with an eye to providing a different life for her sons, Ethel continued her account of obtaining a teacher in "The 3 Rs":

For several months we were without a teacher. Then Miss Janice Gardner came from Denver, a pretty, laughing girl with dark brows and, in the style of the day, puffs of blond hair on each side of her head.

School achieved new glamour. Word flew over the country. Cowboys and others made trips to the ranch. Even John revived his quotations from Burns:

Her 'prentice han' she tried on man,

An' then she made the lasses, O. . .[1]

Sixty years later, David paid tribute to Janice in "Our Last Country Schoolmarm":

Janice Gardner came to us in February, 1925, perhaps through the Fisk agency which had brought Mother to Wyoming 20 years earlier. A natural catalyst, she attracted interesting people and restored our faith in teachers.

About 22 years old, she had a Normal School diploma, but had never taught before. Nor had she any experience in rural living. I suspect that Janice had grave misgivings when she got off the train in Moneta in mid-winter to be met by a grizzled rancher—Dad shaved at least once a week—who drove her to our ranch in an open buggy across a prairie with no sign of human habitation as far as the eye could see. It must have been a further shock to find that she would have to live without electricity or running water, and use an outhouse 180 feet away. Janice never admitted that this was not what she expected.

The school board had provided pens, pencils, ink, paper, and a few old textbooks, but no other teaching aids such as chemicals or pictures. Patiently Janice tried to determine the blank places in our knowledge as well as our strengths and interests. Science and math were the most finite subjects to us, but Janice had had little training in either subject. Valiantly she grappled to stay ahead of us, while we, in turn, tried to please her in the social and cultural subjects.

With no musical instruments, we had nothing to teach concepts of tone or key. Allan was partially tone-deaf, and I not much better. Although Janice had a nice voice, the three of us, with no masking accompaniment, created an exercise in discord when we tried to sing together. Even with the phonograph, we could not hum to "Thaïs" or shout to "Scots wha hae wi' Wallace bled!" Music theory escaped us completely, as did civics, social studies, and other subjects essential in today's school curriculum. With nothing pertinent in our experience, we remained indifferent.

School was held in the living room of the ranch house or on the porch, which suited the two pupils very well, but was surely very distracting to the teacher. How could she compete when someone rushed into the next room shouting that they were carrying in a cowboy whose innards had been ripped out by a saddle horn, or the biggest coyote ever seen had just been killed out by the chicken house?

There were lighter moments, however. When the sun was warm and the ground dry, we played croquet between the windmill and the storehouse, where there was no sagebrush, while Phoebe cooed from her high chair. On stormy days, we put on masquerades and shadow plays, improvising in content and costumes, Allan and I completely unaware of the double-entendres we naïvely created as we played to a more sophisticated audience. My father would collapse on the sofa, holding his sides, roaring with laughter, as tears coursed down his cheeks. I truly feared that he would die laughing.

The sagebrush telegraph had relayed the news of the charming young teacher at the Love ranch. First to arrive to look her over was Dinty Moore, "from the north of Ireland," he said, in his battered Model T. Dinty was a driller on an oil rig 11 miles airline (20 by road) southeast of our ranch. The crew worked just fast enough to encourage its financial angel, a restaurateur from South Dakota, and slowly enough to remain employed. After ten years, they had drilled only about 3,000 feet, and found nothing.

Short, with broad shoulders and a swagger, Dinty had merry eyes and a gift of blarney. He always arrived in a suit, white shirt, necktie, and shiny shoes, which did not endear him to the cowboys.

Schoolmarm Janice Gardiner and Phoebe Love in front of Love ranch house in 1925. Ethel wrote: "When Phoebe's eyes are smiling," Janice would sing over the baby's basket, "Sure it's like a morn in spring, and when Phoebe's eyes are smiling, you can hear the angels sing."
Love Family Archives

The cowboys and horse runners who drifted to the ranch that spring were lean, hard-muscled bachelors, nearly all in their 20s and early 30s. Born poor, with only a rudimentary education, they accepted their lot, working days which knew no hour limitations but daylight and dark, and weeks with no holidays. Most were homely, with prematurely lined faces, but lively eyes that missed little. None wore glasses; people with glasses went into other kinds of work. Some were already stooped from chronic saddle-weariness or spinal injuries, or bowlegged and hip-sprung, with unrepaired hernias requiring trusses. Some wore heavy 8-inch-wide belts to keep their kidneys in place during prolonged rides.

These shy men, more at ease with animals than people, had their virtues, too. Loyal and dependable, they were courteous and respectful in the company of women and older men. At table their language was a model of discretion, so different from what it would be during the last year the ranch operated. Yet, these men could be holy terrors when they went to town to squander their wages on whiskey and whatever amusement they could find.

An inkling of something new came on Dinty's first visit to Janice: romance! On previous visits, he had been disdainful of us "brats," as he called us. When Janice invited him onto the porch, we followed to sit on either side of her on the swing, while Dinty glared at us from a separate chair. Finally, he motioned us to accompany him around the corner of the house. Choking with anger, he made personal remarks about our small sizes and questioned our legitimacy. When we countered that Dad might like to know what he said, he quickly restored our size and legitimacy, gave us two bits, and promised us a box of candy the next time he went to town—if we would leave him and Janice alone.

But the potential source of quarters quickly evaporated. Suspecting what was going on, Dad required us to return the money and apologize for our behavior. Someday, he said, his eyes twinkling, we would realize that young men and women sometimes want to be alone without small boys hanging around.

In May, three wild horse runners arrived. In return for the use of our corrals, they would brand our colts and help castrate the scrub stallions.

Sunshine (he seemed to have no last name) was lean and hard, silent, a man with a past he did not share. Frequently he carried a six-shooter, rare on the range in the 1920s. Yet, occasionally, his lined, weary face would soften to bubble with wit and laughter, so contagious that everyone around would laugh with or at him—the reason, perhaps, for his name.

Red, with hair to match his name, was the youngest. Big, gentle, shy, his face wore a mass of freckles which parted into a broad and beguiling smile. A naïve dreamer of romantic dreams, he was a natural butt for the pranks of his more worldly companions.

The third horse runner was Rosebud Daly, called "Bud," or there was trouble. Part Indian, he was swarthy and smoky-eyed, with a thin, scarred face and slightly stooped shoulders. The oldest, he planned and directed operations, brooking no back talk. His sense of humor often involved risk and discomfort to his victims.

All three men were dazzled by Janice. Red thought she was an angel to be worshipped. Sunshine wanted to court her, and we were too young to know what Rosebud wanted of her. Flattered by the attention of these men, rough though they were, she was gracious to them. She was also gracious to the riders who came from the Sweetwater, the Rattlesnake Hills, 30 miles to the east, and those from Badwater and Poison Creeks, 20–30 miles to the north. Worst of all, she was gracious to Dinty Moore.

The only social events in the region were the Saturday night dances in Moneta or Shoshoni. With his car, Dinty could arrive at the dances freshly bathed, shaved and dressed with Janice on his arm, while the cowboys had a long, dusty ride on horseback. If they didn't want to dance in their travel-stained riding clothes, they could bathe (for 50¢), and change in the back of the barber shop in Shoshoni, or at the horse trough near the railroad station in Moneta. While whiskey dulled their feelings of social inadequacy, Janice did not approve of drinking, so if they got drunk she would not dance with them. Then they would take out their frustrations in fighting, which she didn't approve of either.

One evening while Dinty waited in the living room to escort Janice to a dance, Rosebud loosened the motor mount bolts in the Irishman's car. The three horse runners then departed on horseback for Moneta. Expecting to find Dinty and Janice stranded along the way, they planned to rescue her by borrowing a car in Moneta, leaving Dinty to fix his Ford on the road, and miss the dance. However, the motor did not fall out on the way to town, so their evening turned to roistering. The motor fell out as Dinty was driving Janice home. The now uninhibited horse runners caught up with the stranded car about five miles from the ranch. Declining their offer of a horse, afraid to remain for fear of what they might to do him, and hesitant to leave Janice with his rivals, Dinty finally trudged ignominiously off into the darkness, reaching the ranch near dawn. Dad rescued Janice in the buggy, escorted by the riders, leaving Dinty to repair his car.

As her teaching term neared its end, Janice decided to have a tea party for the cowboys, horse runners, and Dinty, in appreciation of their kind attention to her. Mother cautioned her that most of these men neither knew what a tea party was nor how to behave at one; there might be spectacular consequences. Janice dismissed the suggestion as a figment of Mother's imagination.

Invitations were mailed to each man, so charmingly written that few could resist. At least 15 cowboys arrived on horseback that beautiful Sunday afternoon. Dinty arrived in his car.

The aroma of freshly baked cookies filled the house. Probably with misgivings, Mother lent her four surviving pink and white flowered Dresden bone china tea cups to the occasion, along with our every-day chipped Blue Willow set.

The only lady present, Janice was the center of attention. My parents found excuses to stay in the kitchen. Despite having been ordered to stay away, Allan and I hovered around, hoping for at least one good fight. The guests sat stiffly around the dining room, glaring at each other as Janice showered her attention first on one then another, oblivious to the tension behind her. The ensuing hilarity and gibes which ebbed and flowed sounded like the chatter of a happy group, yet the sole aim was to create trouble.

Red had been handed one of the Dresden tea cups. Already ill at ease, and aware that this was a precious cup made him all the more uncomfortable. His large hands could only hold the dainty cup by sticking the terminal joint of his little finger through the handle. When he sipped, his other three fingers and thumb fanned out in front of his eyes and nose, evoking snickers from his colleagues. Gradually he realized that the circulation in his little finger was cut off, the pinky too swollen to remove from the cup handle. In pain and panic, he gulped the hot tea, choked, and rushed to the kitchen, concealing the dangling cup in front of him. "Please, Mrs. Love, don't tell Miss Janice I ain't used to these pretty tea cups, and please don't tell the fellers about gettin' my finger caught or they'll never let me hear the end of it. Can you get it offn my finger before I break the handle?"

Hiding her amusement under a guise of sympathy, Mother quickly wrapped a soaped string around and around the end of his finger, beginning at the tip and working toward the handle. Her cup was painlessly removed, intact. "Thank you, ma'am, bless you!" With a deep breath, and head held high, Red lumbered back into the dining room.

To Allan and me the afternoon was long and dull. To the men, it was equally long, although they enjoyed vying for Janice's attention. Finally, stuffed with cookies, awash with tea, and too bashful to make a break for the outhouse, the group began to depart. First to go was Dinty, sensing that he and his car could be prime targets for mayhem. Graciously, Janice accompanied the riders to the barn to watch them saddle up and bid them farewell. They were too respectful of her to start anything, so, to our disappointment, there were no open eruptions of hostility.

However, in the group following Janice, one man was suddenly bumped off the narrow foot-bridge over Bear Creek to crash ignominiously six feet down into the brush below. By the time he came roaring up over the bank, his tormentor was strolling contentedly beside the schoolmarm. A hip swung out at the precisely right instant knocked another man into a fresh cow pie. While Janice was saying goodbye to one cowboy who gazed soulfully into her eyes, another lifted the guest's saddle blanket to slip a branch of thorny greasewood beneath. As the departing cowboy hopped nimbly into his saddle, his horse, irritated by the sharp prickling, lurched wildly out of the corral and began to buck, while the spectators cheered and jeered.

Covered by the noisy diversions were the muttered "you sonsabitches! I'll get you at the next roundup." Like yearling bulls attempting to establish supremacy, these men postured and blustered, but did little actual fighting.

As the weather warmed, the delicate perfume of prairie flowers filled the air. Janice was enchanted. When she expressed the desire to see the flowers on the range, Sunshine invited her to go with him the following Sunday. When she admitted that she had never been on a horse before, he offered to teach her to ride.

The morning of the ride, accompanied by crude and occasionally witty re-marks from his cronies, Sunshine bathed in Muskrat Creek, donned his best clothes, brushed the manure from his boots, shined them, oiled his saddle, polished his pistol, and borrowed Mother's wedding saddle for Janice to use.

Then, on his flashiest mount, Sunshine led his gentlest horse toward the porch, where Janice waited. As they pranced past the long building, Rosebud slipped a large, bristly curry comb under the arched tail of Sunshine's high-strung horse. The result was explosive. Riding "loose" with his legs hanging free, Sunshine had no time to get a firm seat or hook his spurs into the cinch. His horse's tail, sensing the intrusion of the curry comb, clamped down hard. The more frightened the horse grew, the harder his tail clamped. With a squeal, he skittered forward, hindquarters low, like a balloon with the nozzle untied and the air gushing out. Directly in front of Janice the frantic horse began to buck in earnest. Sunshine, normally a superb rider, lost the mare he was leading, then one stirrup, then his six shooter, then his hat, as he fought to keep his seat. From the sidelines, we all watched, waiting, while Red and Rosebud whooped and guffawed.

Sunshine, legs flying, arms clawing the air, was thrown, spectacularly. With a sickening thud he sprawled in the dirt as the dust settled around him. Then up he bounced, still clutching the broken bridle rein. Growling curses, he reached for his six shooter, but the holster was empty. Free of its load, his horse bucked harder. Gaseous emanations, released under intense pressure, cracked like pistol shots. Janice, through the dust, had seen the cowboy's hand flash towards his holster. "Sunshine," she screamed, "don't shoot him!" Rosebud, doubled up with laughter, gasped, "Ma'am, them ain't pistol shots, they're—uh— Oh! God!" Convulsed with mirth, he and Red scuttled back to their bachelor quarters. Half a mile away, Sunshine's horse rid himself of the curry comb and stopped to rest.

Choking back the torrent of eloquence which had made him famous in roundup circles, the battered cowboy suddenly discovered that there were compensations. Running up to him, Janice put her arms around him. "Oh, you poor man, you're hurt!" Putting his arm around the schoolmarm's shoul-ders, he adjusted hers around his waist, and they walked ever so slowly back to the ranch house. From the long house, Rosebud and Red stared in disbelief.

Helping Sunshine to the couch, Janice gently sponged the dirt from his forehead and neck, he savoring each ministration as a caress. She dressed his scrapes with iodine and bandages, fixed him tea and cookies, and kept him quiet until the supposed shock could wear off, while Allan and I snickered from the kitchen door. He might have taken all afternoon to recover if Rose-bud and Red had not appeared to inquire about his health, and offer to teach

Janice to ride themselves while he recuperated. Chuckling with sympathy, they settled themselves companionably on the couch. We will draw the curtain of charity over the rest of the scene.

Despite being needled about "mooning around with sick calf eyes," Red, in turn, grew more and more infatuated with Janice. Finally, he found the courage to ask for a lock of her hair. He would wear it, he said, as a lucky charm next to his heart. Gently she told him that it wouldn't be proper. Overhearing the exchange, a sudden inspiration came to Allan and me, which we discussed with Sunshine. What, we asked Red cannily, would he pay for a lock of hair. "Four bits," he replied, assuming that the lock would be from Janice. Over our lessons, we studied Janice's hair, then looked Dumpling over carefully. A 3-inch lock of shiny, wavy hair was carefully snipped from the dog's flank and tied with a red ribbon. In the presence of Sunshine and Rosebud, we gave it to Red and triumphantly collected our four bits. For a week or more he happily wore it next to his heart. (Dad said that he positioned it more as if it were a liver pad.) Then Sunshine and Rosebud burst his euphoric balloon. Unwilling to believe the lock had come from our dog, Red took it to Janice and shyly asked if he could see where it was snipped off. Highly amused, she admitted it really was a beautiful lock, but disclaimed ownership. Sunshine and Rosebud caught Dumpling and showed Red the unmistakable hair stump.

As June came, with Allan completing the 8th grade and I the 7th, Dad asked Janice if it would be legal for me to take the same exam as Allan. If I passed, could I skip the 8th grade to enter high school along with him? Janice could find nothing in the regulations to forbid it. Then Dad said that if I passed the exam, he would take Allan and me on a fishing trip to Long Creek. With little time to spare, I began a program of intensive cramming.

The day of the exam came. We were all excited and nervous. Janice wanted to see her first two pupils do well, I wanted to go on the fishing trip, Allan wanted to get into high school, and our parents wanted us in the same grade because it made continuing our education so much simpler. We both passed, Allan brilliantly, I with an average grade. Thus, at 13 and 12, we were ready for high school in Lander.

Janice had helped us to establish goals during a formative time in our lives. She taught in a grade school in Lander while we were in high school there. Then she married a Scottish grocer and restaurateur, and adopted a baby girl. As college came and went, then graduate school, then the oil business, war, and finally the Geological Survey for me, and dam and superhighway construction for Allan, we saw less and less of Janice. The last time I saw her, more than 60 years later, she had recently been widowed and her daughter had died of cancer. She still sparkled, trim and lovely, her brilliant gray eyes unforgettable with their steady, no-nonsense gaze, and her ready, easy laugh.

That spring, Ethel wrote a mid-year letter to Miss Hill:

14 June, '25

My dear Miss Hill,

A delightful surprise were your letter and package. How the styles for wee folks change and grow more sensible just as they do for us. The "sweater" is the most adorable little garment, it fits so snugly and comfortably, unlike the fly-away ribboned sacques, and it is the most heavenly pink! Phoebe has hardly worn another wrap since it came. David whittled a frame of wood to dry it upon, when it has to be washed, as such things invariably must. The dress, too, is of a dainty new cut, and I must make her others like it later on. I made only two dresses for her, she received so many beautiful ones. One of those I made has lace sent me made by Greek refugees, and is so fine and lovely, it looks as if made by fairies. Little Phoebe is so fine and sweet herself, I try to keep her so. She has been growing quite normally, and now, still not seven months old, has been calling "mum-mum-mum" whenever she is in trouble, and knows her "Mum" by name. David thinks it odd that she should call me so, when everyone else calls me "Mother." I hope to have a picture of her some time for you, but I have been very dilatory with the Kodak lately.

Since February we have had a very nice young girl to teach the boys. She is pretty and jolly and we all enjoy her. Still it is not very long since she had trouble with long division, and I have had to help them all with their problems. Allan is ready for High School, so it seems quite imperative to make a change soon, but the ways and means committee sees no solution, barring miracles, so I am hoping for a miracle, and I do hope it will be prompt and adequate!

After our very cold weather in December the winter became mild and pleasant. In fact there was hardly a six-inch snow and no rain. Cars went back and forth to town at any time. The sun shone every day. May was really too hot! Over ninety in the shade. Now June is cooler and showery, but there has been so little moisture the feed is poor on the range and the springs are drying.

We've come through the year nicely, without so much as a cold for anyone except the "gude mon," who generally brings one from town.

Cordially yours,

Ethel P. Love

The boys' last summer before high school was beginning. David wrote of it in "The Enchanted Summer":

The summer before Allan and I entered high school was so perfect I called it enchanted.

The first event was the fishing trip, scheduled as soon as the roundup was over, the calves had been branded, and the bulls distributed among the cows. Ralph Clark Jr. was invited to join us. The trip would be a true vacation.

We assembled bedrolls, and packed the wooden "grub box"—"Milwaukee's Finest Beer" proclaiming its origin—with cooking gear and food. Shortly after sunrise on the appointed morning, we departed in the topless buggy.

The sun was bright, and the air still, except for bursts of birdsong, the clopping of the horses' hooves, and the grinding of the buggy wheels in the two-track road. Dad was in one of his rare talkative moods.

About a mile south of the ranch, he pointed to a line of boulders progressing eastward across an upland plain, terminating at a 50-foot cliff cut by Muskrat Creek.

"What do you think they are, lads?" he asked. They didn't look like a natural part of the landscape.

"When the buffalo still roamed the plains, the Indians rolled the boulders there as a barrier. Mounted on fast ponies, they would drive a herd of buffalo up to the edge of the cliff. If the animals faltered, warriors hiding behind the boulders would stand and wave hides to frighten them over the cliff. When the poor beasts tumbled to the creek bed below, those killed or crippled were butchered on the spot, and the rest allowed to go free. This is a buffalo jump. You might find arrowheads or scrapers here. There's another jump near the Beaver Divide."

A few miles farther, an expression of sadness crossed his face. "I've a story to tell you, lads, about a great horse, Big Red. Although the events happened over thirty years ago, they form the foundation of our life on Muskrat Creek. Without Big Red, neither we nor our ranch would be here." Through the years I have reconstructed the story of "Big Red" he told us that day:

Dad first saw the magnificent bay horse when he came to work for the 71 Cattle Company on the Sweetwater River in 1893. The foreman Jimmy Craig said that the horse didn't belong to anyone and if the new hand could tame him, he could keep him. Dad felt the prize was worth the challenge. From different sources, the story of the horse gradually unfolded.

The spring of 1888, Big Red was born into one of the fastest herds of wild horses in the Red Desert country of southwestern Wyoming. His dark red coat was rich and soft, his black mane and tail connected by a narrow black stripe down the center of his back. He was large, even at birth.

When Big Red was only a few weeks old, the men of the 71 Cattle Company pursued this herd in a rough, treacherous badland known as the

Honeycombs. The colt, too young to keep up with the herd, was left by his mother in a dry wash among the colorful clay badlands[2] flanking dazzling white sand dunes.

After two days of chasing the herd, as they returned to the 71, the horse runners found the colt, lying caked with dust and dried sweat where his mother had left him.

"What shall we do with him?" asked one of the men. "He's too young to make it on his own, and his mother may never come back."

"Shoot him if you're up to it," replied George B. Henderson, the hard-eyed manager of the 71. He turned and rode away.

Owned by an absentee Scottish syndicate, the 71 was one of the largest ranches in Wyoming. Its land included most of the big springs and wild hay meadows from the Sweetwater River northward for 60 miles into the Wind River Basin, and extended for 15 miles north of what was to become our ranch.

A large, brutal man, Henderson was disliked and feared by his men. It was whispered that his real name was John Powers and that he had been a hired gunman in the Molly Maguire troubles.[3]

The men fidgeted, hoping the colt's mother would come back, although they knew she would not, and finally rode away.

Far behind the cowboys was the nighthawk, the lowest man in the range hierarchy, who looked after the saddle horses at night to keep them from scattering or being chased away by wild stallions. Driving the weary second-string cavvy before him, he was philosophical about the cloud of dust that enveloped him, liking the horses and being away from the other men. Young, handsome, slight of build, swarthy with black hair, he was known as John (or Jack) Tregoning, or, on occasion, John Smith. His dark eyes were gentle and twinkling, his mouth kind. Seeing his relaxed way with horses, people commented that he must be able to speak their language.

Reaching the spot where the riders had stopped, Tregoning found the colt lying in the dust. Gently he spoke to the animal, as he stroked its bony neck and soft ears, careful to keep his arm away from the sharp baby teeth. Gradually the colt's ears came forward, and its velvety nose began to nuzzle the man. What would Henderson's reaction be if he brought the colt to the 71? Frequently bullied by the ranch manager, Tregoning was terribly afraid of him.

Hampered by his small stature, the nighthawk struggled to hoist Big Red onto his horse's back, the colt thrashing wildly until his head flopped against the saddle skirts and he lay still. Tregoning mounted his nervous horse, and dancing and crowhopping, they rounded up the cavvy, and rode the 40 miles to the ranch.

Reaching the 71 late that night, Tregoning cached Red in an outbuilding. He wrapped the colt in burlap bags, and, pulling its tongue out to one side so that it would not strangle, poured a pint of cow's milk down its throat.

The 71 was one of the few ranches in the area to have a barb wire fence[4] around its horse pasture. Freed by the fence from nightherding duties while at the ranch, Tregoning was given the chores that the "real" cowboys tried to avoid: milking, feeding chickens, and cleaning stables, which enabled him to get the milk his colt needed without raising suspicion. Henderson only learned of the colt's arrival when he returned from a business trip several days later, but remained indifferent so long as the colt didn't interfere with Tregoning's work.

A year passed. No one could approach the young horse except Tregoning, whom he followed like a pup. Halter-broken and learning to wear a saddle, he came when called and would race on command.

As Big Red matured, Henderson's indifference turned to hatred. His lowliest ranch hand had rescued and developed a horse which could well become the finest one in the region. An undercurrent of unease began to grow at the 71 Ranch.

One morning, after a night with the herd, Tregoning returned to the 71 to find Big Red snubbed to a post beside the corral, strangling from the lariat tightened around his neck, while a livid Henderson beat him about the head with a neck yoke, the heavy iron-rimmed wooden bar that crosses the chests of a wagon team.

Racing to cut the rope around his horse's neck, Tregoning faced Henderson, who snarled, "He tried to kill me. Get out of my way!"

Quietly, the nighthawk replied, "You know he's a one-man horse, Mr. Henderson. Don't take it out on him because you don't like me." With a curse, Henderson knocked Tregoning to the ground, delivering several tremendous kicks to the prone body. Suddenly he whirled as Big Red, ears back, teeth bared, bore down on him with a scream at a full gallop.

In a flash Henderson leaped up and over the corral fence, while the horse snorted and whistled in frustration, then nuzzled Tregoning back into consciousness.

As they made their way to the bunkhouse, the nighthawk's hand clutching Big Red's mane for support, Henderson screeched, "You're fired! Clear out! Take that killer with you!"

Tregoning turned. "You owe me several months' wages, Mr. Henderson. I'll be back for them."

In an hour he was gone, leading Big Red, who carried his saddle, bedroll and war bag. Two miles up the Sweetwater, they were welcomed at Con

Sheehan's JJ ranch. No questions were asked; the nighthawk's battered condition spoke for itself. He had no other enemies.

A few days later, when Jimmy Craig came by the JJ, Tregoning reminded him of the money owed him and asked to borrow two 71 horses for a few days to hunt for a job. Big Red was still too young to be ridden very far. Craig agreed. Leaving Big Red at Sheehan's, Tregoning rode to Buffalo, Wyoming, 150 miles to the northwest where jobs were said to be plentiful. However, this was just before the start of the Johnson County War, when the cattle ranchers attempted to drive the homesteaders out of the country, and he didn't stay. He was reported to have purchased a .45 Colt six-shooter there, and threatened to use it on Henderson, threats later used as evidence to support premeditated murder.

Twice more, the nighthawk sought out Henderson to ask for the wages owed. He was finally given a check for $9.00, told that was all he was entitled to, and ordered to return the borrowed horses. However, Tregoning did not return the 71 horses, so Henderson, accompanied by cowboy Pete Stickles, went to get them.

Excerpts from the Court testimony[5] described what followed:

Arriving at the [JJ] ranch, Henderson dismounted . . . and some cowboys told him that Tregoning was in the cabin. Henderson started for the cabin, leading his horse. . . . Stickles rode behind him. . . . Henderson had his six-shooter strapped upon him, but Stickles was unarmed. When Henderson was within about forty feet of the cabin door, Tregoning came out with a Winchester rifle and advanced to the path and a man named Berry also came out of the cabin . . . [also] armed with a Winchester. . . . [Three times] Tregoning called out: "Stop! Mr. Henderson, stop and take off your gun." Henderson then stopped . . . and pointing his finger at Tregoning said: "Smith, put down that gun," and Stickles called out . . . "Two of you have guns; one of us is unarmed . . . put down your guns and talk it over like men."

Tregoning looked back over his shoulder at Berry, then, leveling his rifle at Henderson, he pulled the trigger, and Henderson fell to the ground, exclaiming, "My God, I am shot," and he died almost instantly.

Berry and Tregoning were charged with murder. Two lawyers for the 71, and the prosecuting attorney at the trial in Lander, demanded death for both men. Justice was compromised with a life sentence for Tregoning and 25 years for Berry. Both men were sent to the state penitentiary, then in Laramie, where, after two years, Tregoning escaped, concealed in an outgoing laundry hamper from the warden's quarters. Berry served seven years before he was pardoned.

About six months after Tregoning went to prison, in 1891 my father walked into Sweetwater country and was hired to herd sheep by Jack McTurk.

Dad saw the sheepman's view for two years before deciding to try the other side. Jimmy Craig, now manager of the 71, hired him to work as a nighthawk. Dad was attracted to the company because it was Scottish, and he was home-sick for Scotsmen. Craig soon saw that, like Tregoning, the new nighthawk had a natural way with horses, though Dad had less experience.

When Tregoning went to prison, the 71 had kept Big Red, now five years old. However, he responded only to his absent owner, and was therefore a difficult and unreliable mount for other riders. With Craig's permission, Dad set out to train him.

After the beating with the neck yoke, Big Red had been so head-shy that the cowboys had to choke him down to bridle him. A bag of oats on the ground made him lower his head. With brushing, caressing, and much gentle conversation, he learned to accept the bridle again.

Next came gentling him to ride. At 5'6", Dad almost needed a sidehill to mount, so he taught the horse to stand still until he was settled in the saddle. If ever he were injured or sick, this might mean the difference between life and death.

Dad must have met Tregoning within a few weeks of Tregoning's es-cape from prison. If he had come to get Big Red, he certainly realized that to remain free, he would have to be inconspicuous, and no one would be inconspicuous riding such a beautiful horse. There must have been several meetings, probably around the night herds. Whether any money changed hands, I do not know, but Dad kept Big Red. Tregoning disappeared and was never heard of again.

Several years passed. Finding no future in working for day wages and wanting an outfit of his own, Dad left the 71. Using his meager savings to buy a few head of cattle and sheep, he hoped that by having both he could get along with cattlemen and sheepmen alike, and avoid the warfare which flared between them.

He lived on the range, spending little, managing livestock for others on shares, buying, trading, gradually building and improving his own herds. Wherever he went, Big Red was with him. Envious friends offered him $100, then $500, and finally $1,000—an unbelievable amount for a horse in those days. Dad needed the money, but he needed Big Red even more.

On Dec. 7, 1897, he filed on a homestead on Muskrat Creek.

The summer of 1898, Dad contracted to herd several thousand sheep near South Pass, a rich grazing area in the southern part of the Wind River Mountains. Because of his reputation as a good stockman, the bankers in

Lander offered him a bonus if he could put an extra ten pounds on each sheep before they were sold in November, more for each pound over that amount. If he failed, he would receive only wages for his efforts and pay for any sheep lost or killed.

South Pass is mountain country above 8,000 feet where blizzards can strike any time after September 1. By keeping the sheep in the mountains as long as possible, Dad was sure he could meet the bonus weight. He accepted the challenge, signed the papers, and with Big Red took the sheep to the mountains.

It was a summer of lush grass, good weather, and few losses except to an occasional bear, mountain lion, wolf, coyote, or gold miner. He chose Lem Harold, his most reliable herder, to help.

Dad made plans to buy a large bunch of sheep in the fall to breed and winter at his homestead on Muskrat Creek. If all went well, he would have the income from the spring lamb and wool crop, and a full year with no risks other than weather. He was 30 years old; the will to succeed was strong.

He sent word to the Lander bankers to watch for a good bunch of ewes at a reasonable price. In late October, the response came that a fine herd was for sale in Thermopolis, 125 miles to the northeast. He would have to appear in person by November 1 to close the deal. With no time left to trail the sheep off the mountain before going to Thermopolis, Dad decided to go alone. Lem would slowly work the sheep downward toward the Wind River Basin.

Now ten years old, Big Red was still in top condition. Dad rode him to Thermopolis, 65 miles the first day, 50 the second, sleeping out along the trail. He met with the sellers and found the sheep good. There were conditions. A deposit of earnest money had to be made. He was given seven days to get the rest or forfeit the deposit and the herd. Scottish caution struggled with Scottish daring and love of a bargain.

He made the deposit at five o'clock the evening of November 1. All day snow clouds, whipped by a raw, cold wind, had been scudding across the landscape, catching on the tops of the Owl Creek Mountains, then tearing loose to be replaced by more and lower clouds. Dad had the achy feeling of storm in his bones; the responsibility he had assumed weighed heavily on his shoulders.

He bought a loaf of bread, a hank of jerky, a sack of stick candy, and a quart of oats for Big Red. He donned his buffalo hide overcoat and leather chaps, whose outer side was kinky brown Angora wool, and adjusted his bearskin cap.

The light was fading; the wind was blowing ice crystals directly into their faces. Dad paused to give Big Red a handful of oats, speaking softly as he scratched the horse's ears. Big Red nuzzled Dad's hand and pricked up his ears, impatient to be moving in the cold. The 400-foot climb the first mile west of Thermopolis settled him down to an easy lope.

In 1898 there was no road or trail south through the Wind River Canyon into the Wind River Basin along the present route of the highway and railroad. Instead, the trail to Lander climbed over the Owl Creek Mountains, west of the canyon.

Vertical walls of rusty sandstone on the north flank of the Owl Creek Mountains were dimly visible in the twilight, rising several hundred feet on both sides of the trail. Big Red slowed to a trot, picking his way through the angular boulders which had fallen from above. He seemed to sense which trail to take, perhaps smelling traces of his passing two days before. Clots of gray fog drifted past, more felt than seen.

For the rest of the night Dad and Big Red traveled through the wind-driven snow, up over the Mexican Pass, stopping only for water at Nostrum Spring and again at an intermittently occupied roadhouse, called "The Mexican Place."

Sixty-two miles from Thermopolis they swam the Wind River near the trading post of Kinnear.[6] A bleak dawn was breaking by the time they reached the next river, the Popo Agie, 27 miles farther, following it southwestward to the Wind River Reservation, whose few ranch buildings and tepees were scattered among the cottonwood trees. Here, the trail had become a well-traveled wagon road, muddy and slippery from the water-saturated, churned-up dust.

As the weary rider and foam-lathered horse clattered down the main street of Lander about seven o'clock, the few early risers turned to stare. They had come 94 miles, over a mountain range in a blizzard, in 14 hours, but there was no time to tarry.

The gray landscape changed to colorful, linear cliffs of folded sandstone, red, purple, orange, and white. Here they took the well-used military route from Lander to Fort Stambaugh on the Sweetwater River and the access to the gold mines at South Pass and Atlantic City in the Wind River Mountains. Fourteen miles south of Lander they entered Red Canyon, whose red and orange-layered cliffs tower 600 feet above the valley floor to the east. When dry, this road gave off clouds of choking red dust; when wet, the upper three miles of the canyon became a mire of gumbo. This day it was wet.

Mud-spattered and blowing, the weary horse floundered up the grade, his muscles quivering whenever he stopped for breath. At the broad flat head of the canyon they had an easy mile across a surface of gold-bearing gravel, pock-marked with old placer workings.[7]

By now they had come 117 miles. Dad patted the mud-streaked shoulders in front of him; Big Red eased into a slow trot. Reaching Twin Creek Canyon, they climbed 1,000 feet in three miles. Volcanic ash made the mud chalky gray and sticky, balling up on the horse's hooves so that he had to kick his feet to dislodge it. At the summit, to the west, Beaver Meadows showed through the snow clouds, beautiful with lush grass, willows and evergreens on both sides.

The cavvy came into view, the sheep, the herder's white tent, a plume of smoke rising from the stovepipe, and Lem Harold waiting. As Dad dismounted, his legs gave way and he clung to Big Red for a moment. The horse, too, was spent. They had come 125 miles; the last 30 had taken seven hours. It was two o'clock in the afternoon. The snow began in earnest.

"Figured you'd be along about now," said Lem. "The sheep are bunched and ready to go. Hot food in the Dutch oven in the tent. I'll rub Red down and grain him, and saddle you another horse. We can move out in an hour." Dad nodded, appreciating the difference between a top hand who looked ahead and the average worker who did not. The prospect of hot food suddenly seemed very, very good.

In an hour they were headed back down the trail that Dad and Big Red had just climbed. Free of his trappings, the tired horse followed behind, snatching grass that had escaped the sheep.

Allowed to feed along the way, the sheep reached the weighing corrals in four days, exceeding the bonus weight by an average of ten pounds per animal. The bankers were pleased to pay the bonus.

Except for some stiffness, Big Red was none the worse for his long trip. He was still needed for one more. With only one day remaining to complete the purchase of the sheep, in the wee small hours of the seventh day from the time he'd originally left Thermopolis, Dad and Big Red were on their way back, going the 95 miles from Lander nonstop, meeting the deadline. As he rubbed the horse down in the livery stable late that night and gave him the customary handful of oats, emotion blurred Dad's Scottish accent: "Aye, Red, we make a great team."

Dad trailed his new sheep in easy stages to the ranch on Muskrat Creek. He bought bucks, bred ewes, hired men, and made preparations for winter feeding and spring lambing. He also purchased sheep wagons, freight wagons, and a few horses. In the mild weather that spring, lambing was very successful. Shearing went well, the wool yield was high and the prices good. For the next few years, winters continued mild, the market rose, and the world looked very good.

Dad first built barns, sheds, and corrals; protected stock ensured good income. He lived in a two-room dugout cave, carved in the gray clay bank about 100 feet northeast of the present ranch house. Pine poles and clay formed the roof. A door and window gave light and access to a room with pole bunk beds along one side. It was adequate—warm in winter and cool in summer, but unpleasant in wet weather. He lived in the dugout for ten years.

One morning, the summer of 1903, as Dad and Big Red were riding near the Owl Creek Mountains north of the ranch, they heard a cry for help over the rush of the Wind River flowing nearby. Topping a ridge, they saw in the swirling water a spring wagon, whose team had lost its footing and was being washed downstream. Wading Big Red into the river, Dad lassoed one of the lead horses and dragged it to solid footing, saving the team, the wagon, and the driver. "This man," Dad told us, "was Nelson Horatio Darton, a mapmaker, the first geologist I ever met."

Several bands of wild horses roamed around Castle Gardens, more in the badlands to the south, free to the riders with the skill to capture them. Dad's ranch now needed good saddle and work horses more than anything else.

He built a "blind corral," now known as Corral Draw, about four miles southeast of his ranch. The draw was dry except during flash floods, which had guttered out vertical clay cliffs 10 feet high. These cliffs, 20 feet apart in some places, narrowed upstream to merge, creating three sides of a natural enclosure. Not visible unless one was almost on top of it, this trap could hold at least 50 horses. Where the cliffs became gentle slopes downstream, Dad and his men built wings of cedar posts and stout wire netting to funnel wild horses into the draw.

Around a kink in this wash, Dad built a pole fence of tall cedar posts set in pairs, eight inches apart. Horizontal poles could quickly be slid into the slots between these posts after the horses had passed, preventing their escape. Frightened horses could not injure themselves against the clay walls, and there was no wire in the pole barricade to cut them. After a couple of days in the corral, they could more easily be subdued and taken to the ranch for training.

For several years Dad used this corral so successfully that he built up a small herd carrying his flatiron brand. However, one band of exceptionally fine horses, led by the glorious sorrel mare known as "Old Essie," continued to elude him, as we boys had later seen when Dad was so seriously injured a few years before.[8]

The fall of 1903, Dad set out to capture Old Essie and her band. Big Red was now thirteen years old, and although no longer as fast as he once had been, he was still sound enough to be a match for the wild horses. As sure-footed as his wild ancestors, he had never been known to stumble or fall.

Dad stationed riders along the approximate circle he knew the band would make. As the wild horses began to tire, he and Big Red would head them toward the blind corral while the other riders chased them into it.

As predicted, Old Essie followed the circle, outrunning each rider in turn, coming in sight of Dad and Big Red about six miles south of the ranch. As the corral was three miles to the north, Dad had to divert them. As if sensing the strategy, Old Essie suddenly bolted southward. Big Red raced after them. For some distance he had better footing than they, and as their paths converged, they were neck and neck, about 50 yards apart. Dad's weight on a fresh horse just about offset their weariness.

On the right, bordering Muskrat Creek, was spongy, hummocky ground, dotted with greasewood and riddled with drainage tunnels typical in this type of soil. On the left was a flat with low salt sage. Old Essie, with the advantage of good footing, crowded closer and closer, forcing Big Red to run in the greasewood or drop back. If he could keep his speed just a 100 yards more, he could turn her, and her band would follow.

Their flaxen manes and tails streaming, the wild horses thundered along the ground, twenty or more sorrel mares, two-year olds, yearlings and colts, and a fiery young stallion matching Old Essie step for step.

With a surge, Big Red lept ahead, turning the band. Breaking stride, the herd faltered in confusion. As Big Red bounded over a giant clump of grease-wood, both front feet broke through the roof of one of the concealed tunnels with a terrible crash. Catapulted from the saddle, Dad hit a spongy bank 20 feet away, and the light went out of his world.

A long time later, the light came on again, dimly, red-rimmed, with needles of pain driving into his head. Through the haze he reached for Big Red and found nothing—no sound, no motion, only soft powdery ground. Dad tried to call him, but his voice was only a bubbling croak. His mouth seemed to be filled with rocks. He spit out a few of the objects and found that they were splintered teeth. Cautiously he tested his arms and legs. The soft dirt had spared him more serious injury. Slowly he staggered to his feet, but there was no horse standing near him.

As his vision cleared, Dad saw what he had been afraid to find. Big Red lay where he had fallen, both front legs broken, his head turned under his body at an odd angle. Mercifully, he had died instantly.

Gently Dad pulled the great head out straight, felt for the pulse, and found none. Crumpling to the ground, he sat with his hand on Big Red's dust-covered, but still beautiful head. The dark eyes were open, but no longer luminous. Great shuddering sobs racked Dad's shoulders. Remorse and self-accusation followed. This magnificent horse had given him service, prestige, material success, and above all, unquestioning loyalty in good times as well as on dark and dangerous trails when the human spirit was apt to falter.

Dad did not say how long he sat there, but as the shadows lengthened and a chilly breeze began to blow, he roused. The other men would not come to look for him. They would follow instructions and wait at the blind corral. With great effort, he removed the bridle and pulled the saddle loose. He lingered, trying to say farewell, but could not speak, and nothing he thought seemed adequate. From his face so swollen he could not close his mouth, blood dripped slowly onto his shirt.

Draping the saddle blanket over his shoulder, he slung the heavy saddle on his back, and with the bridle in his other hand, started the long walk back to his dugout.

As our buggy approached Corral Draw, Dad heaved a great sigh and showed us where Big Red had fallen and died. Seldom did my father show grief, but a clue to the depth of his feelings was revealed later quite by accident. In his desk drawer I saw an old, battered bit and asked him about it. He said it had belonged to Big Red. Young and unsentimental, I commented that it still looked usable, so why didn't we use it? For a long moment, he looked at me. "Laddie," he said, finally, "It won't fit any other horse."

In silence we progressed southward, the road climbing steeply from 5,675 feet at the ranch to 7,311 feet to cross the Beaver Divide. As we passed through Indian Grove, Allan and I eyed the chokecherries, relieved that they were still small green nubbins.

From there we turned southwest, crossing a gentle upland plain, to reach the meadow through which Long Creek flowed. This narrow, sluggish creek hardly looked big enough for the trout we hoped to catch. We unloaded the buggy, hobbled the horses and turned them out to graze.

That evening, Dad dipped several small trout in cornmeal and fried them in bacon fat. He boiled some potatoes and we ate supper with genuine pleasure. Dad cleaned the 20-30 remaining trout, and placed them in the dry pit he had dug adjacent to the cold spring flowing into the creek. The next morning, he packed them in wet grass, wrapping the bundle in canvas to stay cool beneath the buggy seat during the hot trip home.

A world of awakening had begun for me on this trip. I began to share Dad's interest in the terrain, the quality of the water, the fertility of the soil, the types of vegetation, the distribution and variety of wildlife, the well-being of the livestock, the effects of weather on everything. Dad's own experiences in the region took on new value. I asked endless questions: Were there good maps of the region? No? Why not? Why was the Sweetwater

River on an upland plain more than 1,000 feet above where we lived? Why didn't Long Creek flow downhill into Muskrat Creek? Why did Long Creek and the springs at Indian Grove have water without alkali, whereas Muskrat Creek had a lot? Why did the well under our kitchen have less alkali than the creek 100 feet away? Why did the Beaver Divide have more snow than we did at the ranch? Why did the wind blow from west to east? Why did the rocks at Castle Gardens tilt north? Why did they look so different from the horizontal cliffs at Indian Grove? (Years later I nearly lost my life on a crumbling ledge there trying to answer this question.)

Dad showed no impatience at my questions. Often he referred me to our *Encyclopædia Britannica* because he did not know the answers. Not know? We had assumed that he and Mother knew everything. Near the end of our trip he remarked that I sounded like his uncle, John Muir. What a compliment! Muir was even then a legendary figure.

The rest of the summer was idyllic for me. Lacking the endurance to ride on long roundups, I had few responsibilities other than helping Mother. Allan, however, was big enough to participate with the men. The riders were a tough group whose conversation was revolting and revealing. Allan passed on what he learned to me, but I was more interested in discoveries of my own.

Day after day I explored on foot, making crude maps of the terrain showing where the rock outcrops were, where the roads and my secret trails led, where I had discovered Indian artifacts and bird nests. I studied the birds— redwing blackbirds, blue herons, killdeer, fly catchers, yellow warblers, night hawks, meadowlarks, hummingbirds, marveling at the construction of their nests, watching the egg-to-chick-to-adult cycle of each species. The Northern Shrike, or "butcher bird," was my only enemy. I had seen the young birds of other species, and even grasshoppers, impaled on greasewood thorns by the shrikes, so I destroyed their nests whenever I found them and shot the adults with my .22 rifle.

Ants fascinated me as well; their habitats ranged from cone-shaped piles of grit and sand in the center of 6-foot clearings, to mounds of sticks. The tiniest ants built doughnut-sized circular mounds with an entrance pit in the center. The black "stick ants," as I called them, measuring one-half inch, were the largest and fiercest. The red "grit-cone" ants were equally ferocious, but smaller. I observed these two species in combat, their fighters streaming to the battlefield, and carrying back the dead and wounded. Were the battles among the ants and those of the soldiers who fought in World War I exercises in futility?

I pored over the books in our overflowing book cases: *The Encyclopædia Britannica, Book of Knowledge* and others on birds and mammals, whose descriptions of various life forms were similar, but never identical to what I had observed. I was content to learn just the broader story.

I mapped the pocket gopher and prairie dog colonies, and observed their social habits. I was especially fascinated with the tiny burrowing owls which lived in some of the burrows with prairie dogs. Each day was a journey of discovery, and by evening I was so enthusiastic I could hardly eat supper. My parents never belittled my discoveries, but Allan did. Openly contemptuous, he considered my adventures a waste of time, especially a means of avoiding the chores, which, in my absence, he had to do.

One glorious day I hiked the four miles to the "Chalk Hills," a small area of red and white candy-striped badlands, unlike any other area in the region. In a thin layer of clay I found a dozen or more tiny, black, shiny, and perfectly preserved teeth of some small mammals. *Elements of Geology* described similar teeth, and I guessed correctly that they were tiny ancestral horses.

As I became more and more aware of the limitless richness of what had seemed a very drab world around me, I began to see the interrelation of the myriads of living organisms, their mutual dependency upon each other, the weather, the temperature, the precipitation, the soil. I could see for myself how my father, by building dams and plowing up the virgin sod had altered entire plant and animal communities. His dams had changed the stream course of Muskrat Creek, and he had paid the penalty: when the dams were washed out, the accumulated silt in the reservoir areas was flushed out to destroy a field which had formerly grown badly needed grain. The floodwaters incised the stream bed. What had formerly been a grassy bottom became a broad sandy-bottomed channel flanked by steep banks. (The channel has gradually reverted back to a narrow, non-sandy grassy slot, which will probably again become a grassy bottom.)

My parents had been wise enough to let me roam freely to study the natural wonders around me. That opportunity for self-development gave me the strength and balance I needed to deal with what was ahead.

The summer ended abruptly in September when Mother took us by train to Lander to enroll Allan and me in the high school there. Well aware of our social and academic limitations, she and Dad felt that we needed at least one parent to supervise the drastic transition. Mercifully, we boys were unaware of the trials of high school that awaited us.

We packed trunks with cooking utensils, dishes, linens and clothes, and Phoebe's highchair wrapped in burlap sacks to be shipped on the train.

In "Our George," Ethel described the next phase of the family's experience:

I went house hunting, carrying Phoebe in my arms. We rented a furnished house there and moved for the school term.

The Frasers' farm was four miles distant. Friends often drove us there in their car. We all shared Lizzie's delicious Christmas dinner. We often saw George Rushton, who was quietly taking a respected place in the neighborhood. The ranchers began calling him "Old George." He stopped in town when he could to see Phoebe and to talk to John. For John found many reasons to be in Lander. He accepted jury duty for the first time, and attended long trials. He had a man staying on the ranch, so he could get away. At first a sheepman from Lander brought him to town. The next year John was persuaded to buy a second-hand Buick car. Under severe nervous and vocal strain, he taught himself to drive, alone on a wide expanse of level ground. Automatically he called, "Whoa there!" as he had to our horse Dan, when he wanted to stop. He spoke in a superior fashion of the stockman who had chopped his car to pieces with an axe when he and it had a disagreement.

Summers we returned to the ranch.

As the family began this next phase of their lives, John's parting advice echoed in David's memory over the following years. Their formative life on the ranch, the

Ethel Waxham Love at Love ranch, 1925.
Love Family Archives

importance of family, persistence in the face of difficulty, and self knowledge stem-
ming from experience became part of the family legacy:

Often I remember Dad's words as we hugged him goodbye at the Moneta railroad station, leaving him and our childhood behind: "Mind your mother, lads, and take care of her and Phoebe. And no matter how difficult it gets, we Loves aren't quitters. Remember who you are."

Notes

1. From a song by Robert Burns, "Green Grow the Rashes," (1784). In *English Romantic Poetry & Prose*, ed. Russell Noyes. New York: Oxford University Press, 1956: 142–143.

2. Geologic formations with no grass, game, or good water. Difficult to cross.

3. According to George W. Hufsmith, "Henderson had earlier been a Pinkerton detective and a skull-cracking strike breaker in the Molly McGuire coal mine upris-ing in Pennsylvania." *The Wyoming Lynching of Cattle Kate 1889*. Glendo, WY: High Plains Press, 1993: 180.

4. Barbs had been hand-crimped to a strand of heavy wire, salvaged six years ear-lier from the transcontinental telegraph line that followed the Oregon Trail along the Sweetwater River. A 17-year-old by named John Kirk did much of the crimping. In 1870, the 71 was the first ranch in Wyoming to have barb wire fences. J.D. Love, personal communication.

5. A.J. Mockler, *History of Natrona County Wyoming 1888–1922*. Chicago: R.R Donnelley & Sons Company, The Lakeside Press, 1923: 274.

6. This crossing was not where the present town is. The town was run by a civil engineer of that name, who, in 1880, had opened one of the few coal mines in the area.

7. Today, when travelers drive northeastward on Highway 28 from Farson to Lander, the sudden beauty of Red Canyon invariably makes them want to stop to admire the color, the sweeping varicolored lines of rock, the broad expanse of the Wind River Basin, and the Owl Creek Mountains, shimmering blue in the distance.

8. A generation later Allan and David, with their best horses, went after "Young Essie's" descendents, but could only get them to within 100 yards of the corrals before they escaped.

~

Epilogue

Allan and David attended Lander High School for two years before trans-ferring to University Prep in Laramie, Wyoming, where they boarded at Sherwood Hall, a home for children run by the Episcopal Church. Following graduation in 1929, both boys enrolled at the University of Wyoming and went on to earn advanced degrees, Allan becoming an engineer, working on major engineering projects in Wyoming, New York, New Jersey, and Labra-dor. David, a geologist with a PhD from Yale, made a career with the U.S. Geological Survey in Wyoming. Toward the end of his life, among many other honors, David was named a "Legendary Geoscientist" by the American Geological Institute.

When the boys went to school in Laramie, Ethel and Phoebe returned to the ranch until Phoebe was old enough for school. Mother and daugh-ter then spent the winters in Casper, Wyoming, while John stayed on the ranch. Ethel was active in many civic organizations in Casper and was the founding state president of the American Association of University Women. She attended some Wellesley reunions and maintained life-long friendships with her classmates there. Phoebe also graduated from the University of Wyoming, earning a master's degree in natural science. She later worked as a reclamation specialist on projects around Casper.

With their children grown, John and Ethel remained on the ranch until 1947, when age and ill health caused them to retire. They enjoyed some winters in Arizona, and spent their last years living with David's family in Laramie. John died in 1950, and Ethel passed away in 1959, leaving a legacy of stories and family history. The Love ranch stayed in the family until it was sold in 2012, still waiting for the mirage to materialize. None of the children, grandchildren, or great-grandchildren have become ranchers, yet. While the descendants have followed their own dreams into careers in science, education, and the arts, they retain their connections to the isolated ranch on the Wyoming plains and the couple who made it their home.

Bibliography

Unpublished Sources

Love, Ethel Waxham, Undated Writing:
"The Cats"
"Dumpling"
"Election Day"
"The Equalizer"
"Flotsam": "The Wooden-legged Man," "Old Mica," "Bert Austin"
"The Gospel Wagon"
"Hats and Gloves"
"Jack Peterson"
"Marlinspike"
"Mirage"
"The Old Indestructible"
"Our George"
"Panorama"
"Pigs"
"Porch Chair"
"Red and Blue"
"Roll, Jordan, Roll"
"Rome Was Not Built in a Day"
"Roundup Time"
"Someone Will Come Along"
"The Story of Allan and David"
"The 3 R's"

"Too Much Wild Duck"
"Wagon Wheels"

Love, Ethel Waxham, Undated Poetry
"Dark Dawn"
"Earth Changeling"
"Jig Saw"
"Outlasting"
"The Year Has Cast His Cloak Away"

Love, J. David, Unpublished Writing:
"Big Red" (1969)
"Bill Grace and the Rattlesnake Dinner" (1995)
"The Broken Plank" (1972)
"Childhood without Music" (1999)
"A Christmas at the Ranch" (1967)
"Dreams, Dams, and Disasters, 1908–1913" (1989)
"Earned, Not Given" (1975)
"The Enchanted Summer" (1990)
"First Memories" (1988)
"The Foot Race" (1996)
"From Father, Christmas, 1901—The Gold Watch" (1982)
"Going, Going, Gone" (1981)
"Haying at Mud Spring" (1999)
"Hypothermia" (1985)
"More Speed, To Hell with Direction" (1981)
"Our Last Country Schoolmarm" (1973)
"Our Last School Meeting" (1991)
"Peace on Earth, Good Will to All" (1982)
"Ride a Cock Horse" (1970)
"The Runaways" (1987)
"The Scar" (1981)
"We'll Rebuild, Again" (1997)

Love, M. Jordan, "Christmas Stories Revived: The Origin of the Love and Galloway Families," unpublished family history, 2015.

Published Sources

Blunt, Judy. *Breaking Clean*. New York: Vintage Books, 2002.
Burns, Robert. "Green Grow the Rashes" (1784). In *English Romantic Poetry & Prose*, ed. Russell Noyes. New York: Oxford University Press, 1956: 142–143.

———. "Scots Wha Hae" (1793). In *English Romantic Poetry & Prose*, ed. Russell Noyes. New York: Oxford University Press, 1956: 166.

Cowper, William. "The Solitude of Alexander Selkirk." In F. T. Palgrave's *The Golden Treasury of English Songs and Lyrics*, ed. Oscar Williams. New York: Mentor Books, 1961.

Dowling, Bartholomew. "The Revel (East India)." In *Victorian Anthology 1837–1895*, ed. Edmund Clarence Stedman. Boston: Houghton Mifflin, 1895: 101–102.

Healy, Cathy. *An Improbable Pioneer: The Letters of Edith Holden Healy 1911–1950*. Worland, WY: Washakie Museum & Cultural Center Legacy Collection, 2013.

Hendricks, Cecilia Hennel. *Letters from Honey Hill: A Woman's View of Homesteading, 1914–1922*. Boulder: Pruett Publishing, 1990.

Huntoon, Peter W. "The National Bank Failures in Wyoming, 1924." *Annals of Wyoming*, 54 (Fall 1982): 34–44.

Ives, Stephen. "One Sky above Us." *The West: Episode 8*. The West Film Project, Inc./Greater Washington Educational Telecommunications Association, Inc., 1996.

Jefferys, Charles. "Mary of Argyle." Philadelphia: A. Fiot, n.d. circa 1850.

Jordan, Teresa. *Riding the White Horse Home: A Western Family Album*. New York: Pantheon Books, 1993.

LeConte, Joseph. *Elements of Geology*. New York: D. Appleton and Company, 1889.

Love, Barbara and Frances Love Froidevaux, eds. *Lady's Choice: Ethel Waxham's Journals & Letters, 1905–1910*. Albuquerque: University of New Mexico Press, 1993.

Love, Ethel Waxham. *The Record of the Class of 1905 of Wellesley College*, vol. I (1905–1910) 58, vol. II (1910–1915), vol. III (1916–1921), vol. IV (1920–1925) 96. Wellesley, MA: Wellesley College.

Love, Ethel Waxham. "Wyoming Wolf Drive," *Writing at Wyoming*. Laramie, WY: Department of English, University of Wyoming, 1958: 46–55.

Love, Ethel Waxham. "At the Twin Creek School," *Let Your Light Shine, Pioneer Women Educators of Wyoming*. Ed. Alpha Xi State Delta Kappa Gamma. Sheridan, WY: Wyoming Print Shop, 1965.

McPhee, John. *Rising from the Plains*. New York: Farrar, Straus, Giroux, 1986.

Mokler, Alfred James. *History of Natrona County, Wyoming 1888–1922*. Chicago: R.R. Donnelley & Sons Company, 1923.

Moore, Thomas. "A Ballad: The Lake of the Dismal Swamp." *Thomas Moore's Complete Poetical Works*. Boston: Thomas V. Crowell & Company, 1895: 129.

Mother Goose. "Ride a Cockhorse." *Poetry Foundation*. https://www.poetryfoundation.org/poems-and-poets/poems/detail/46955.

Rankin, Charles. Introduction to *Lady's Choice: Ethel Waxham's Journals & Letters, 1905–1910*. Ed. Barbara Love and Frances Love Froidevaux. Albuquerque: University of New Mexico Press, 1993: xiii–xix.

Read, Mary L. *The Mothercraft Manual*. Boston: Little, Brown and Co., 1916.

Scott, Walter. *The Lady of the Lake*. Glasgow: Wm. Collins, Sons & Co., 1810.

Sedgwick, Theodore. "A Church Wagon in Southern Wyoming," *The Spirit of Missions*, Vol. 2, No. 11 (Nov. 1910): 924–925.

Stewart, Elinore Pruett. *Letters of a Woman Homesteader*. Boston: Houghton Mifflin, 1914.

Ward, Geoffrey C. *The West: An Illustrated History*. Boston: Little, Brown and Co., 1996: 409–416, 421–425.

Waxham, Ethel. "I Know A Land" and "Earth-Changeling." *Sagebrush Classics*. Ed. Betsy Bernfeld. Lincoln, NE: Media Publishing, 1990: 87–88.

Waxham, Ethel and John G. Love. Selected letters 1906–1909. *Women's Letters: America from the Revolutionary War to the Present*. Ed. Lisa Grunwald and Stephen J. Adler. New York: The Dial Press, 2005: 443–445.

Wynn, Ed and F. S. Smith, publishers, *Shoshoni Pathfinder* (No place of publication or publishing company given), 1906.

About the Editors

Frances Love Froidevaux (left) (1942–2011) graduated from Cottey College (AA French 1961) in Missouri and the University of Wyoming (BA French 1966). While spending her junior year at the University of Neuchâtel, Switzerland, she met and married geologist Claude Froidevaux, with whom she raised three children and lived in Singapore, Indonesia, and Oklahoma while he worked for Phillips Petroleum. During their years in Bartlesville, Oklahoma, she taught French and ESL at Bartlesville Wesleyan College, was an advisor to the Oklahoma State Department of Education for Certification Recom-

mendation of Entry-Year French Teachers, and was the founder and coordinator of the Bartlesville Elementary Foreign Language Program, the school system's first foreign language program. She was a skilled knitter, weaver, and musician. With her sister, Barbara, she edited *Lady's Choice, A Wyoming Courtship: Ethel Waxham's Journals & Letters, 1905–1910* (1993).

Barbara Love (right) (1949–) graduated from Wheaton College, Norton, Massachusetts (BA English 1971), and earned MA degrees from the University of Colorado (Linguistics/ESL 1979) and the University of Wyoming

(English 1984). She worked as an archaeologist on sites in Wyoming and Switzerland (1971–1974), and was assistant staff archaeologist for the Colorado Department of Highways, 1975–1979. Along with raising two sons, she taught ESL and English at Western Wyoming Community College, Laramie County Community College, and the University of Wyoming before becoming the Director of Academic Programs for Mukogawa Fort Wright Institute in Spokane, Washington, 1990–2001. After moving to Pennsylvania to join husband, Stephen Cutcliffe, she worked as Writing Coordinator for Northampton Community College in Bethlehem, 2001–2015.